Dear Reader:

P9-BTN-203

The book you are about to read is the latest bestseller from the St. Martin's True Crime Library, the imprint *The New York Times* calls "the leader in true crime!" Each month, we offer you a fascinating account of the latest, most sensational crime that has captured the national attention. St. Martin's is the publisher of bestselling true crime author and crime journalist Kieran Crowley, who explores the dark, deadly links between a prominent Manhattan surgeon and the disappearance of his wife fifteen years earlier in THE SURGEON'S WIFE. Suzy Spencer's BREAKING POINT guides readers through the tortuous twists and turns in the case of Andrea Yates, the Houston mother who drowned her five young children in the family's bathtub. In Edgar Award-nominated DARK DREAMS, legendary FBI profiler Roy Hazelwood and bestselling crime author Stephen G. Michaud shine light on the inner workings of America's most violent and depraved murderers. In the book you now hold, THE DARKEST NIGHT, acclaimed author Ron Franscell explores a shocking story of abduction and murder.

St. Martin's True Crime Library gives you the stories behind the headlines. Our authors take you right to the scene of the crime and into the minds of the most notorious murderers to show you what really makes them tick. St. Martin's True Crime Library paperbacks are better than the most terrifying thriller, because it's all true! The next time you want a crackling good read, make sure it's got the St. Martin's True Crime Library logo on the spine—you'll be up all night!

Charles E. Spicer, Jr.
Executive Editor, St. Martin's True Crime Library

Praise for
THE DARKEST NIGHT

"Few authors understand what makes a true crime book stand out like a beacon from the mass of prosaically gruesome re-telling of police reports. Ron Franscell does! *The Darkest Night* explores the true story of this unholy sacrifice of youth and misplaced trust in a gripping, throat-tightening way. It will make you cry honest tears. The victims deserve no less."   —Ann Rule, #1 *New York Times* bestselling author of *The Stranger Beside Me*

"Ron Franscell's *The Darkest Night* gets everything right: Casper, Wyoming, in the boom-town 1970s, the effect of an unspeakable crime on an entire generation of residents, and a diligent search for why it happened when the only answer can only be true evil. I know he got it right because I was there. I remember Amy Burridge and Becky Thomson before the crime and Becky after. I remember the names 'Kennedy and Jenkins' spoken only with naked hatred and contempt. And I remember where I was when I heard how Becky dealt with the horror and violence after so many years. *The Darkest Night* is a true story that you wish wasn't true because it will haunt you long after you've read it. A remarkable achievement."   —C.J. Box, bestselling author of *Free Fire* and *Blue Heaven* and Wyoming native

"Ron Franscell has penned a true-crime book reminiscent of Truman Capote's *In Cold Blood* . . . a grim reminder of ubiquitous violence. . . . As a testament to the depth of evil and an elegy for a simpler time, *The Darkest Night* delivers a crackling story of lives and innocence lost."   —*Bookmarks* magazine

"On more than one level, *The Darkest Night* rises above most books in the true-crime genre, mostly because it searingly depicts a type of evil not too often exceeded. In an elegant and powerful voice normally seen only in fiction, Ron Franscell captures the sights, sounds and smells of this Wyoming saga and masterfully gets inside the emotional marrow of its participants."—Vincent Bugliosi, #1 *New York Times* bestselling author of *Helter Skelter*

"Read it in broad daylight, because *The Darkest Night* is going to chill you like no other true crime book you've ever read. Lock your doors, make sure your kids are safe in bed, and pick up this horrifyingly absorbing memoir."

—Terri Schlichenmeyer, syndicated reviewer

MORE . . .

"Amazingly well-written, this is an important story for America today, maybe for the world."
— Louie Free, talk-show host at WWOW-AM, Cleveland

"Ron Franscell's investigation into a town scarred by evil strikes some unexpectedly resonant chords. A true insider, Franscell's insight into the case is more than equaled by his insight into the tight-knit town, making windy Casper, Wyo., one of the book's most mysterious characters . . . [his] reportorial vigor, fine pacing and moral center carry the grim story, and he's also capable of great moments of eloquence."
—*Publishers Weekly*

"*The Darkest Night* is one of those rare true-crime books that crosses genre lines into what is simply dramatic literary nonfiction at its best. In the vein of *In Cold Blood*—and perhaps even more meaningful with the author's personal connection—it is a deep and moving tale about the impact of a crime on a small town, written with the flair of a novelist, and a journalist's eye and ear for truth."
—Steve Jackson, bestselling author of
Monster, *No Stone Unturned*, and *Partners In Evil*

"In a style similar to *In Cold Blood*, Mr. Franscell captures, from start to finish (if there is ever a finish), this terrible saga. He went to enormous lengths to provide vivid and unforgettable narrative . . . The end will floor you. If it was fiction, no one would believe it could happen."
—Ken Blum in *Publishers' Auxiliary*

"What sets the book apart from others in the true-crime genre is that Franscell grew up next door to the victims. It is also serves as a grim reminder that random, senseless crimes happen regularly and can never truly be explained or understood."
—*Free Press* (Winnipeg, Manitoba)

"Suspenseful narrative and amazing detail . . . a classic tragedy about how the past never really separates from the present."
—*Daily Times* (Rawlins, WY)

THE DARKEST NIGHT

*Two Sisters, a Brutal Murder, and
the Loss of Innocence in a Small Town*

RON FRANSCELL

St. Martin's Paperbacks

Previously published under the title *Fall*.

THE DARKEST NIGHT

Copyright © 2007 by Ron Franscell.

Cover photo of bridge and cover photo of Amy Burridge from memorial plaque © Ron Franscell.

Library of Congress Catalog Card Number: 2006923962

ISBN: 0-312-94846-8
EAN: 978-0-312-94846-7

Printed in the United States of America

New Horizon Press edition / January 2007
St. Martin's Paperbacks edition / March 2008

St. Martin's Paperbacks are published by St. Martin's Press, 175 Fifth Avenue, New York, NY 10010.

10 9 8 7 6 5 4 3 2 1

I remember you on this bridge, staring down into the void, but it can't be a real memory.

I wasn't here.

More like a belief, the faded ghost of something I never actually witnessed, a still life reappearing through layers of other memories painted over it. It's part of me, just deep down; real, just out of focus. And as I stand here tonight, thirty years later, I animate the whole heartbreaking movie, frame by frame through a time warped lens. I have the unnerving sensation, for a newspaperman, that I am hoping beyond hope to see what nobody saw, to watch a nightmare somebody else dreamed, to hear words unspoken, to walk paths journeyed only in another heart, to recall what almost nobody remembers.

But I remember you on this bridge.

And though I wasn't here, I asked about you later, about the color of the sky, the sound of the wind, and the light and dark in your heart.

Now the time is all mixed up for me. I have lived in your life for a long time now, and I'm not sure when I cross the border between you and me, this present and that past.

This is your story, but it is also mine.

Ron Franscell
On Fremont Canyon Bridge

TABLE OF CONTENTS

Part One

Chapter 1 DARK END OF THE SKY 1

Chapter 2 THE JOURNEY 9

Chapter 3 THE DAY 20

Chapter 4 AFTER 33

Part Two

Chapter 5 THE PROSECUTION 85

Chapter 6 THE DEFENSE 117

Chapter 7 THE VERDICT 149

Part Three

Chapter 8 THE NEXT LIFE 175

Chapter 9 UNTOLD DESTINY 205

Chapter 10 CLOSURE 256

Endnotes 279

Acknowledgments 281

"For once, I want to know what bones know—what we can only know after we have died. I have many fantasies that I cannot achieve in life as I have known it—including being able to breathe under water and to fly—that I may only be able to know after death."

Anne Arden McDonald
who photographed a series of images
on Death Row in Wyoming's Frontier Prison

Part One

Chapter 1

DARK END OF THE SKY

September 25, 1973

T he cold and the dark and the fear of death kept her awake, praying for first light, for another morning. Just one.

The long plunge into the black river had crippled her somehow. Her legs didn't work. Maybe when she'd hit the rocks. Even at eighteen, she'd never had a broken bone, but she now believed her legs were broken. They protruded from her frozen hips, useless and thick with pain.

They hadn't let her put her panties and brassiere back on, just her light sweater and jeans. When they dumped her off the bridge into the infinite darkness, she slammed hard into a stone ledge, but not the bottom. Her long, lithe body caromed off the wall and spiraled down again, seconds that seemed like forever, not knowing what was below. Then she hit the water, in the eye of a liquid detonation that embraced her rather than vaporized her.

Her body plunged deep into the river, like a knife through soft flesh. Her lungs smoldered, and water filled her sinuses and mouth, crashed against her eardrums, and trickled into her lungs. She wanted to scream, to exhale, to inhale, to know she was alive, but in the water down there in the dark, half blinded already by the beating she'd suffered before the fall, she couldn't know the way to the surface. She sank farther, but there was no bottom.

Then she stopped. She clawed against the water with her hands, unable to make her legs obey. The weight of water

pulled her down, and she fought against it so hard her pants
slipped off her useless legs. She felt she might be a hundred,
a thousand, feet below the surface, and her lungs would burst
before she found air, but she clawed at it, raged against it.

When she burst through the placid surface of the deep
river, the night air swept into and over her. It was near freezing but still warmer than the water and felt like her mother's
hand on her face . . . *It's all right, baby, breathe, breathe* . . .
but her mother wasn't there.

She was alive. She managed to paddle to the rocky granite slabs beside the river, where they formed not a soft shore,
but an insurmountable curb. Dragging her deadened legs out
of the black water into the black night, she wormed across
the sharp stones, naked below the waist, beaten and bruised,
in shock. What blood remained in her kept her heart beating
and served only the most primitive part of her brain, where
survival came before all else.

She grasped for purchase among the river stones, and a water rat skittered across her arm. She stifled a shriek, but she
worried more about the two men who might be waiting above
than any other vermin below. The autumn wind swirled in the
bottom of the canyon, trapped like she was, chilling her naked
skin. Silent.

Stones carved her flesh as she dragged herself toward
softer, flatter earth. She collapsed in a clump of river brush
rooted in the loose talus between two boulders, protected
from the churning wind, from the Wyoming temperatures
that fell abruptly after midnight, from the view of anyone
who might come looking for her—even in the dark.

She folded herself into her stone womb, pulling her dead
legs against her body with her hands until she was balled
tightly in a fetal position. She draped her long brown hair
across them, then covered herself with uprooted bushes, and
waited.

Don't fall asleep. Her mind flashed out some ancient wisdom of warm-blooded humans in desperately cold climates.
I won't wake up. Fall asleep and die.

Then she heard the voices from the lip of the canyon, more than a hundred feet above. Two men talking and laughing. It was them, she knew. All was black. Even if her left eye hadn't been swollen shut and throbbing, she couldn't see her own hand in front of her face, and they would not be able to see her, but she knew they were there and they were trying to see her. She made herself smaller and wished she were invisible, part of the earth itself. Unseeable. While it was dark, she was as close to invisible as she could be, but at dawn . . . would they still be up there, watching?

Don't fall asleep.

As the analgesic shock trickled away, pain seeped through her like some poisonous liquid. Her hips pulsed and oozed with a deep-down ache, and her stunned heart pumped pain into the rest of her. She wanted to cry, but dared not, for fear of them hearing. The more it hurt, the more she wanted to slip into unconsciousness, but not to die. To be freed from the unknowable pain that was slowly saturating her, from the fear and from the thought that her little sister might be there, within a few feet.

Maybe alive.

Maybe a corpse.

I love you, Becky, was the last thing Amy had said. Becky bit her lip to keep from crying as a deeper hurt rose in her chest.

She tasted blood in her mouth, and wild, algae-fouled river water. She began to tremble, and the trembling constricted her breathing. She tried to pray, but she'd never done it much, and she didn't know what to ask for. Her mind just played and replayed the endless loop of what had happened, and what might happen still.

Only stars shone. The slivered moon kept low to the horizon, never appearing in the open gash above the canyon. All else was black, without form, detail or depth. Just black.

Suddenly, high above, headlights reflected off the steel buttresses of the bridge as a car passed over it. Were they leaving? Was it some other peculiar traveler out here in the middle of the night? Was it a trick to get her to reveal herself? Or were they satisfied she was dead? She couldn't know.

No matter. Dawn was a few hours away. She'd wait for the first light. Maybe she'd gather enough energy to find a way out. First light.

Just don't fall asleep.

First light.

As if she had not been betrayed enough, the heavens deceived Becky, too.

First light was an illusion.

Fremont Canyon is as narrow and profound as a grave. And in the hours before dawn, deep inside the slow-green guts of the gorge, the night sky is as black as the inside of a coffin lid. To look up from its depths is to glimpse infinity through the slender, claustrophobic frame of towering canyon walls.

At night, when a full moon is directly overhead, the gorge is illuminated in eerie blue like a boxful of moonlight. In winter, when the sun slants in from its lowest point in the sky, light might only hit the bottom for a few minutes every day.

But long before sunrise in the heart of Wyoming's autumn, false dawn appears. False dawn is not the first vestige of morning twilight, a glow that precedes the sunrise. It's different. Sometimes known as "zodiacal light," it can be seen two or three hours before the sun comes up, a faint and eerie cone of light in the predawn sky. It manifests briefly only in the eastern sky in autumn, the west in spring.

At its zenith, false dawn rivals the Milky Way in brightness, but it usually remains the sky's secret, hidden by the haze in our own atmosphere. Nonetheless, Fremont Canyon—far removed from city lights and all the rest that civilization entails—acts like an enormous camera obscura, focusing the light on its floor, blocking the light pollution from all other sources, even most of the stars in the sky.

And what is almost never seen—because human eyes are drawn to the light in a dark sky, not away from it—is false dawn's counterglow. It appears at the dark end of the sky, the west, as a faint oval of light amid a streak of bright stardust. But it is almost always camouflaged by that stardust, the Milky Way, thirty-thousand light years away.

Thirty years.

She'd fought off sleep and pain and fear and the terrifying, endless replays of what had happened a few hours before. She avoided imagining that Amy might be down there with her, unseen, perhaps within reach. She tried in vain to sort the lies from reality. But she couldn't stop the second-guessing, going back and trying to make it end differently. *Oh, God, how could I have stopped it?*

In the night, although the black hole absorbed most sounds, she heard otherworldly noises. Not just the coyotes howling far away, stones falling from the cliffs, or fish splashing in the unhurried river. When the night was darkest, she heard a low moan, a sound like someone blowing across the open neck of a bottle, somewhere up the river. She didn't know if it was an animal, the wind swirling inside the canyon, or one of her tormentors trying to frighten her. She wasn't even sure it was real. There in the dark, alone and gravely injured, she had too little to believe.

Then a fragile light rose in the east, a delicate glow above the black canyon wall. The foretelling of dawn. Twilight in the morning. Light like the cavalry coming to the rescue, still distant, but coming. A pale triangle of the coming day hovered above the canyon, and she imagined dawn was less than an hour away. It was not yet enough to illuminate a path out of the canyon, but she took it as a promise that, from this moment, there would be more light, not less. Yes, the light would disperse whatever demons hovered above, she was certain.

She was wrong. The light was false dawn, a trick of the season. The sun wouldn't rise for at least two hours, and after that, the canyon would remain dark and cold for another two. And no amount of light would scatter her demons, ever.

Barefoot and naked below the waist, she gathered herself for the most difficult journey of her life, harder even than falling one hundred and twenty feet into a black, bottomless river. A few seconds. No, this journey would be longer and harder.

GOOD OPEN-WATER DAYS were dwindling as Wyoming's brief autumn exhaled its last relatively temperate breaths, so Carl and Dorothy Strasser rose at dawn on a cold but clear Tuesday morning to go fishing.

It wasn't the elderly couple's habit to escape their quiet life in town on a weekday, but they had the day off, and as the days grew shorter for them and for the season, they stole such moments to be together in the open air. They left Casper just after sun-up.

Although the state highway was faster, they drove the more scenic "lower road" to Pathfinder Reservoir, past Alcova. The blacktop ambled through the rocky, dun-colored landscape pocked by scrub cedar and ruddy buttes that both absorbed and reflected the sweet morning light.

In the morning light, the magnificent landscape unfurled before them, horizon to horizon. The deceptive emptiness contained a kind of beauty that was both alluring and vicious. Without so much as a stone being moved, the perfect design of this ancient landscape could be tranquil one morning, horrific the next.

The road rose slowly and curled through the highlands, skirting the edge of the Fremont Canyon until it crossed the narrow but deep gorge on an old, sixty-foot-long steel bridge.

As the Strassers' Ford rumbled over the bridge a little after eight o'clock, they saw a flicker of color at the other end, a scrap of bright crimson out of place in this severe landscape.

And it was moving.

A brown-haired girl lay in the dirt at the end of the bridge, waving her arms. Her bright red pullover was torn and dirty, but she was nude from the waist down. Carl Strasser hit his brakes, leapt from the car and ran to her. The girl was pale, dirty, cold, exhausted and bloody. He could see the traces where she'd dragged herself across the gravel from the edge of the canyon.

It was near freezing. Dorothy retrieved an old blanket from the trunk and covered her, but she needed more help than a little warmth. Her face was caked with dried blood. Her left eye was swollen shut, the side of her head engorged and purple. White strips of fat and blood congealed around a ghastly gash on her left hip. The lower half of her body was badly flayed, and her dust- and blood-spattered legs didn't work at all.

"My God, what happened to you?" Carl asked, astonished.

"I was raped and thrown off the bridge and my little sister, too. She's down there someplace and I think she's dead. And I'm sorry for . . ." the girl covered her exposed genitals with dirty hands. Carl took off his Pendleton jacket and tied the arms around the girl's waist, to cover her nakedness.

"Can you walk?" he asked. She couldn't.

The Strassers lifted her into the back seat of their car and turned the heater up full blast.

"Are you sure," Carl asked her, "your sister is down there someplace?"

The girl said she was, so Carl ran to the bridge railing and leaned way out, looking down. He didn't want to waste time looking for a body that might not be there, but he didn't want to leave the young girl if she needed help, too. He saw nothing.

Back in the car, he sped toward Sloane's store, a one-room roadside market about ten miles back down the road, where weekend fishermen usually filled their trucks with beer, bait and gas.

On the way, shivering and crying, the girl asked for water and drank some hot coffee, which the Strassers always carried on their fishing outings. She told them more of the story, details about the abduction, the rape and plunge from the bridge. Down there in the dark canyon and the frigid water, she'd called out to Amy, but got no answers. As she crawled up the sheer rock face, she remembered seeing a splash of blood on a rock near the water. She feared it was Amy's.

"I'm not worried about me anymore," she said. "Just Amy and my poor mother."

Not knowing who this Amy was and in shock herself, Dorothy tried to comfort the girl, but couldn't find the words. She was a mother, too. From the front seat, she caressed the young girl's tangled brown hair and tried to keep her warm.

At the store, Carl ran inside to call the sheriff's office while Dorothy tended to the injured girl in the Ford.

About twenty minutes later, the ambulance arrived, just behind Sheriff Bill Estes. The sheriff himself quickly questioned the girl—her name was Becky Thomson—to confirm if she was one of the two girls reported missing the night before. While paramedics prepared her for the thirty-mile ride back to town, she repeated her story. Then Becky turned angry. She burned to get the men who killed Amy, she told the sheriff, and it was all she'd thought about as she lay in the bottom of the canyon all night, protected from the cold only by her long brown hair and some sagebrush.

It was her only thought as she dragged her broken body, inch after inch, out of that evil place.

They'll pay for this, she thought, *those animals will pay . . . but only if I survive.*

Chapter 2

THE JOURNEY

A my's dead."

That's how the news came. My mother spoke it matter-of-factly as I came through the front door after high school football practice that night, just sort of let it fall as if a distant cousin's hamster had died, not Amy Burridge, the eleven-year-old girl who lived next door.

"Becky was with her," she added.

Becky Thomson was Amy's older half-sister. Just a couple grades ahead of me in school, she had graduated the previous May from the high school where I was a recently minted junior. Because she was older than me and the rest of the neighborhood boys, because she wore eye makeup and her chestnut-brown hair long, because she drove her own car and actually spoke to us, she'd long been the stuff of our innocent adolescent fantasies.

"What happened?"

"A couple guys picked them up from the store and took them out to some bridge and raped them and threw them off."

But I was a naïve kid, even at sixteen. I hadn't yet defined for myself the act of rape, much less murder. To be honest, I wasn't exactly clear on the concept of "rape," but I didn't want my mother to explain it to me. Sex of any kind was uncharted territory for me. After that day, it was different.

"What about Becky?" I asked. I'd seen her earlier that day, in her driveway, before school. She'd waved.

"She's hurt bad. She's in the hospital. But she knew the

guys or something, and I guess they arrested them today. That's all I heard."

The news had come to her, just as it had come to me, in lowered voices. Other parents at my little brother's junior high football game were talking about it in the bleachers. Undoubtedly, they huddled together with their meager assortment of facts, embellished them to suit their personal purposes, and fanned the grassfire of rumor. That's how news spread in a small town. In whispers.

It was the autumn of 1973. We were growing up in a close-knit neighborhood on the far southern edge of Casper, Wyoming, a modest little cow-and-oil town on the brink of the Great Plains, unaware of what lurked in plain sight. I didn't know Death. I didn't know evil.

The war in Vietnam seethed for most of my childhood, but our wars were fought in dirt forts with plastic soldiers. War was a card game and a rock 'n' roll band. Boys a few years older than us, boys who had once attended our grade school, were fighting and dying in Vietnam, but sucking chest wounds and disembowelment-by-booby-trap were only discussed when children weren't around. Like sex.

Kennedy and King were assassinated, but we didn't really understand the abstractness of murder. Our PE teachers showed us movies about how to survive an atomic blast, advising us to wipe the radioactive dust off the lids of food cans and to drink water from old Clorox bottles.

But we thought we were invincible. None of us had died. We understood the theory but dismissed the reality. In that way, we were probably not much different from most small-town kids in the guiltless years before videogames, twenty-four-hour cable news, Columbine, the Internet, graphic prime-time violence, embedded war correspondents, gangsta rap and mass cynicism.

In the idealized hometown of my memory, a tall sissy bar and a long front fork on your Stingray bike was an emblem of rebellion. It made you look like a cool bad-ass biker when all you were was a small-town kid in a pair of muddy Chuck Taylors and white socks. We genuinely believed chugging

Coke and Pop Rocks would cause your bowels to explode. Some of us sneaked tie-dyed T-shirts to school, because our parents had forbidden them. And that was courting trouble.

Even in the world of fantasy, evil and murder were abstract, distant concepts. Movies like *Deliverance* and *The Exorcist* were just movies, not real, not reflections of fact. We had no concept of a world where crime and horror might be one and the same. That a man would rape another man seemed as unlikely as a child's head spinning on her neck like a haunted carousel.

The most trouble I ever heard about was when a kid sneaked out his bedroom window one summer night and was caught skinny-dipping in a public pool. He feared he'd get held back a grade, because to us, that was as cruel and unusual as the death penalty. To us, it *was* the death penalty because it was socially fatal to repeat a grade while your friends moved on.

In our innocence, the punishment tended to far exceed any crime we might commit. But when it was all said and done, the sentence carried out, that boy knew the feel of wind on a naked body. And he never forgot it.

But, of course, this was a place and time that doesn't really exist anymore. Now that I think about it, maybe it never did exist, except in my memory.

Oh, the houses I often rode past on my bicycle on summer nights are still there, but they no longer open their windows wide enough that passing boys can hear the life inside and smell suppers cooking. The old sandlot was long ago gouged up for new homes, but when I think of those nightfall games when our baseball became a moving piece of twilight, I still smell chlorine and dust on my skin.

The waves of settlers who passed through here believed, deep in the heart of their hearts, there was something beyond what they called "the Big Empty." On the other side waited remedy, Oregon, prosperity, a great ocean, escape, restoration, a place to set down roots, a new start, perhaps Heaven. Certainly, Death awaited some, but these were sanguine people. Death and hope were in conflict.

(Still today, one finds the oldest Western cemeteries on

hills, because they would be a little closer to Heaven. By the same token, it was common for outlaws, scoundrels, desperadoes, rustlers, ruffians, rogues, thugs and other scofflaws to be buried eight feet or deeper, a little closer to Hell than most.)

So the road doesn't always lead where we'd like to go. It's just a road, and it just goes. All roads are connected. No road begins and ends without crossing another. And there's no road someone hasn't traveled before me. But sometimes the roads get all tangled up.

But roads are also symbols. And some journeys take you farther from where you started, closer to where you come from.

When my twenty-year marriage fell apart, I literally hit the road in a new job as a wandering writer for *The Denver Post*. On an abandoned stretch of old Route 66 in a far corner of the Arizona desert, I met a woman who lived alone in a big house. She cherished a rusty old Model A Ford. As she told me stories about the car, her slack-jawed hired hand stood nearby. For the moment, he was her guardian and never spoke, but he clearly wasn't normal.

When it came time for me to go, she put her hand on his hulking shoulder and smiled.

"He has the mind of a five-year-old," she said, "but he's a good man."

The old car wasn't important to me anymore. Instead, for the next thousand miles, I pondered the significance of being a good man in a lonely place.

THE TOWN WHERE I grew up was a lonely place.

A one-train cow town in its early days, Casper's roots were barely deep enough to hold its place in the unremitting winds that swept down from the mountains. A mercantile, a bank, a small hotel and some liveries were sustained by a feeble local economy, built almost entirely on beef and mutton.

But its great riches were under the soil. Oil—the precious product of death, rot and time—existed in great lakes and ponds beneath the crust of the earth, and Casper was situated perfectly as a gateway between the undrilled crude and an oil-addicted world.

Because civilization is always attended by vice, other businesses thrived, too. Boomtowns are just worse. Taverns sprouted along Casper's main street, then some whore-houses out back. Casper was nobody's destination in those days, but for libidinous cowboys and sheepherders who'd grown as hot as a two-dollar pistol out in the bleak, lonely badlands, it was an oasis.

For a long time, women were allowed to walk only on the east side of Center Street, the main avenue through town. That's because the west side of the street was literally lined with pool halls and saloons—at one time, nine taprooms were shoe-horned into a single block.

Casper's first murder was so unexpected that the body was laid out on a saloon's billiards table for two days while a hasty coroner's inquest was convened.

Besides bone-rattling winters, the area's only other fear-some natural feature was the North Platte River, which regu-larly flooded in spring. The town was settled on high ground above the riverbanks, but fear of the river remained strong. Not even the fertility of its banks could lure settlement, which would certainly be swept away next spring or maybe the spring after.

By 1909, the federal government had finished Pathfinder Dam, fifty miles upstream from Casper, harnessing the North Platte's furious spring floods. The dam itself spanned a deep granite chasm known as Fremont Canyon—named, like Pathfinder Reservoir and its dam, for the legendary explorer John C. Fremont. The dam shunted its water through Fre-mont Canyon, whose vertical red walls rise as high as five hundred feet from the surface of the narrow river in some places. Carved over millennia, the seven-mile canyon is deep and astoundingly narrow, like a colossal prehistoric grave.

But even the inflexible granite of a modern dam couldn't quell the town's apprehensions overnight. The riverine low-lands became a dumping ground for both humans and trash.

A few squalid, tar-paper sheds known as "pest shacks" were erected on the river bank a safe distance from town—if not the river—for unlucky citizens with communicable diseases.

Then in 1914, Casper's first great oil boom swept in like a great wind, transforming the economy and the landscape just as World War One exploded in Europe—and another, bigger boom was close behind.

Two oil refineries were built and were soon processing a total 55,000 barrels of oil a day, much of it shipped to American allies fighting on Europe's Western Front. A second railroad laid tracks along the northern edge of the town, between its blooming downtown and the all-but-vacant river bottoms.

But that was just the beginning. In 1917, as America teetered on the brink of joining the Great War, a huge new oilfield virtually hemorrhaged just east of Casper. Millions of dollars' worth of oil was literally spurting from nearly every hole drilled in the vast field. Suddenly, the place was awash in hard-working dreamers—and assorted boomtown rats. Hookers, gamblers, bootleggers, grifters and other colorful parasites surfed the human wave of oilfield roughnecks, refinery workers, carpenters, teamsters, speculators, railroaders and boilermen.

And they all needed places to sleep and play. One speculator quickly snatched up twenty-six acres of the river bottom known as the Sandbar for one dollar and platted 257 lots where only a shanty-town of tents and cheap pest-shacks then stood.

Farther downriver, across the railroad tracks from the town, more bottomland was being settled. Burlington Railroad workers who had been living in vacant boxcars quickly moved into thirty hastily built company houses in what they called "North Casper," where more than 190 houses were built in fewer than six months.

But the river's ghost still haunted Casper.

The Sandbar and North Casper were quickly settled, but not by people who could afford better land on the proper side of the tracks. From the very start, they were districts for the desperate, the marginal, the itinerant, and the poor who hoped for but likely wouldn't see riches in their lifetimes.

Where many of America's ghettoes and slums would devolve from grander days, North Casper would start mean and stay mean.

And just off the northernmost end of Center Street, as close to the river as anyone dared to get in those days, a tiny four-room house was built for a railroader's family. When they moved away during the inevitable bust after the Great War, they sold it to a Prohibition-era bootlegger who hid a still in a crawlspace beneath the wooden floor of the front room and hung a strand of barbed wire along the top of his fence, for security from revenuers and thieves.

In 1935, in the darkest days of the Depression when booze was legal but nobody could afford it, the bootlegger quit his still. He rented out his little house for twenty dollars a month to a small-town mechanic who was moving his new wife to the big city and dreaming of a better life they'd never find. The ill wind that was blowing through their young lives at that moment hadn't yet intensified into the tempest that would eventually lay waste to a whole family.

I REMEMBER THE wind.

Wherever the wind begins and wherever it goes, Casper is just one of those unlucky places along the way, where the anarchic wind rushes by like a freight train passing a bum.

Casper's wind is incessant. It plays the bass line in the soundtrack of local life: low, constant, moving noise always thrumming in the background.

Wind is a natural consequence of meteorological push-and-pull. It is not caused by the turning of the Earth, nor does it grace every spot on the globe equally. Casper takes a perverse pride in its "Chinook" wind, an atmospheric affliction (which includes the occasional June snow and January heat wave). The locals joke it takes years before a native goes somewhere else and learns to walk upright. The Chamber of Commerce has been absurdly jealous in asserting Casper is windier than anyplace else in the Lower Forty-eight, including the so-called Windy City, Chicago.

Chinook is an old Indian word for "snow-eater." The thawing wind rushes out of the southwest, sometimes up to a hundred miles an hour, usually in winter, melting snow and sapping moisture from the soil. Old-timers say the rushing wind is so fraught with positive ions, it can electrify wire fences, electrocuting cattle who brush up against them.

Casper's chinook is a "witch's wind." In fact, back in the Seventies, some university researcher postulated that Casper's unrelenting wind contributed to the town's high per-capita suicide rate. Tiny electric particles in the air—negative and positive ions—were capable of arousing a community-wide feeling of well-being on calm days . . . or, if the positively charged wind were blowing, totally inexplicable fits of anxiety, depression, physical illness and bottomless despair.

Wind has almost never been shaped by man, but it has helped shape men and their places.

The steel veins of railroads carried essential nutrients to build the American West: wood, food, supplies and more settlers. Towns tended to be planted beside the rails, and then spread outward. Eventually, those rails divided the more prosperous half of town from the poorer half, "the wrong side of the tracks."

What made one side of the tracks "wrong"?

Wind.

Etymologists surmise that sometime in the nineteenth century's Western railroad expansion, the phrase referred to that side of the tracks which, because of prevailing winds, usually received most of the locomotives' black, sooty smoke. The town's more genteel, fashionable citizens would not willingly choose to breathe such pollution, nor to have it soil their clothing, so would build their homes upwind of the tracks.

But poorer folks would willingly trade a little stink for cheap land. Along with the scrofulous denizens of the "wrong side" came the saloons, gaming houses, bagnios, and loose women who would be tolerated only if they congregated away from the society folk.

Wind helped rails become boundaries of privilege in my hometown, too.

North Casper was a neighborhood literally on the "wrong" side of the tracks from the tree-lined streets on the south side where swells settled after the turn of the last century. The prevailing winds from the south and the west would have embraced all the airborne garbage of the growing town—the smoke, soot, dust and odors—and blasted it through the narrow, often unpaved streets of North Casper before exiting to wherever wind goes.

And in Casper, anything not weighted down by prosperity drifted up on the other side of the railroad tracks, whether it was smoke or families. Or children.

But Casper's wind was a great equalizer, even if it helped carve the social landscape. No man, woman or child on either side of the tracks escaped it. The bridges across those tracks were few, but they existed. Hard work was one. Crime was another. And Death, which erased most social boundaries in my town. In our cemeteries, the dead were mixed. The limits that existed above-ground could not be taken below.

So to grow up in Casper was to grow up windblown. It was to know the sound of loose windows clattering against their frames, to lift the hem of your coat over your head to make a sail that would glide you home from school, to always carry a pocket comb, to dig a tunnel from your front door through two-story drifts, to laugh at dogs who howled when they heard the wind whistle in chimney flues, to grow up with more grit than most in the dead end of your gut, to hear your outlander grandfather say, while visiting on vacation, "goddamn fucking wind."

TWO MEN, TWO girls, one night, and nothing is the same. We all changed.

On the last leg of a long flight home from the Middle East, where I'd been dispatched to report in the first weeks of the 2001 Afghan War, I couldn't sleep. I don't know why, but I can't sleep on planes. A little bleary, I thumbed through a European news magazine, but I felt as if I were staring a thousand yards beyond its pages. Then one photograph jerked me back into the moment: Two people falling from the World Trade Center on Sept. 11, barely two months before. They were holding hands.

I wondered who they were as I watched them fall. I wondered what they were feeling as they plunged toward oblivion. I wondered if they even knew each other. Or if holding hands made it easier to die.

I closed my eyes, but my mind continued to unreel that grotesque movie. I imagined my own plane exploding. I felt myself plummeting through the dark sky of my imagination toward the Atlantic below, and how at that height, I'd never know the exact moment I'd hit the water.

And right there, at forty thousand feet and almost thirty years later, Becky and Amy fell through my reverie, too. How odd that they would appear. How odd it seemed to me that this particular memory survived so long.

Although I tried, I couldn't remember many details of the crime, just the skeletal facts, which I couldn't seem to forget. Their abductors' ruse, the bridge, Becky's desperate climb out of the canyon . . . like everyone else, I knew what I *thought* I knew, but nothing was clear anymore. Everything had changed, and time had scattered its lies throughout my memory.

By the time I landed in New York, I wanted to know what really happened that night in 1973, to piece it together. I wanted to understand why this one event haunted me, even thirty years later. I needed desperately to see the pictures, to read the reports, to hear Becky speak again.

I had to make a passage of the heart, knowing full-well that some journeys take you farther from where you started, closer to where you come from. Maybe I wouldn't find what I was looking for.

But I knew small towns have long memories. I had to go home again.

I had to tell the story.

OFFENSE REPORT

NARRATIVE: Sometime after 9:00pm Sept. 24,
1973 Becky Thompson and her sister Amy left
their home at 2150 Glendale. Becky was
driving her Ford station wagon. The two girls
went to the Thrift Way Store located at 12th
and Melrose. The girls went into the store
and when they returned to the Ford they found
the right rear tire flat. They then called
home and advised their mother that they would
use some of the grocery money to have the
tire repaired. When they went back to the
Ford they were offered help by the two above
suspects. The suspects started to make
motions of jacking the car up. Then one
suspect produced a knife and advised the
girls to get into their car. They were then
driven to the Casper Mountain Road. The
suspects then drove the girls to the area of
Fremont Canyon near Pathfinder. At the point
where the bridge crosses Fremont Canyon the
suspects stopped the car. One of the suspects
then took Amy out of the car and Becky was
held on the floor of the back seat. The
suspect then returned to the car with-out
Amy. Becky was then taken out of the car and
raped by each suspect. After being raped
Becky was then taken onto the bridge and
thrown over the side.

INVESTIGATING OFFICER(S) Dovala DATE 9-25-73

Chapter 3

THE DAY

September 24, 1973

Chera Jenkins was her daddy's girl. She was only a year old, but when her daddy started moving around in the morning, she scrambled out of bed to find him.

A little after 7:00 a.m. on this late-September Monday morning, Daddy stirred. Jerry Jenkins was getting ready for work at the gas station where he'd been employed for a few weeks. Chera toddled into her parents' cramped, under-furnished bedroom and hugged one of her father's squat, flabby legs.

Her mother, Darci, was up, too. Today was the day Chera's infant sister, born only one month before, was coming home from the hospital. She'd come down with encephalitis and, after hovering briefly near death, the baby was being released after more than a week in the intensive-care nursery.

Chera had naturally enjoyed her father's undivided attention while her sister was in the hospital. Just a couple weeks before, Jerry had brought a tiny black toy-poodle puppy home and told Chera it was hers. Together, they fed the puppy cookies and hotdogs under the table, and that's all the dog ever ate when Chera and her daddy were doing the feeding.

While Chera and Jerry waited for Darci to fix some cereal—Darci was eighteen, and still a teenager herself, she wasn't inclined to fix big breakfasts on workdays—they ate cookies and some candy. Whatever Chera ate, Jerry ate.

But Jerry's gray station wagon had a flat he'd never gotten around to fixing, and since he needed to get to work, he borrowed Darci's white Impala, his gift to her when her sister was born. It had really been his car, but he signed the title over to her. Fact is, he didn't have anything else to give her, and no money to buy a proper gift.

While he slurped his cereal milk, Jerry casually mentioned he was having some trouble at work. He just wasn't happy there, he told Darci.

She'd been with Jerry long enough to know what that meant. He was quitting, if he hadn't already. He'd promised he'd find a job and stick with it, but this was the old Jerry now, the Jerry who never kept a job long, who hated to be told what to do, who always wanted to be having fun instead of putting food on the table. He was twenty-nine, lazy and irresponsible.

Besides, he knew other ways to make money.

"Jerry, you promised," Darci snapped. "You said you'd stick it out. I should have known you wouldn't."

Jerry didn't want to fight. He scooped up Chera and rolled around with her on the floor as she giggled in delight.

"Look," he said, "I gotta go to work. I'll come back around one, and we'll go get the baby."

"You can't take off work. You should have fixed your car."

"Yeah, I can," he said. "I want to take off. I'll fix it later. But I'll just come and get you at one and we'll pick up the baby, okay?"

Jerry left, and Darci spent the rest of the morning getting the apartment ready for the baby's homecoming. She fed Chera some lunch and dressed to see her baby daughter.

But 1:00 p.m. came and went.

No Jerry.

Another hour passed. No Jerry. And no call.

At 2:00 p.m., she called the gas station where her husband worked. Jerry never came to work that day, the boss said. In fact, he hadn't been to work in several days.

"So is Jerry quitting or what?" he asked. "I haven't fired him yet, but I can't keep a guy who won't come in."

Darci was fuming. She promised to talk to Jerry, but she really didn't give a shit. Even though she'd grown up here, she was done with Casper, with the life she was living. With Jerry.

It just wasn't what she'd expected. A blunt redhead who had a penchant for boyfriends her parents didn't like, Darci was a rebellious high schooler when she met Jerry in 1971. He was twenty-six and she was sixteen. She knew he was wild and liked to party, but she didn't learn until too late just how wild he'd been.

When she got pregnant her senior year in high school, her parents flipped. They threatened statutory rape charges against Jerry, and he left the state for a while. When she was five months along, Darci was gently asked to leave school. It was a matter of policy, they said.

The baby, Chera, was born in June 1972. A month later, Jerry sent a message to Darci that he wanted to see his baby. Fearing he'd stalk her forever if she didn't, they met secretly. Two weeks later, they were back together, and two months after that, they sneaked away to a small town nearby and got married without her parents' approval.

They moved around a lot in that first year but finally settled in a cheap apartment in an industrial section of town. Across the street was a welding shop that spewed sparks and the smoky-metallic odor of electric fusion well into the night.

Darci supported the family, for the most part. She worked as a nurse's aide, a waitress, any job a teenage girl might be able to do, mostly at minimum wage. Jerry took jobs as a grease monkey, but they never lasted long. Instead, he'd stay home and watch soap operas on television, and when she got home at night, he'd spill out all the deliciously tangled plot lines like a fishwife in a beauty salon.

They had few friends, but among them was a Pentecostal couple who often dropped in to see Jerry while Darci was working. Their visits grew frequent and purposeful: Twice a week, they'd come and study the Bible with Jerry, intent on saving his soul from inevitable damnation. Darci called them the "door-knockers," but Jerry was filling with the Spirit. After some convincing, she and Jerry were baptized at a local church. And when the "door-knockers" were sent to South America as missionaries, Jerry began to dream about a life as a traveling evangelist in a foreign land—if Darci would do it with him. But his passion for preaching, like everything else, soon passed.

Darci briefly saw her marriage as a new kind of freedom, a ticket to the "white-picket-fence life"—maybe on a farm with lots of kids and animals—that she always imagined living. Jerry was usually out of work, but he treated her well. He was a stay-at-home dad before the term became fashionable, and he liked it. Until he started hanging around with Ron Kennedy, he came home by 10:00 p.m. every night, even if he was drinking with his friends. He hardly made any money at all, but they got by. He never lifted a hand against her, and they were good in bed together.

But now, one year and another child later, she had decided to leave him for good. She planned to move to Colorado, where her parents had recently relocated. She'd leave that night, as soon as Jerry got home with the only working car they owned.

She only grew more determined when a friend visited later and told her he'd seen Jerry and his no-good punk friend Ron Kennedy drinking and playing pool around the time Jerry was supposed to be home to get his baby girl out of the hospital. Darci called the shabby, tough bar on the edge of town, but they said Jerry wasn't there. She called a few more places. No Jerry.

Things were bad between her and Jerry's family, and she didn't want to call asking for their help. So her friend drove her to the hospital to fetch the baby. Back at home, she laid the baby in the bed and started packing.

AFTER SCHOOL THAT day, Amy Burridge walked home with her best friend, Danny Nemitz. Danny damn sure wasn't her boyfriend, because she'd never truly transitioned from tomboy to a feminine little girl. Danny lived across the street in their intimate little neighborhood on the edge of town.

Plus, they were in the same sixth-grade class. And Amy was always just more comfortable with boys than girls, more at home outside than in, more alive at recess than in the classroom. She'd come home from her first day of kindergarten exasperated. When her mom asked what she'd learned on her first day of school, Amy replied: "I learned one thing for sure. You can't teach 'em a thing."

One time, she emerged from her dentist's office fuming.

"That son of a bitch," is all she said as she stormed through the waiting room. The dentist soon followed with bloody knuckles.

But even if Amy showed a rough face to the world, she had a core of softer stuff.

Her mother once found an outgoing letter in the mailbox on her porch. It was addressed, in Amy's familiar boy-like scrawl, to the Baptist summer camp she'd recently attended. It wasn't stamped, so Toni opened it to see what it said.

"I'm sorry I broke a plate at your camp," Amy wrote to whomever would open it. "I'll pay for it."

Amy would rather ride a dirt bike than play with a doll. When the other neighborhood girls were playing house and dress-up, Amy was in the sandlot with the neighborhood boys. She was wiry, small and eager, but in the game of work-ups—where a batter earns his right to hit—her enthusiasm wasn't enough. She usually spent most of every game in the outfield, an expanse of snake grass, prairie-dog holes and alkali muck.

But Amy owned the outfield. The bigger boys, some three or four years older, prowled the infield. The pug-nosed and pugnacious Tommy Browning liked to pitch as much as he liked to brawl with his twin brother Billy, but everyone—Rick, Danny, Mike, Steve, Bimbo, Brad, Lance, me, and anyone else who wandered through—yearned to bat. The farther we hit into the mythic waste-land we called a ball field, the better. Some fences were automatic outs because the homeowners hated kids, and only one of us ever hit a ball over the house at the far end of the field Amy patrolled. The rest must be snatched from the mud bogs and wild shrubs that dotted "the yard," and that was Amy's job.

Once, while they were both shagging fly balls, Amy couldn't miss—and Danny dropped a few. Danny's older brother Rick hollered from home plate, "You gonna let a girl beat you?"

"She's not a girl," Danny shouted back. "She's Amy."

That September Monday, Danny and Amy tossed a foot-ball and talked together until the sun had gone down, then they sat on the lawn, already going yellow for autumn. They hated going inside. They never wanted any day to end, espe-cially if they could be outside.

Amy's older half-sister, Becky, came out of the house with her car keys a little before nine p.m.

"Mom wants me to get some stuff at the store," Becky said. "Why don't you come along?"

Amy got up and turned to Danny.

"You wanna go? We can get some candy."

Danny ran to ask his mom, who looked at the clock. Nine p.m. on a school night. No, it was time to come in for the night. Some other time, she said. Not tonight.

Danny pouted. Amy and Becky had pulled up at the curb in front of his house, waiting.

"Can't go," he said, purposely letting the storm door slam behind him. "But I'll see you tomorrow."

Amy shrugged and waved, and Becky smiled.

Then they drove away.

Tomorrow, everything would be different.

JERRY JENKINS LEFT his apartment that morning and went straight over to his buddy Ron Kennedy's place in north Casper. He needed a favor and knew Kennedy would help. Kennedy didn't have a job, lived with his wife at his mother's house, and he wanted to spend as much time on the street as possible to avoid work or chores.

Jenkins had skipped work for a few days, but it was payday. He wanted Kennedy to go down to the station, feed the boss some bullshit that he was sick or something, and pick up his check. Kennedy agreed and they took off, on the prowl for a good beer buzz and any other distraction that might cross their paths.

After some pool and beer at the club, Jenkins hid out at a local truck-stop café while Kennedy lied for him.

Kennedy delivered Jerry's paycheck, and some bad news. While he was at the gas station, Darci had called the boss. Jenkins knew he was in deep shit, but he didn't care. Instead of calling his wife or going home, Jenkins drove Kennedy around for the next five or six hours, cruising for girls, bullshitting each other, and stopping at local bars buying beer by the case and drinking it as fast as they could before going back for more. At one point, after sharing a case of Schlitz beer, Jenkins decided he didn't like Schlitz, so they switched to buying cases of Coors.

Around 9:00 p.m., the nicotine-addicted Jenkins crumpled his empty pack of cigarettes. He needed more. Plus, he was hungry.

Up ahead was a convenience store, just in front of a bigger grocery store. Perfect for a chain-smoking food junky who'd been drinking and driving all day. Plus, he still had a little of the paycheck he'd cashed that afternoon. He'd worry about feeding his family tomorrow.

Jenkins pulled off the street and parked at almost the same time as a white station wagon. A tall, dark-haired girl and a little pigtailed kid got out. The older girl was beautiful, slender and young—but old enough.

"Oooh baby, look at that!" Kennedy said. "I'd like to meet her."

"Why don't you just go up and talk to her?" Jenkins asked, more interested in cigs and doughnuts than the girls for the moment.

"Nah," Kennedy said. "I've got a better idea. Switch me places."

ALMOST NINE-THIRTY, Amy was on the phone.

"We had a flat and two nice men are gonna give us a ride home," the little girl said from the convenience-store pay phone.

"OK, be careful and hurry," her mother, Toni Case, told her. "I'll wait up."

Toni was already in her pajamas, and although she was unsettled by her daughters' unexpected delay, she now knew they were safe. They should have been home in less than thirty minutes, and the girls were already late when Amy called. The store wasn't more than a mile away, and Toni hadn't needed much that night, just some little things. The cupboards were understocked because they'd just come home from Mexico, where they'd visited Toni's husband Jack, the girls' stepfather, who was working on a drilling project there. The next day was a Tuesday, a school day, and Amy was up past her bedtime.

Calmer now, Toni settled in and watched some television. Almost forty-five minutes passed, but the girls didn't come home. She started worrying again.

Toni took off her pajamas and hurriedly put on some jeans, then drove to the convenience store. She went slowly, taking the back streets, thinking she might come across them walking. It was dark, hardly any moon, but maybe, she thought, just maybe the ride never materialized. Maybe they had to walk. Maybe they were taking it slow, freighted with a bag of groceries. Maybe they had stopped along the way to rest or to play or . . . or anything.

As she pulled into the store's parking lot, she saw Becky's car still parked there. Its rear passenger tire was flat, but the girls were nowhere to be seen. She opened the unlocked door and looked inside, but there was no bag of groceries, and no girls. The parking lot was otherwise empty, the store closed.

Toni drove up and down the streets between the store and their home on Glendale Avenue, peering into the shadows, slowing for every fleeting shred of movement she caught in the corner of her eye. For almost two hours, she hunted in vain for her daughters.

A little past twelve-thirty in the morning, she abandoned her search and called the police. A dispatcher took the report and alerted the two or three Monday-night cruisers to watch for the two girls, but no investigator came on watch until eight in the morning. It was, after all, a small town that didn't need many cops on the street in the wee hours.

Toni's fear and dread mounted. Since Jack was still in Mexico, she called a friend to spend the night.

She slept only fitfully that night, listening for the sound of a car in the driveway, or the front door opening.

But all she heard was the wind.

THE WIND SWEPT down from the high places above the canyon.

The girls didn't know where they were, but when one of their abductors, the vicious guy who called himself Kenny, opened the car door, the wind rushed in and swirled over them in the backseat. They had been forced to lie down and shut up for the past two or three hours as the two men drove them around aimlessly, beating and terrorizing them.

The girls asked more than once what was going to happen. Were they going to be killed? The two guys only laughed at them, or slapped them, or told them to shut up.

The girls were scared. As they drove, the guys told them they were going to meet a man who would decide what to do with them.

They crossed a bridge and stopped. Pushed down on the

seat, they couldn't see much, but in the reflected glow of headlights, they saw a roof. *The man must live here,* one of them thought, *and we'll ask him to be merciful. And maybe this nightmare will go away.*

The skinny guy with the crazy eyes, Kenny, got out of the passenger-side door and pulled the seat forward. He reached for the little girl, the young one.

"You first," he said. "You can't go in together."

The girls both begged him to take them together to see "the man."

"Oh, please let me go in first and talk to these men," the older girl said.

Kenny's freakish eyes were empty and black.

"No. I want the little one first," he said.

DRIVING HOME FROM Rawlins that night, Don Chapin took the state highway that served as the back door to Casper, crossing nothing but badlands through only semi-inhabited places like Muddy Gap and Lamont, where only a few stubborn loners lived. A Casper lawyer who specialized in the lucrative, unmessy transfer of land and other civil—in the most literal sense of the word—legal matters, Chapin had been in Rawlins on business. He was eager to get home, so he left after the late meeting and drove back to Casper after sunset.

As his car hummed down the lonely blacktop, through seemingly endless square miles of prairie and badlands, he cursed the encroaching night. His headlights lit only as much highway as he needed to keep moving. He could see no moon.

It was the darkest night he could recall in a long time, he thought, but maybe it's just because he was so far from the lights of settlement.

Civilization was bright, comforting even after dark. Out here in the middle of nowhere, the night was menacing.

JERRY HAD BROKEN several unspoken rules of Darci's, and

she didn't even try to rationalize for him. Saving their marriage was the last thing on her mind. Getting far away from Jerry and this town was first.

She wasn't mad. She was crazy mad.

And rather than wait for the Impala, she decided she'd make a clean getaway. Maybe leave a note on the table, or scrawl "fuck you" in lipstick on the dirty bathroom mirror, or maybe not say anything at all. But she wasn't going to wait for her slothful slob of a husband to pour himself in and try to beg her to give him another chance. He'd had plenty.

She visited some friends in the next apartment and asked them to help her fix the station wagon's flat tire. While they changed the tire, she started throwing everything she owned in cardboard boxes and shopping bags, then loading them into the back of their spindly car.

After dark, she had second thoughts. It wasn't her style to sneak away from a conflict. She decided she'd hang around until he got home, to look him in the eye and tell him he was history—and maybe take his once-prized white Impala with her, too.

So she waited.

The hours passed. She couldn't sit still. When the girls went to bed, she went to see the neighbors who'd helped her fix the old gray car, sipping coffee with them and venting about Jerry, about life and every other thing that had rotted out from under her so soon in her young existence. The neighbor lady stayed up with her that night, making more coffee every time the pot ran dry.

Sometime after 2:00 a.m., Darci went back to the apartment. Jerry was already there. She erupted like a storm that has been building for a whole season. And the storm lasted for hours.

Jerry just sat there on the ratty couch, his head in his hands. He said nothing. A good thing, since it would only have made the storm more inclement.

When she had said what she wanted to say, she asked for the keys to the Impala. He refused.

"I don't want you to leave tonight," he said.

Darci laughed at him. She didn't want to stay, and he couldn't make her.

"I never asked nothing of you before and this will be the last time I ever ask anything of you again," he said, on the verge of tears. "You can leave or whatever you want in the morning, but I need you to stay here tonight."

He was begging her. The night was almost over. The sun would rise soon. But he was begging her to stay. In previous fights, he always defended himself against her tempestuous outbursts, but tonight was different. He was strangely spent, sad and unprotected.

But Darci thundered anew as she secretly cursed her decision to confront him.

"Why? So we could just scream and fight more?" she yelled at him. "And besides, what difference would it make if I left now or a few hours from now? Just give me the fucking car keys!"

"I don't care if you scream all night," he said, without raising his voice, "just stay. I need you here. I'll give you the keys in the morning."

Enraged and defeated, Darci couldn't control herself any longer. She snatched a glass ashtray from the coffee table and flung it at him. It glanced off the table and shattered in a spray of glass shards. She was ready to fire another volley when she noticed blood streaming down Jerry's face.

In all their passionate fights, it had never gone this far. Darci waited for her husband—a sometime stranger she now knew to be a veteran criminal—to cut her to pieces.

But he didn't. Jerry just got up from the couch and went to the bathroom. Darci waited for him to say something, anything, but he didn't speak.

Ashamed and frightened, she went to help him. It wasn't a deep wound, but a piece of glass had sliced his temple. Blood had splattered on the white porcelain sink and the floor. She helped him staunch the bleeding, then wiped up the bloodstains.

"Are you mad?" she asked, half-afraid of his answer.

"No," he said. "Will you please stay 'til morning?"

Darci nodded.

Just before dawn, after a night of storms and blood, they undressed and went to bed. They didn't have sex, as was their habit after most fights, but many years later, Darci would recall that Jerry held her painfully tight for the rest of the night.

THE SUN FINALLY came up, but that night would never end.

Four lives had converged on a cold, steel bridge over a deep, secluded gorge in the middle of a black September night.

All four died that night.

But three of them didn't know it.

Before the Earth had made a single rotation around the sun, everything had changed.

The ripples sent forth by the plunge of two bodies into the slow, dark river would echo in the heart of an entire community for more than thirty years.

And a handful of people directly splashed by the crime's incongruous sadism and heroism would never be the same. Some wished they could go back to a different time and place. Some wished it hadn't happened, and others wished for swift vengeance. Because Amy and Becky lived next door to me and played among us, I wished I hadn't learned so young how close evil could come.

But wishing is like talking to the wind.

Chapter 4

AFTER

Investigator Dave Dovala still hadn't shaken the chill of an autumn morning in Wyoming when he arrived back at Natrona County Memorial Hospital.

He parked his unmarked blue station wagon in a police space behind the hospital.

Even the rush of artificially warmed air past the hospital's glass doors, freighted as it was with the barren tang of antiseptics and floating fragments of infinite affliction, prickled on his skin.

He held the door for Becky's mother, Toni. He'd been sent to bring her to the hospital, to meet the ambulance when it arrived. She knew what he knew: Becky was found out near the bridge. She's in shock and badly injured. They don't know where Amy is, but they're looking.

Nothing about this work, this case, comforted him. But he was a cop and he wanted answers more than comfort. He made some mental notes about the interview, in case Becky could speak. *Breathe,* he thought. *Evidence, not emotion.*

Dovala was thirty-five, a father of two teen-agers. He wanted to surrender to the emotion, but after twelve years as a cop, he fought it.

He'd grown up a blue-collar kid in Parma, Ohio, a sprawling Cleveland suburb. His father was a mill worker there, his mother a secretary in a doctor's office. After graduating from high school, he'd gone to work for Ohio Bell, married, was laid off and fled west to Wyoming, where his

family had often visited on summer vacations. He took a refinery job, but was laid off there, too. Not yet twenty-three,
with a wife and two small kids, he needed work.

There was a patrol job at the Casper Police Department,
so he applied and got it. Over the next eight years, he took
night classes, earned a criminal justice degree, and was pro-
moted to investigator in 1972. He'd been a street cop for
eleven years, and he was still settling into the less adrenalized routine of his days. He'd liked the beat, and some days,
he missed the rush of a hot call.

When he arrived at the squad room that Tuesday morning, Dovala was assigned the missing-persons case from the
night before because no detectives had been working when it
first came in. He and a uniformed cop went to Toni Case's
home a little after 8:00 a.m., gathering information about the
two girls' home life, to rule out runaways. He checked their
rooms and found some money on the dressers. Nothing
seemed to be missing.

He had joined the team of cops canvassing the area
around the store when a back-channel call came on his
walkie-talkie to phone the police department, a bad sign.
When a dispatcher didn't want information to go out on public airways monitored by civilians with police scanners,
she'd typically ask field officers to call on a secure land-line.

Over the phone, Dovala was told Becky had been found
alive, but her sister was presumed dead. He was ordered to
meet Chief Investigator Bill Claxton at the hospital, but the
ambulance hadn't yet arrived when he got there, so he was
dispatched to break the bittersweet news to Becky and
Amy's mother and bring her to the hospital.

Even good news gave way to foreboding. Yeah, Becky
Thomson was alive in the back of an ambulance speeding
toward him now, but what about Amy? Where was she? Was
Becky conscious? Could she tell them who did it, or anything? Why was she found out by the lake, no, near a remote
canyon beyond the lake, thirty miles from town?

He watched Toni prowl the emergency room. The blood
in her veins impelled her to fight or flee, but she could do

neither. Dovala had long ago learned to sit back on the adrenaline buzz, to counter the imbalance of such frozen moments with weightless patience. His armor was his badge, which acted like some magical shield against this shit, but Toni stood stark naked in a storm of it. A small-town house-wife with four daughters, a good woman who never imag-ined she'd get a call from Amy after bedtime on a school night . . . *we had a flat and some boys are going to help us and we'll be home real soon* . . . and never hear her voice again. But she was imagining it now.

For Toni, the questions—or maybe the answers—sliced through her softer tissue like a razor.

Dovala needed hot coffee to think. He didn't like the taste these questions left in his mouth. *Some boys* haunted him. This wasn't a couple little girls staying out all night on a lark. Not these girls. *Some boys* . . . He was certain it was abduction, maybe rape. But by whom?

And, goddammit, where's Amy?

While Toni paced, Dovala dropped some coins into the waiting room's droning hot-drink machine and leaned against it while the little paper cup filled with coffee-like sludge. It tasted like hot chocolate and chicken soup. Good enough for a cop, he thought. Nothing good comes easy, and nothing easy comes good.

The ambulance arrived at 9:40 a.m. They hadn't been waiting more than twenty minutes.

Paramedics wheeled Becky through the manual double-doors on a gurney, gliding across the polished tile floor to-ward a private examination room prepared for her. Toni slid up beside her and held Becky's mud-streaked hand tightly.

Becky was awake and frightened, but safe.

Dovala knew the ambulance guys, like he knew all the firefighters in this small prairie town, and they knew him. But they were distracted, busy, and said nothing.

While doctors examined Becky, Detective Dick Fields and Lieutenant Claxton jotted down a few questions that would determine if a crime had been committed and, if so, by whom.

They didn't intend to wait much longer.

A nurse led them down the sterile hallway past a few empty beds and silent silver equipment to a tiny room where a doctor and a nurse were helping Becky get comfortable after X-rays. They'd cleaned her up a little, but her hands were still caked with blood and mud. Her face was swollen and bruised, her left eye the color and shape of an overripe plum. Her good eye was tired and empty, her hair a tangled nest. She had scrapes and bruises on her arms and neck, and she held her hospital blanket close, as if it might protect her from any further harm.

The injuries they could see were nothing compared to the hidden wounds.

Claxton clicked on his cassette recorder. Despite her injuries—doctors would later learn her pelvis had been broken in five places—Becky was calm, hurting but determined. And she never cried, except when Amy's name came up.

She told how she and Amy had gone to the Thriftway, a small neighborhood market, to buy some groceries for their mother a little after 9:00 p.m. It was dark when they left, and they parked in the weak light near the store's front door.

Fifteen minutes later, they got in Becky's Ford station wagon and backed up a few feet, but Becky soon realized her right rear tire was flat.

It angered her, she said, because she'd just gotten it fixed a couple days before. To avoid damaging the rim, she pulled back into her parking spot beside two guys in a white car who'd seen her predicament.

She stood beside her car, cussing the tire and her luck.

"Do you need any help?" the driver asked. He was fat, with greasy blond hair, and wore a denim jacket. She thought his name might be Jerry.

"Well, yeah, sure," she said.

"Do you have a spare tire?"

"Well, yes, but it's also flat."

"We'll help you anyway," one of them said.

Jerry and his passenger, a lanky, wild-eyed beanpole who

called himself Kenny, rummaged in Jerry's trunk for a jack. They jacked up her car a few inches, then stopped.

When she described her assailants, Fields and Claxton exchanged a knowing glance. Just from her spare description—a tall, bug-eyed guy named Kenny or maybe Ronnie (she'd heard Jerry say that name, too), and a short, greasy, fat guy named Jerry—they knew exactly who they were looking for. Ronald Leroy Kennedy and Jerry Lee Jenkins were small-time hoods, joined at the hip, probably because neither fit anyone else's idea of a good buddy, even among other outlaws. Every cop knew them and didn't much care for them.

"We're going to go to another station and see if they can fix your tire real fast," she recalled they told her.

"That'd be really great," Becky said.

"Okay, we'll leave our jack with you. You just sit here and make sure it doesn't get stolen or anything."

"Okay, that's fine."

Becky told Amy to dash over to a nearby convenience store to call their mother, to tell her they had a flat but "some nice men were going to help us and we'd be right home."

The two guys left, but they were back within five minutes, even before Amy returned from the convenience store. They wanted Becky to go with them to the station.

"Just a minute," she said. "I've got to go get my little sister."

Amy had dawdled after the phone call, buying some candy. Becky hurried her, and together they went back to her car.

The Kenny guy with the crazy eyes sidled up beside Becky and stuck a knife against her ribs.

"Get in the car," he said. His breath was boozy, stale.

Startled, Becky glanced around, praying someone was close enough to see what was happening, to save her and her sister. But the light was dim and aloof. Even if a shopper had come out of the store, nobody lingered in the fall air.

It wasn't a good night for angels.

When Toni Case finally was allowed to visit her daughter,

doctors and nurses were still working, and police were peppering her with questions. She only wanted to hold Becky close forever, but she couldn't get close enough. She began to think she might never again get close enough.

Becky turned to her mother, broken in spirit as much as body.

"Mama, I don't think Amy's coming back," she said, almost apologizing as she wept. "I knew I had to make it so I could tell you what happened."

While she comforted Becky, a doctor removed a contact that had been trapped in her swollen left eye. She didn't know it then, but that contact—or rather its missing mate—would soon link Becky to her assailants in an undeniable way.

LITTLE DOUBT EXISTED about whom the cops would be hunting: Ron Kennedy and Jerry Jenkins. But for good measure, Investigators Dave Dovala and Bill Claxton arranged a photo lineup for Becky. She picked out Kennedy and Jenkins without hesitation.

The cops knew these guys all too well.

Jenkins was in and out of jail. Oily and fat, he looked more harmless than he was. He always chatted amiably with the cops who rousted him on the street or picked him up for his many lapses. He'd graduated from drunken delinquent to sneak thief with a few prison stretches, but a few years before, he'd been busted for his part in a gang-rape. Charges were dropped when the victim refused to testify against him.

Kennedy was a skinny, pop-eyed kid, a little younger than Jenkins, but no less shifty and dangerous. He'd done prison time, too, and he remained one of only a few good suspects in the bludgeoning murder and robbery of an all-night gas-station clerk, Ed Peckham, the year before. He'd known the sixty-six-year-old Peckham and regularly stopped at the station after midnight just to talk. Based on the location of the body and other evidence, investigators were certain Ed Peckham knew his killer.

A little before noon, Dovala himself staked out Kennedy's

house—or rather his mother's house, where Kennedy was living at the time. When Dovala heard on the police radio that both Kennedy and Jenkins had been spotted together in Kennedy's old green pickup on the nearby interstate, Dovala broke off his surveillance to join the hunt, but before he went very far, the pursuers had lost Kennedy's truck.

Dovala was about to return to his stake-out when, to his surprise, he saw Kennedy's truck going down the street away from him. But Kennedy was alone. If Jenkins had been with him, he'd gotten out of the truck sometime in the past couple minutes. The veteran cop swung his unmarked car around and followed Kennedy for a few blocks, desperately trying to break through a logjam of radio traffic to call for back-up. But he couldn't get through.

Luck doesn't wait for back-up. After several blocks, Kennedy stopped at a stoplight on the town's main street, ironically in front of the county courthouse. A few pedestrians crossed at the light, right in front of his truck.

Dovala leapt from his car and lit out down the center of the main street to Kennedy's open window, drawing his Smith & Wesson nine-shot, semi-auto, nine-millimeter handgun as he ran. In a single, instinctual move, he swept open the punk's driver-side door and dragged Kennedy out onto the asphalt of Center Street. The engine was still running.

Spread-eagled across the fender of his truck, Dovala arrested Ronald Leroy Kennedy, who was swiftly hustled by other surprised cops into the police department barely thirty paces from where he was busted.

Years later, Dovala reflected on the dramatic arrest at high noon on the main street, almost literally on the courthouse steps—and the personal tumult that would follow for many people.

"If I could have seen years ahead," Dovala would say thirty years later, "I probably would have shot him."

FRED KLEIN'S CARDINAL rule for his search divers, his inviolable demand, was "never go alone." But when he arrived at the remote Fremont Canyon Bridge late that Tuesday morning, none of his team had yet arrived. And nobody—including Fred—wanted to wait another minute to search for Amy in the cold, murky dark water under the bridge.

He had been puttering around his mountaintop cabin when Sheriff Estes phoned through dispatch. The sheriff's voice was urgent, shaken.

"Fred, you ain't gonna like this one," Estes said, skipping the usual pleasantries.

"What you got?"

"There's a little girl down in the water off the Fremont Canyon Bridge. You gotta get out here. Fast."

Klein, a former ambulance driver, didn't ask any more questions and certainly didn't wait for answers. He hung up and ran out the door. His diving gear was already stowed in his Blazer, so he peeled off on a dirt back road, down the windblown backside of Casper Mountain, hurtling south and west toward Fremont Canyon.

He'd only dived into the canyon's deep, sluggish water once before, earlier that same summer, searching below the Pathfinder Dam for the corpse of a suicide. But there was no body. The guy was found a few weeks later, alive and reasonably happy, shacked up with a girlfriend back East.

Forty minutes after the sheriff's call, Klein rolled onto the cold steel bridge, where the sheriff, his deputies, some paramedics and a few gawkers milled around, helpless to do anything but wait. He hated the crowds that inevitably gathered at death scenes like hungry flies. Where did they come from? Did horror have an odor that drew them like fat flies to a rotting carcass?

But none of his divers, all volunteers who worked day jobs in town, had arrived.

Parking his rig off the far end of the bridge, Klein quickly stripped off his street clothes and squeezed into his wet suit, keeping an eye on the blacktop for any of his team as the sheriff briefed him.

He knew he was looking for a little girl named Amy, possibly raped and thrown off the bridge by her abductors.

Maybe she floated downstream, maybe not, but the search for her corpse had to start someplace.

Klein also knew the North Platte here was as slow as it was deep, as cloudy as it was cold. He was reluctant to break diving's unbreakable rule—*"never go alone"*—but Amy was down there because bigger rules had been broken. He was forty-six years old. He had already plucked eight corpses from various lakes and rivers in his time as a rescue diver, and he had a daughter about Amy's age.

He decided to go in alone.

The North Platte River under the bridge was deep, green and viscous. Only a few steps from the edge, it plunged thirty feet to a rocky bottom. It eddied and purled in vast pools as it snaked through the precipitous canyon, a ragged gash across the Wyoming prairie that choked to barely a hundred feet wide in some spots. In some places, the river curled like liquid smoke, swirling endlessly in place, defying natural laws and the irresistible tug of distant oceans.

In Wyoming's brief, almost ceremonial fall, when summer often surrenders unconditionally to winter in a matter of days, lakes such as Pathfinder Reservoir begin to "turn over." As the warmer surface water cools, it sinks, forcing the cooler bottom layer to well up thick with silt, algae and whatever other microscopic particles of the life-and-death cycle sink to the bottom. In late September, the water passing beneath the Fremont Canyon Bridge was almost opaque.

Klein was an experienced mountain climber, but he slid several times as they lowered him by a tether down a steep vertical gutter laced with loose rocks and gravel. Two deputies waited for him below on the shore—little more than a slender ledge of half-submerged rock—and when he arrived safely, his oxygen tanks, regulator and buoyancy control device were lowered on another rope.

The deputies lifted his double tanks and steadied him on the stony shelf in his awkward flippers as he adjusted his straps. Again, he looked up the sheer walls of the canyon toward the staging area. No other divers had arrived, but it was too late anyway. No waiting now.

Fuck the rules.

The air was warm for late September, mid-fifties, but the water was numbing. His bare hands were chilled, and even a wet suit couldn't keep the cold from trickling in at first.

Directly beneath the bridge, deputies guarded a bloody splash on the rocks, the spot where Amy had likely crashed before slipping beneath the water. Searchers had already found a pair of black panties on the secluded road just above and two bright pink hair bows floating in the water near shore.

Klein squatted on a flat boulder and cleared his mask before pushing out into the deeper water.

Barely two body lengths from shore, he pitched down about thirty feet. Even in the middle of the day, the water grew darker and colder as he went down, and he heard only his own breathing and the escaping bubbles of his breath.

He could barely see his own hands as they explored the smooth stone river-wall, seeking any place to grab, pulling him forward and downward into the colder, darker water.

Then he saw it, a ghostly white artifact settled on the bottom, otherworldly in the primeval brown-green soup. It was a white tennis shoe. A little girl's size.

He'd been in the water less than a minute.

Klein picked up the shoe and held it close to his mask. Dropped in a yawning pool away from the current, it had settled to the bottom almost exactly below the lip of the bridge one hundred and twenty feet above. If it had come off Amy's foot when she hit the water, then she, too, might have sunk nearby. She'd been in the cold water less than fifteen hours, not enough time for the decomposition gases to float her toward the surface and away from the splash site. And without a current to sweep her away, her lifeless body—he hoped desperately she had not been conscious—had quickly descended to the bottom.

He was right.

A few feet farther, he found Amy hovering on the bottom; face down, limbs floating rigidly and awkwardly from her torso. He saw her feet first. She was fully clothed in jeans and a tee-shirt, except for one shoeless foot.

Klein touched her. Rigor mortis had stiffened her and the cold river congealed her blood and muscles. Buoyed by the water, her wrecked body had no more weight, no more pain. *Like a little angel*, he thought.

He carefully knotted a nylon rope around her torso, just under her unfolded arms, then tugged it to signal the men on shore to pull her up.

Klein surfaced near shore, guiding Amy's body to the surface. As he kneeled on a smooth rock at water's edge, the deputies rushed into the water up to their knees. Gently, he handed over her stiff little body, still nearly weightless even though she was no longer submerged.

"Anything else down there?" one of the deputies asked as they wrapped Amy in a brown wool blanket.

"A shoe," Klein said.

"Get it."

Klein went back into the murky river and retrieved the shoe. By the time he emerged again and took off his flippers, Amy's body was laid out on the rocky shore for a police photographer. Her dark, wet hair covered her face, and blood that seeped from her mouth and nose made it look like a gory veil that hid her eyes. A silver ring hung on a slender leather shoelace around her neck. Her skin was blanched watercolor-white, and her tender young hands had crumpled into a washerwoman's.

Later in the day, hospital X-rays would reveal that the left side of her rib cage was crushed. Her spine had literally been driven like a deadly spike deep into her brain.

In a few minutes, they covered her with a blue tarp and hauled her up the precipice in a yellow raft, protecting her already-broken body from any more damage on the steep slope.

Up on top, Estes thanked Klein for his work, but Klein wasn't in any mood.

"Never call me again," he growled to the sheriff, then cursed Amy's killers and went home.

He got drunk that night and tried to put it all out of his mind. In the next few days, as word of Amy's murder and

Becky's miraculous survival seeped deeper under the small town's skin, some folks would call and ask for gory details, but he gently put them off. Somebody even called to ask if he'd contribute to the suspected killers' bail fund. Bailing them out, the caller explained, would make them an easier target for vigilantes and was safer than storming the jail-house.

Older and tired of spending more than ninety-nine percent of his life awaiting brief, adrenalized moments of barely controlled panic, Klein left the search and rescue team soon after he found Amy. She was the last victim he ever found.

And never, not once, did he ever dream of her or the dive. He preferred to keep this memory in his waking hours, out in the light.

POLICE OFFICERS ROD Jacques and Dave Cashel escorted Ron Kennedy to Police Chief Robert Zipay's cramped office in the courthouse basement, a couple dozen steps from the holding cell where he'd been cooling his heels since his arrest less than one hour before.

The chief's secretary occupied a tiny anteroom, barely twenty inches wider than her desk. As if it weren't already cramped enough, her space functioned as a waiting room and storage area for office supplies. The ancient wooden phone booth in the outer hall, outfitted with a wooden seat and sliding glass doors, was roomier.

The chief's office, all desk and dark paneling, was slightly bigger, but not much. Already crowded inside were Zipay, Lieutenant Bill Claxton, who supervised investigations, County Attorney Jack Burk and his chief deputy, Dave Lewis.

Lesser criminals surrounded by six cops and prosecutors in a dark, confined space might have been shaken, but Kennedy was cool. Only twenty-seven, he'd been a law-breaker longer than any of these guys had been cops or lawyers. He knew the drill better than they did.

Claxton asked the patrolmen to unlock Kennedy's handcuffs and then invited the lanky, cocky kid to sit down as he read him his Miranda rights. Kennedy listened and acknowledged he understood his rights completely.

"What's the charge?" Kennedy chirped.

"Murder, rape, assault and kidnapping," Claxton said, skipping the grisly details.

"How are you gonna prove it?" Kennedy asked. "You've got no witnesses."

Claxton stood in front of Kennedy and looked him in the eye.

"Well, we have a surprise for you, Mister Son-of-a-bitch," he said. "One of them is still alive."

KENNEDY WAS BUSTED, but the hunt for Jenkins continued.

His car had been spotted in North Casper but, peculiarly, it was driven by Kennedy's wife, who was delivering it to Jenkins' apartment. At one point, when she realized she was being followed, she pulled to the curb and confronted the cops.

But Jerry Jenkins simply couldn't stay lost. He was spotted on foot, headed to a neighborhood liquor store—ironically, one he'd burglarized just a few years before with Ron Kennedy. The two cops, City Patrolman Ohly Callies and Sheriff's Deputy Mike Johnson, pulled up in a city cruiser beside him and told him he was under arrest.

Jenkins stood dumbfounded.

"What's going on?" he asked the two cops.

With little explanation beyond the suspicion he was involved in a rape and murder, they read him his rights and cuffed him. Patting him down, Callies found a pocketknife in Jenkins' trousers, the same knife Kennedy had used to abduct and terrorize the two girls the night before.

THE SECRETARY AT the Casper Police Department always got up early.

Most mornings, she got out of bed, shook off her sleep and did some extremely light housework—domesticity was not her calling—maybe some laundry, whatever busywork could fill a couple hours before showering, dressing and doing her hair just right before starting her day as a secretary for all of Casper's police detectives in the downtown station. In her twenties and unmarried, her mornings were her own, and she savored them.

But today was already different.

Investigator Dave Dovala had called early and told her he had a missing-persons case, two girls, and it just didn't smell right. He wanted her in as soon as she could get there.

She skipped the domestic chores and showered quickly. She fixed her hair, slipped into a skirt, blouse and high heels, got into her red-and-white Cougar convertible and cranked up the radio. The drive from her apartment to the cop shop took only seven minutes.

She loved this town, not just for the shortness of her daily commute, but because she'd grown up here. She knew every square inch of Casper, and it comforted her to know something so well.

At that time the Casper Police Department was, to observers inside and out, a small-town outfit. Housed in the frigid, cramped, dimly-lighted courthouse basement, with dark tile and walls, cops joked that you needed a flashlight just to see if the lights were on.

At one end of the long, gloomy hall was the investigation division, the bullpen where three windows offered a sweeping vista of the courthouse's concrete window wells. The extraordinary panorama was framed by steel gratings intended to prevent suspects from escaping out the window.

Every piece of furniture was old and ugly, but functional. The metal desks were gray or brown, their matching metal chairs gray or brown, the cabinets, tables, shelves and faces . . . gray or brown. But not the floor nor the walls. Detectives spent their days on heinous orange-brown indoor/outdoor carpeting and, inexplicably, all the walls were painted yellow.

Typewriters clattered constantly. Unoiled chairs groaned. And the rustle of activity in the hall droned ceaselessly through the day, especially during the two-month period when Wyoming license plates were renewed and the line from the Motor Vehicle Office stretched down the hall, through the police department, up the stairs and out the door. Perps, cops, lawyers, impatient motorists, guns and evidence were thrown together for sixty days every year like feedlot cattle in a foul mood.

At one end of the room was a long table with several telephones on it. This was the "office" for five or six junior investigators. Their secretary was one of the chosen: She was given an ugly metal desk at one end of the long table, and her own phone.

Part of the investigators' wall enclosed a sewage pipe from the county jail three floors above. One night, a prisoner crammed his bed sheet in his toilet, flooding the investigation office with three inches of raw sewage.

Detectives dressed as they pleased, although their mufti never included jeans. The men generally wore leisure suits, and the secretary, who was treated like one of the boys, always preferred a dress or suit at work. She often thanked her lucky stars she wasn't in the records section, where the women always wore ensembles of polyester, royal blue uniforms with red or mustard-yellow turtlenecks, with a Casper Police Department patch sewn on the vest—all hand-made by one of the investigators' wives.

Only a thin wall separated the detectives' bullpen from the interrogation room, an afterthought space never designed to hold much of anything or anyone. It was filled by a dark gray metal table, maybe six feet long, in the center of the room, with four or five gray metal chairs squeezed around it. A single light hung overhead, with no windows. Two ventilation slits merely channeled the dead air from between the walls.

Today, Claxton had asked the secretary to take notes at an interrogation, which she often did, so she followed him to the interview room.

A little after 12:35 p.m., Jerry Lee Jenkins was brought into the interrogation room in handcuffs. He kept his head down. He'd been in police custody less than an hour, kept in a holding cell at the other end of the basement hall. The cell itself was fronted by a garage door, and prisoners who'd earned "trusty" status could raise the garage doors for the privilege of washing the cop cars on the other side.

AT TWENTY-NINE, JERRY Lee Jenkins already knew the criminal justice system better than any rookie cop.

Lumpy and dumb, he never found a good reason to go to school. He was a poor student and had a discipline problem. He didn't want to be there, and the school didn't want him there.

His real education began just before he dropped out of the tenth grade in 1960. He ran away from home four times when he was fifteen, always returned to his parents until the last time, when he was turned over to juvenile probation officers.

His father, Edgar Jenkins, was a tough-ass truck driver, an Army sergeant in World War Two—and a taskmaster who was too-often away from home. His lone transgression against the law had been a speeding ticket, and it chafed him for years. Edgar believed he'd licked a terrible drinking problem by limiting himself to only occasional cocktails. He worked hard to support his wife Dorothy and four kids (a fifth, Barbara Ann, had died at birth) and, when he came home from the road, he wanted no trouble.

But trouble abounded. The Jenkins family was a mess. Booze and fights were common. The father beat the mother and the kids ruthlessly. They moved frequently from one overcrowded hovel to another. The kids got into drugs and worse when they were still young, and none of the four of them ever warmed up to schooling.

Jerry didn't run from his family's turbulence. He embraced it. He thrived on the tumult and mayhem.

Once, fed up with Jerry's delinquency, Edgar drove his

eldest son to the Casper city limits, handed him a ten-dollar bill and told him to get lost.

But Jerry, ever the bad penny, came back.

Over the next two years, when other kids his age were going to proms and studying algebra, Jerry was studying for the only career he'd ever have: crime. Other kids went to the soda shop together; Jenkins fell in with local hoodlums, stole cars, stayed drunk and lived a life beyond the petty limits imposed by his father, his town or the law.

His jobs were usually menial and brief: Busboy, dishwasher, grease-monkey, fruit-picker in the Pacific Northwest, janitor, ditch-digger and dirt-hauler. The only thing Jerry Jenkins did regularly was break the law—and almost as regularly, he was caught.

But his real talent was for drinking and carousing. More than once, his brother Roy had watched him—and sometimes accompanied him—as Jerry stayed up three straight aimless nights, oozing from basement parties to after-hours bars to sweaty catnaps in strange beds. And while he debauched, the opportunistic—and usually drunk—crook always kept one eye out for easy marks and cheap thrills at someone else's expense.

Jenkins was arrested nine times before he turned eighteen—public drunkenness, careless driving, vagrancy and hit-and-run. He served two stretches at the Wyoming Boys' School, a reformatory for juvenile offenders in Worland, Wyoming.

At eighteen, Jenkins wheedled a parole from his last stint at the Boys' School by telling the board of pardons he wanted to join the U.S. Army. He passed the test, his mother vouched for him, and the Army recruiting sergeant in Casper was officially notified he'd soon meet future Private Jerry Lee Jenkins. But as soon as the reformatory turned him loose, Jenkins went AWOL before he was even inducted. Crime, not the military, was his bag.

Two months later, he was busted for auto burglary after a cop caught him sucking gasoline out of a car's fuel tank. He was arrested and arraigned before Justice of the Peace Alice

Burridge—whose new granddaughter, Amy, had recently been middle-named "Allice" in her honor. This time, Jenkins was sent to the Wyoming State in Rawlins for thirteen months, but after an abortive escape attempt, he finished out almost two years in solitary confinement, "The Hole."

Less than two months after he walked out of prison, Jenkins was popped again. After his 1965 conviction for check-forgery, a probation officer assessed the twenty-two-year-old Jenkins' future as dim.

"He has demonstrated in the past that he will not respond to supervision," Jenkins' pre-sentence investigation said, "and will probably continue this path of doing a life sentence on the installment plan."

Jenkins was paroled a little more than a year later. Even though he'd finally earned his high school diploma while behind bars, he quickly fell back into his old habits with old friends, namely another hood named James Kennedy.

On a hot summer night in 1968, Jim Kennedy and Jerry Jenkins got drunk and cajoled a nineteen-year-old divorcee into their car, supposedly to get a soda at a local diner. Instead, they drove her to a deserted road west of town, parked beside a deep irrigation canal, and raped her. They later dumped the woman, alive, behind an apartment building in town and threatened to kill her if she told the cops what happened. But she did, and they were quickly arrested.

Jim Kennedy's trial was first, and despite the victim's ferocious cross-examination by defense lawyers, he was convicted of first-degree rape. But before Jenkins' trial could start, the raped woman decided she had suffered enough in courtrooms. She refused to testify further. Jerry Jenkins walked.

Jenkins might have thanked his lucky stars if he weren't already in trouble again.

Even before his rapist partner Jim Kennedy was sent to prison, Jenkins had been arrested in a bungled liquor store heist. Drunk but still thirsty, Jenkins smashed the front window of a liquor store and grabbed an armload of whiskey bottles. But in his drunken retreat, he stumbled on the curb, dropping the bottles and losing his glasses. An accomplice—Ron Kennedy—helped him snatch up the booty and they fled, but not far. Both were arrested the next morning.

Again, they faced Justice of the Peace Burridge in their initial court appearance. She was growing weary of seeing Jenkins in her court. "I guess you're just gonna have to kill somebody before we put you away for good," she chided him. Legendary for her creatively harsh application of the law and her quick tongue, she had no idea at the time how prophetic those words would be, four years later.

At trial, his own lawyer admitted Jenkins' long rap sheet was best attributed to "too little thinking and too much whiskey." Jenkins would serve almost two years for the boozy burglary, mostly because it was his third major felony conviction in six years.

His twenty-two-year-old buddy Ron Kennedy—the younger brother of Jenkins' rape cohort and his constant companion when he wasn't in jail—got off easier, because it was only his first adult arrest. He drew twelve-to-eighteen months in prison but served only nine.

Jenkins got out of prison, but prison never got out of Jerry Jenkins.

In his first free spring in a few years, Jenkins was popped again after a cop caught him stealing money from vending machines.

On the way to jail, Jenkins casually asked when he could expect to appear in court. The cop shrugged.

At his booking, Jenkins asked again, curious whether he might be able to see the judge sooner rather than later. Again, the cop demurred and suggested he talk to his lawyer. An hour later, as Jenkins was taken to his cell in the county jail, he asked if there were any chance his court appearance could be hurried.

"You know the drill, Jerry," his jailer said. "What's your big hurry?"

"Well, next Friday is softball try-outs at the Pen," Jenkins explained, "and I'd like to make the team."

＋＋＋

JENKINS STUNK OF cigarette smoke and nervous sweat.

His dishwater-blond hair was greasy, as if coiffed with lard. His posture would have made a first-grade teacher wince. He wore jeans and a puke-colored, short-sleeved shirt, with the sleeves rolled even higher like some street-corner pug he must have seen in a movie.

His paunch and old-fashioned horn-rimmed glasses— even though he was still quite young—might have made him look harmless in the world outside, but in here, looks didn't matter. He was a suspected rapist and child-killer.

Once the cuffs were removed, Jenkins was seated with his back to the worthless ventilation slits, with Lieutenant Bill Claxton at one end of the table, Deputy Ernie Johnson at the other. The secretary chose the chair farthest from Jenkins, across the table from him. Although a tape recorder sat in the center of the table in front of the suspect, she brought her notebook to take shorthand notes of the interview.

The secretary started scribbling his words in shorthand, a secretarial skill she picked up in teacher's college. She struggled to transform this fat, stinking asshole into a voice; a sound in the room that she could reduce to inky symbols on a page. She tried to keep her eyes on the pad in front of her, to hear the sound of the ballpoint skittering across the paper, to see the ranks of hieroglyphs march across the little lines. Her powers of concentration had always been impenetrable, but Jenkins repulsed her.

She knew she'd have to get it right, every word. This was a big case, she knew. Later, she'd have to transcribe her notes, to make Jenkins come alive and be a reality so everyone would know what he did.

Claxton read Jenkins his Miranda rights and asked him to sign a card acknowledging he'd been advised he could stay quiet, have a free lawyer if necessary, and that anything he said could become evidence against him. It was a necessary formality, of course, but Jenkins had been here before; he could warble Miranda like a show tune in his sleep.

After a few perfunctory questions to establish a foundation, Claxton wasted no time getting to the heart of the crime, and Jenkins wasted no time playing his con.

"Did Ronnie let the air out of the tire?" the detective asked.

"I didn't do it," Jenkins replied. "I didn't let the air out of the tire."

Claxton asked again.

"Did Ronnie let the air out of the tire?"

And Jenkins answered again, no less vaguely. "I didn't do it. We pulled up to the store and saw them come in the store behind there."

"The convenience store?"

"Yeah, Ronnie said he wanted to meet her. So I told him to just go up and talk to her if he wanted to meet her, but he said no, he had a better way."

A better way.

Jenkins pulled in behind Becky's car, he said, and Kennedy got out. He couldn't see what happened next, but he guessed Kennedy slashed the tire, because it flattened fast.

The two retreated to the shadows at the edge of the parking lot and waited for the two girls to come out of the store.

"Then what happened?" Claxton asked.

"They came out and we was going to help them fix the flat, only my wrench didn't work with her nuts," Jenkins explained. "The jack was up under the car and the car was jacked up and my wrench didn't fit. I put the jack back in the car."

Claxton pressed for more. Jenkins made no eye contact with anyone. As he spoke, his eyes darted around in empty spaces, and his hands swept the table pointlessly, as if they might uncover a good answer on its scarred top.

But he was composed, emotionless, stone-like.

"Well, the little one went and called her mother and said she had a flat tire. We said we would give them a ride home and everything started happening."

He didn't even know their names, Ash thought.

"What do you mean, 'everything started happening'?" Claxton continued.

"Ronnie became out of his gourd."

"Did Ronnie have the knife?"

"Yeah, it was in the glove box," Jenkins said. "He knew it was there 'cause I always kept it there."

Kennedy had unfolded the cheap pocketknife and, holding it against the older girl's ribs, forced the girls into the backseat of the two-door sedan.

"We started driving up the street, and just—boom," Jenkins said.

"Just boom?"

"Yeah, just boom. Everything went boom."

"Did Ronnie ever tell you the reason why he started hitting them in the car while you were still not very far from the grocery store?"

Jenkins shrugged and looked down at his sweaty palms.

"No, he didn't. But being with Ronnie a few years, I think back, in his own mind, I think he hated girls," Jenkins said. "I think that's because . . . he had no reason really as far as I know. He didn't know 'em and they didn't say nothing to upset him."

"Had you discussed this before the time you picked them up?" Claxton asked.

Jenkins answered abruptly, as if the randomness of the abduction were somehow more defensible than a premeditated conspiracy.

"No."

They headed toward Casper Mountain, a sparsely settled and mostly wild mountain that rose three thousand feet over the town, a hulking beacon for kids with a hankering for keg-beer and sex. Its switchbacks stitched a path to a few year-round cabins, campgrounds, a small ski area, and Crimson Dawn, where locals gathered at the summer solstice every year to hear witch stories.

On the trip, Kennedy leaned over the front seat to slap and slug the girls with his fist, but Jenkins was keeping an eye on his temperature gauge and fretting about his bald tires. His old Impala was overheating, so they abandoned the steady uphill climb and drove back to town.

"I figured we'd just drive around and maybe calm him down and talk to the girls and try to scare them real good, and if they were scared, maybe they would shut up," Jenkins said.

"Did they happen to tell you what their names were?"

"I think they told me, but I can't remember. We'd been drinking since four o'clock and were pretty well wasted."

Jenkins cruised through town while Kennedy continued to terrorize the girls, forcing them down on the back seat.

"Ronnie told ''em to lay down so they laid down on the seat and they stayed down until we got out of town. And the oldest one asked me if she could get up and I said 'Yes,' but that's when Ronnie said, 'No, just stay there.' So instead of getting him all riled, I just kept my mouth shut."

"Are you physically afraid of Ron Kennedy?" the investigator asked.

"No, it's not that. I just figured that if I got him riled up again that he might start in on the girls again. I figured that if I just kept quiet and talked to him that things would work out."

Jenkins told the investigators he asked his buddy Kennedy what he planned to do, but Kennedy didn't know, or didn't say. He suggested calming the girls down and recalled Kennedy saying, simply, "Okay."

"I started driving out towards Alcova, and just kept going, and we got there and Ronnie said he would talk to them one at a time."

Alcova, known locally simply as "The Lake," was some thirty miles southwest of town, and even less populated than Casper Mountain. It was actually one of four successive Depression-era reservoirs built to control the erratic flows of the unpredictable North Platte River as it raced from the eastern slopes of the Rocky Mountains toward an ocean most people in Wyoming had never seen. Two dirt roads meander around the edges of the lake toward the remote gash—and they cross at the Fremont Canyon Bridge, a dizzyingly high steel bridge across the gorge, one hundred twenty feet above the water.

At night, the blackness seeped like ink into every crevice of Wyoming's isolated corners. This night was no lighter. The moon was dark and old, a sliver two days away from new, but the sky was clear.

Jenkins crossed the bridge and steered the Impala onto a dirt road jutting toward nowhere at the far end. The beer buzz was beginning to wear off.

At that point, he told Claxton, they were only talking to the girls. He believed they were only trying to scare them into silence.

"We was sitting there giving them a line."

"What kind of line?"

"We were telling them a buddy of ours got hurt, and they were the ones that did it and they were gonna have to pay and all of this, and it was their fault and we wanted to talk to them and all this. Ronnie told the little one that he wanted to talk to her first."

"Did he just tell her to get out of the car?"

"Yeah. We was there about five minutes at the most and Ronnie opened the door and told the little girl to come on."

"What was the little girl's response to this? Was she afraid?"

"I think she was a little afraid, but her older sister told her everything would be all right, and I told her not to worry, nothing was going to happen."

Did he know he was lying? the secretary wondered. Or was it just in his blood to lie?

"Could you see him after they left the car?" Claxton asked.

"No, it was dark as midnight out there."

Kennedy wasn't gone long, a few minutes.

"During the time the younger girl was out of the car with Ronnie, didn't you hear her call for help?"

"No, I was talking to the other one in the car. . . . Anyway, he came back and the girl didn't come back with him. I asked him about it, and he said, 'She's over there thinking,' and then he told me . . . He told me that we didn't have to worry about her talking."

"What did you figure he meant?"

"I just figured what he meant."

"What did you figure happened to her?"

Jenkins said nothing.

Somebody knocked on the interrogation room's door. Claxton ignored it and asked another question, but the knocking was insistent.

Sitting nearest the door, the secretary heard somebody whispering to Claxton, and the lieutenant left. In a few minutes, he came back. His jaw was set and his face stern, empty.

Searchers had found Amy's body in the cold water under the bridge, he'd just been told.

And John Ackerman, the town's new public defender, was waiting outside in the cramped, crowded hallway, asking to see Jenkins.

"There's a lawyer outside, John Ackerman," Claxton told Jenkins. "Is he your attorney?"

Jenkins shook his head. "No."

"Do you want to talk to him?"

Jenkins shook his head again.

Claxton resumed his questioning. He bristled at the word "interrogation" and always preferred to call it an "interview."

Trying to get a clear picture of the crime scene, he asked Jenkins where the Impala was parked—and inadvertently snatched a key admission from Jenkins.

"Where were you at this time? On the bridge?"

"No, right on that little road."

"The road to the right or the road to the left?"

"To the right."

"Do you know where the rape took place?"

"That was on the left side of the road," Jenkins answered helpfully.

But just as quickly, perhaps realizing what he'd just said—what he'd just *admitted*—Jenkins retreated into Miranda.

"Did both you and Ron Kennedy have intercourse with the girl?" Claxton pressed.

"I'd rather not answer that."

"All right. Did Ron?"

"I'd still rather not answer that."

Claxton moved ahead to Becky's last moments with her two abductors.

"Did Ronnie then take the other girl out of the car or did you both take her out?"

"He got her out, and started walking towards the bridge," Jenkins recalled without emotion. "I got out of the car and followed them and we just pushed her over. It was just like a sack of potatoes."

Nobody said anything. Jenkins had just confessed to an attempted murder as if he were unloading groceries from his car.

"Okay now, were you aware of what was going to happen to the older girl when he started walking her toward the bridge? Did you have an idea what he was going to do?"

Jenkins shrugged.

"I think in the back of my mind, but I don't think I wanted to accept it," he said without emotion, but his mind and tongue were tripping in time and space, confusing his present and his future. "My mind at that time was fighting with itself. I didn't know what to do, which way to go. What I wanted to do when we first left there was turn onto the bridge and come on back to Casper, but then, I pulled a few years in the joint and I was scared of going back. It's not that I feared the joint. I just don't want to pull no more time."

The investigator tried a different tack.

"So then basically you didn't know when he was walking the eighteen-year-old onto the bridge that he had, in fact, thrown the little girl off?"

"No," Jenkins replied. "The only thing was I couldn't figure out where she was and I just figured maybe he had her down there and he might have done something to her. I didn't know until they told me what had happened when they picked me up."

"All right now, on your conversation when you were coming back to Casper, did he tell you what he had done to the little girl?"

"No," Jenkins replied. "The only thing was I asked Ronnie, I says, 'Well, what are we going to do?' and he said, 'Just keep our mouths shut,' and I told him I don't think I could do it and that was the only thing that was said about it 'cause I had my own thoughts."

Of all the things Jenkins had confessed, admitting that he was actually thinking at any moment, that he'd done *anything* independent of Kennedy, seemed the least credible to Ash.

Nobody asked Jenkins what he'd been thinking, but he continued.

"I was thinking what I was going to do and if I could live with it or not, and I didn't want to talk to him because I figured he might just tell me something that would get me upset and then there'd be more . . . I just figured I'd do my own thinking and more than likely turn myself in."

Jenkins described how they drove back to town, dumped Becky's purse and other evidence off another bridge, dropped Kennedy at his house, and got home sometime after 2:00 a.m. His wife wasn't home at the time, but when she arrived, they fought until after dawn.

The next morning, groggy and still a little drunk, Jenkins had another beer. He told Claxton he'd contemplated surrendering to the cops.

But while driving around, he saw Kennedy. Over coffee at a truck stop on the edge of town, he confessed to feeling guilty and wanted to spill his guts to police. Maybe they'd go easier on them if they came forward on their own.

But Kennedy blew up and told Jenkins "if I did, I'd never get out of the joint."

Claxton had a few more questions, and then wrapped it up. Jenkins had been in the interrogation room for about forty minutes.

"Will you be willing to talk to us at a later time?"

"Yes, I guess so," Jenkins replied. "How is the other one doing?"

He won't say her name, dammit, the secretary thought.

"She's going to be fine."

"Will you be seeing her?"

"Yes."

"Will you please tell her I'm sorry?"

"Okay, I will do that," Claxton said.

"If that little one is dead, I hope they reinstate the death penalty 'cause I don't think I could live with that. What really tore me up is when I got up this morning and saw my little girl. I think that if I knew what he was going to do, I would have tried to stop him, I don't know. It's hard for a man to say what he would do. You know, I've been a mess-up all my life, but I ain't never hurt nobody."

WITHIN HOURS OF Kennedy and Jenkins' arrests, word had spread through Casper the way wildfire creeps through the roots of a forest, quickly and invisibly.

The girls had been abducted Monday night after the morning newspaper had gone to bed and after the local TV station's evening news; nothing more was known about their disappearance—even to police—until Becky was found the next morning. Local reporters wouldn't get their first taste of the news until after noon on Tuesday, and for the rest of the day, sketchy radio broadcasts provided the only media coverage until the five o'clock news.

But Casper was a small town. The news unfolded in the ancient way: mouth to mouth. Everybody knew everybody, and if they didn't, they knew somebody who knew somebody else. Over back fences and on street corners, in grocery stores and schoolyards, on the phone and in whispers, the town thrummed like a vast party line.

No names had yet been named officially, but anonymity wasn't as precious in the underground scuttlebutt. Before the day was over—before the news confirmed any identities at all—almost everyone had already heard the names of both the girls and their assailants.

The rumor mill was in high gear, spinning out fabulously detailed variations of a story that was, at best, unclear to anyone. Terror, rape and murder were shocking enough, but they assumed monstrous proportions when spoken in the soft voice of gossip. Every hour that passed, the story mushroomed and warped and stewed in a small town's disbelief and, soon, its venom.

Tension grew palpable. The phones started ringing relentlessly at the sheriff's office and the police department. Investigators knew public sentiment might soon turn from sympathy to fury, and they wanted to say something publicly, if just to quell some rumors and fears.

County Attorney Jack Burk and Chief Investigator Bill Claxton gathered a few reporters in a cramped office at the police department and shared the essential details: Two girls were reported missing by their distraught mother the night before. One of them was found by fishermen that morning near Fremont Canyon Bridge, and the other was confirmed dead. At least one of them had been raped by two men before both were thrown off the remote, lofty bridge. And two men were in custody.

The suspects arrested only an hour before—a twenty-nine-year-old gas station attendant named Jerry Lee Jenkins and a twenty-seven-year-old unemployed hood named Ronald Leroy Kennedy—were to be arraigned later in the day, Claxton and Burk said.

As if news of a brutal abduction, rape and murder in a small town wasn't dreadful enough, nor their arrest comforting enough, prosecutor Burk added a significant tidbit. He'd heard Becky's horrific story only a couple hours before, and it ate at his guts. The law might be complex, but his choice was simple and unapologetic.

Kennedy and Jenkins, he assured reporters, would be the first suspects charged under Wyoming's new first-degree murder law, which was unambiguous when a cold-blooded murder was committed to conceal the killer's identity, to hide evidence or to cover up another crime. Death was the only choice the jury had, and Burk hoped the prospect of an execution would assuage the mounting rage.

Reporters got their first glimpse of the suspects that afternoon. Four hours after their arrests, Kennedy and Jenkins were taken into a small courtroom on the second floor of the Natrona County Courthouse. Both wore jail coveralls, unzipped halfway down their pale chests. Neither was shack-led. Jenkins wore boots, but Kennedy was barefoot and smoking a cigarette as they were led by public defender John Ackerman and jailer Slim Hollembaek through a gauntlet of reporters and gawkers in the hallway.

Although no significant media reports had yet circulated, except on radio, the courtroom and the outer hall were packed with spectators, many of them friends and relatives of the two accused killers. Before the hearing started, a woman pushed her way through the crowd and held out a pack of cigarettes to Kennedy, but they were intercepted by a bailiff, who exam-ined them before handing them to the skinny, bug-eyed punk.

The arraignment was brief, although the courtroom at-mosphere was electric. Justice of the Peace Robert McCrary set bonds of $250,000 for both men on the murder charges and heaped on another $25,000 in the rape charges. He scheduled their preliminary hearing in three weeks.

Kennedy and Jenkins were led out of the courtroom and back through the swarm of photographers and curious by-standers. Spotting a television camera in the crowd of on-lookers, Kennedy smiled and raised his middle finger, an insolent gesture of his contempt for them and their world and their morbid inquisitiveness. They wanted to see a bad-ass, and he obliged them.

Nearly every television in town was tuned into the dinner-hour news that night, and what viewers saw infuri-ated them: An accused kidnapper, rapist and killer, a piece of shit who'd throw an eleven-year-old girl off a twelve-story bridge after god-knows-what perversions he might have inflicted on her, a greasy and twisted beanpole with crazy eyes, smiling and giving the finger to the world.

DURING THE INVESTIGATION, several other women came forward with eerily similar stories about recent encounters with two men closely resembling Kennedy and Jenkins. In each case, the two approached strange women who were alone and vulnerable.

A high school sophomore told investigators she and a friend were walking home from school one day in early September when two men in a white two-door car pulled up beside them on the street. The skinny, dark-haired guy in the passenger seat asked if she and her friend knew a girl—he forgot the name—who went to their school. While they chatted, she saw beer cans in the back seat. After a few minutes they left.

Later, when shown pictures of Kennedy and Jenkins, the girls both positively identified them as the men who stopped and talked to them.

Around the same time, another woman was sitting in a city park when she was approached by two suspicious-looking men. They drove a white Impala with a temporary sticker in the rear window, and they were drinking beer from a quart bottle.

Whatever intuition she had about these two guys was aroused.

The dark-haired, taller one, wearing a red shirt, made small talk and asked her name.

"Buzz off," she said. "My name isn't any of your business."

"Well, I don't want to know your name anyway," he said and sat down near her. "My name is Ron."

"Buzz off," she snapped. "I don't want to know your name."

But he wouldn't leave. As she walked off, the skinny punk grabbed her arm.

"Buddy, if you don't let go and leave me alone, I'm just going to crack you a good one," she snapped at him.

He released her but made a proposition.

"Why don't you go with me and my friend Tom?"

"I don't know Tom from the man in the moon," she said sternly, "and I don't know you, and I don't want to go."

The guy got in the car and left, but they continued to circle the park until she left.

Again, when police showed her mug shots of Kennedy and Jenkins, she positively identified them as the masher and the Impala driver at the park.

Just a couple months before the incident at Fremont Canyon Bridge, a woman driving alone in the open countryside west of town had a frightening encounter of her own. An antiques dealer from the small mountain town of Ten Sleep, eighty miles northwest of Casper, she was on her way to a show in another small town, and she needed to pass through Casper on the way.

On the two-lane state blacktop west of Casper, she was stopped by road construction. A tubby man with black glasses and greasy hair, driving an old green pickup, pulled up on the shoulder beside her and offered to show her a detour around the construction. Running late and eager to bypass the bottleneck, she agreed and followed him down a dirt road into the open prairie and badlands, miles from any real settlement.

After a few miles in the wrong direction, she panicked. She stopped and turned around. Suddenly, the fat guy in the green truck was behind her again. She went faster, and before she reached the pavement again, he'd peeled off and disappeared in a cloud of dust in the other direction. She told a flagman what happened, and the kid promised to tell a highway patrolman if he saw one. No report was ever made.

Kennedy owned an old green pickup, and the woman's description of the driver matched Jenkins. Had Kennedy been out there in a remote, isolated dead-end, waiting to ambush an unsuspecting woman with Jenkins' help? If she had been killed, who would have known where she was? Had she narrowly avoided a shallow, undiscoverable grave in the vast emptiness of Wyoming?

More haunting to think about, had they already done it to anyone else? Who would know?

And the police never knew about some of the close calls with Kennedy and Jenkins.

Thirty years later, Ron Kennedy's former sister-in-law told how he had stalked her and her sister—his soon-to-be ex-wife. One night after dinner at a cheap café, the two women came out to find the rear tire on their car was flat. But before they could even open the trunk, Ron Kennedy unexpectedly pulled up behind them and offered to help. They refused and argued briefly before he sped off.

Later, a gas-station mechanic told them the tire was sliced by a knife.

Ron Kennedy, it seems, had stumbled upon a trick that would put him close to women he wanted.

AFTER SPENDING SOME time alone with Becky in her room, Toni stepped aside as an orderly wheeled Becky to X-ray. While waiting outside the X-ray room, another cop appeared down the fluorescent hallway, coming slowly toward her. *The news isn't good*, Toni knew from his slumping shoulders.

Amy had been found.

She was dead and her body was being prepared for the long trip to town.

Toni's knees buckled. She had been up all night. One daughter was raped and brutalized; the other was dead. She needed to go someplace, to be alone, to let this nightmare run its course. To wake up so everything could be all right.

There was nothing more she could do at the hospital, they told her, so she went home and tried to nap. Sleep didn't come, but later that afternoon, a policeman arrived. He'd been sent to take her back to the hospital for the one task no mother wants to do. She had to identify Amy's body in the hospital's morgue.

At the hospital, she was led into a small room in the basement, beyond secure doors that keep out the living world and keep in the antiseptic stink and the ghosts of the dead.

A coroner's assistant peeled back a sheet covering a small lump on one of the metal tables. Toni looked directly at the little corpse for a long, painful moment.

"Yes, that's my baby," was all she said.

Less than forty-eight hours after they were handcuffed, Kennedy and Jenkins were marked men.

Hate is impatient. The law is slow and complex; revenge is faster, simpler. Word was starting to circulate that a shadowy group of men was quickly gathering enough money to bail the two accused rapist-killers out of jail, just to get a clearer, safer shot at them.

Two nights after their arrest, somebody ignited a blanket against the front door at Jerry Jenkins' apartment in a dark, decaying part of town. His eighteen-year-old wife Darci and two young daughters were asleep inside.

The arsonist was never caught, but police immediately began protective surveillance at the homes of Kennedy's and Jenkins' other relatives. The community was seething with revenge, and the cops wanted only to keep a lid on the barely contained rage.

Nobody could get to the third-floor jail in the courthouse without a key to operate the elevator or unlock the double-doors at the top of the stairwell. Any attempt to break-out Kennedy and Jenkins, whether by friend or foe, would be far more dangerous and costly than old western movies portrayed.

But lynchings weren't only the stuff of cowboy movies. Less than ten years before, an angry mob tried to break into a jail in Jackson, Wyoming, to kill Andrew Pixley, a drifter who'd raped and slaughtered two young girls in a local hotel. Pixley escaped, only to be executed legally a few months later in the Wyoming gas chamber.

And in 1901, while cop-killer Charlie Woodard awaited his execution at dawn, vigilantes broke into the Casper jail, bound and gagged the jailer, then hanged Woodard a few hours before his formal appointment on the gallows. They left him dangling for all to see, a note pinned to his blouse: "Process of law is a little slow, so this is the road you have to go. Murderers and sinners beware! People's Verdict."

At least Charlie got a trial. Two earlier accused cattle rustlers, Ella Watson and Jim Averell, hadn't been so lucky.

Watson, known locally as Cattle Kate, and Averell were homesteading sweethearts who lived about forty miles southwest of Casper. Averell was a popular local rancher who might have been building his herd almost exclusively on "mavericks," or unbranded stray calves. Such business was considered rustling by the big operators.

Averell also ran a roadhouse and general store beside the old Oregon Trail, but the only passersby in the late 1880s were drifters, drovers and the occasional dreamer who'd merely gotten a late start. His neighbors in this isolated part of the territory urged him to import some feminine companions. One day, he literally bumped into Watson in town and persuaded the reputed "soiled dove" to relocate to his lonely badlands.

Once settled, some historians say Watson plied her trade for cowboys and neighbors, cooked meals at Averell's roadhouse and started building her own herd by enticing horny cowboys to put her brand on calves in return for certain female favors.

On the morning of July 20, 1889, six local ranchers had had enough of the rustling. They rode to Averell and Watson's homesteads with fake arrest warrants and dragged them into a hidden canyon near the Sweetwater River. There, they hanged Jim and Kate from a tree that still stands today.

Their corpses were eventually buried together on Averell's homestead, an unmarked gravesite now occasionally flooded by the backwaters of Pathfinder Reservoir. Although the lynchers were well known to almost everyone, and common folks were enraged at the killers' audacity, none was ever charged with a crime.[1]

Natrona County Sheriff Bill Estes wasn't going to wait for a mob to show up on his courthouse steps.

Shortly after midnight Wednesday, in the dark, cold hours before the sun came up, two sheriff's cruisers rolled out of the courthouse garage. Ronald Kennedy rode in the back seat of one; Jerry Jenkins in the other. And neither knew where they were going.

Although the Natrona County jail roster continued to list Kennedy and Jenkins among its inmates for the next couple weeks, they weren't there. Kennedy was safely hidden one hundred fifty miles west in the Fremont County jail in Lander, Wyoming, under the watchful gaze of Sheriff PeeWee McDougall; Jenkins was sent one hundred thirty miles away to cool his heels in the historic spa town of Thermopolis,

Wyoming, while authorities in Casper tried to quell the over-heated hostility that simmered openly back home.

ONLY A FEW hours after Amy's body was found in the river, her sixth-grade classmates gathered after school in the Fairdale Elementary gym for volleyball practice. They didn't know why she wasn't there, but they missed her. She was the sparkplug.

It was a small town, but word simply hadn't seeped among the children yet. Many parents knew about the crime, and a few even knew it was Amy and Becky who had some-how been caught up in a grotesque crime, maybe a rape, cer-tainly a murder.

And the Fairdale volleyball coach, a young teacher her-self, knew why Amy wasn't there, but she knew of no way to tell the children.

Amy had been absent all day, but when she didn't show up for volleyball practice, her teammates thought she was *really* sick.

"It's just not the same when Amy isn't here," one of the little girls complained.

The coach spoke softly, almost inaudibly.

"It'll never be the same again," she said.

A FEW DAYS later, after they learned the terrible news, Amy's mother asked her volleyball teammates to come to her house before the funeral, the last time they'd ever visit their little friend's home.

Toni Case sat on a kitchen chair in the middle of her liv-ing room, in the heart of her modest tri-level house at the end of Glendale Avenue, and the girls gathered around her on the carpeted floor.

They talked about sports, and how good Amy was at everything. How good she might have been if . . .

They talked about Amy's irrepressible zest for every-thing, her way of energizing the air, like lightning. She'd been game for anything, a bundle of electricity, color and vitality. She was fresh in spirit and personality, like a bucket of new rain. They shared little stories about her, the way little girls remember other little girls, in color and in times when life was warm and safe.

Maybe they didn't know it, but they also talked about her courage. But courage isn't courage for little girls, just the thing that makes them play with boys. And win. But they'd never played in the sandlots like Amy, nor mucked through stock ponds slithering with salamanders and water snakes, nor imagined and built earthen forts in the caliche with stolen shovels and scrap lumber, nor glided full-tilt into a right field dangerously land-mined with prairie-dog mounds and stubborn stumps of sage and veined with fissures carved by rains and run-off.

They talked about Amy's favorite things, like the way her hair bows always matched what she wore, and the colorful, hand-embroidered vest she was fondest of and wore to school almost every day. Or at least that's the way they recalled her.

Toni listened, and they cried together when it felt like the right thing to do. And Toni decided to bury Amy in her vest, with matching hair ribbons.

That's what Amy wore. Her casket was open to mourners, to the world, as she had been open to almost everything. But none of her little teammates would see her that way, at least in death.

Such were the times, when parents protected children as much as they could from the intrusion of death. Death was hidden from view, from the touch, not like the old days in these parts when a dead sister or mother or son might be laid out in the back bedroom until the time for burial. No need to frighten the children now. Funeral homes, hospitals and shiny hearses kept the sights, smells and feels of it safely distant. So distant, death might never be truly understood.

And so it was for Amy's teammates. The open casket would be as sickening and macabre as an open wound, their parents thought. None were allowed to say goodbye that way, not to see her, nor to touch her. All of them stayed home on that day. They were all too young yet.

Let them believe dying was simply a little oblivion, a brief moment of black that would be illuminated, eventually, by the fading of memory, the way a stick of kindling dissolves into bright light as it burns. From darkness, light. From something broken and dead, warmth.

The girls who helped choose Amy's funeral clothes didn't say goodbye that way. One doesn't mourn when switching off the lights, does she? She was electric, and electricity doesn't die, does it? The storm ends, but rain never stops, does it? A spark flies into the sky and disappears, but do we mourn the cold, black ember that falls when the light is gone?

Someday, as grown women, they would think about loss and death and forever. But back then, the little girls just didn't say goodbye. They didn't really know how long Amy would be gone.

OVER SEVERAL DAYS in December, Ronald Kennedy dispatched various jailers with messages for Natrona County Undersheriff Ray Clark, who ignored them.

Clark knew Kennedy "professionally." The long-limbed, long-suffering former state trooper had crossed paths with the veteran lawbreaker maybe a half dozen times in the past, mostly on lesser beefs. And Clark had a reputation among all the "guests" in his jail for being a stand-up guy.

Clark was raised in the microscopic eastern Wyoming farm town of Albin, a stone's throw from the Nebraska line. His father was a traveling debt-collector for the International Harvester Company during the Depression, dunning hard-up farmers who'd bought their implements directly from the factory and couldn't pay. When he was old enough, Clark enlisted in the U.S. Army Air Corps in World War II. Flying as a nineteen-year-old radioman in B-29 bombers raiding mainland Japan, he was shot down three times in 1944.

He came home from the war to Albin and started slowly going insane. The manic terror of battle, the emotional turbulence of life and death in a foreign place, and a new view of the world from above the clouds had jangled his rhythms. He simply couldn't survive the transition from the arousal of war into the flaccid bosom of a quiet, Southern Baptist town on the edge of nowhere, even if his roots were there.

Rather than settle down and farm the rest of his days, Clark took to the road, literally. A friend told him the Wyoming Highway Patrol was expanding its ranks, so Clark applied and got a job. A few weeks later, he was surprised to be assigned as a "training officer" to a handful of slightly greener recruits, including a newly married former grain hauler named Bill Estes.

Clark, at this point, was fifty years old. Whether war had chastened him or he'd already seen everything a crook had to offer, he'd become a phlegmatic cop. Just back from a training stint at the FBI Academy in Quantico, he was easy-going and laconic, not given to boasting, and dry of wit, in the mold of mythic western lawmen who might never have really existed except in Gary Cooper movies.

When he felt he could no longer shirk Ronald Kennedy's increasingly desperate requests for a meeting, Clark ambled over to the jail to visit him on a Thursday afternoon before Christmas.

Kennedy was animated, smiling as if they'd been friends for years.

"I need your help," he told Clark.

"To do what?"

"To get my bond reduced," Kennedy said. "I know this town and if I can make bail, I'll find out what sick mother-fucker really did this."

Clark contemplated Kennedy's seemingly heartfelt appeal. He'd never heard the guy sound so genuine.

"Not a bad idea," he responded. "Me and Judge Daniels are pretty close. I could ask him for some special consideration. Sure, I'll help. But it's gonna take some time. It might be next Tuesday before we hear anything. There's lots of talking and paperwork, you understand, but if you're patient, I think we can do it."

Kennedy smiled broadly and nodded. Time was no problem. He seemed pleasantly surprised he'd get a shot at freedom.

"And I gotta get down to the paper and take out an ad, and that takes time, too," Clark continued.

Kennedy's smile wilted into a confused grin.

"An ad?"

Clark nodded.

"Sure," he said. "I gotta put an ad in the paper before we do it."

"Why?"

Clark clapped the accused killer on the shoulder, old buddy that he was.

"Hell, Ron, I got a whole lot of people out there who want to know exactly when you walk out of this jail," Clark said. "And I wanna get some good odds on just exactly how long you'll last out there on the street."

As far as Ronald Kennedy was concerned, that wasn't a friendly joke at all.

"LORD, MAKE ME to know mine end, and the measure of my days . . ."

Amy Allice Anthea Burridge was eleven years old. The measure of her days was reduced to the hyphen between those dates on her gravestone in Casper's Highland Cemetery.

Eleven years, ten months, one week and most of one day. Four thousand three hundred and thirty days parsed out to 103,920 hours, one autopsy, hundreds of fly-balls into an infinitely deep right field, maybe a thousand Jolly Ranchers, a handful of clandestine jaunts on a forbidden mini-bike, and 142 full moons.

The Rev. Jack Williams, pastor at the First Presbyterian Church, struggled with his eulogy. Amy's mother and stepfather weren't members of the church, but Williams had been asked by a friend if he would comfort Toni and, when the time came, conduct Amy's funeral.

But he wasn't sure what he should say—or not say. He knew there were those among the mourners who wanted blood revenge, men in the pews who would gladly kill the bastards. He knew there were others who hoped the accused killers' lives would be stained forever with pain and suffering.

He also knew many would wonder: Where was God that night?

He prayed for an epiphany. He felt deeply for Amy, for Becky and their family. But he didn't want to judge anyone, even in such a monstrous moment.

Amy was buried on a Friday. The day of the funeral, almost two weeks after the crime because of the necessary forensic inspection of her little corpse, the five hundred-seat church was filled to overflowing, but there were few children. It was an open-casket funeral on a school day, and inside Amy's casket were her baseball mitt and a transistor radio, two of her favorite things.

Reverend Williams spoke from the heart. His eulogy was not written down. His invocation asked God to lift them all above the sadness and shadow of mortality, and then he recited the Twenty-third Psalm . . . *yea, though I walk through the valley of the shadow of death, I will fear no evil, for thou art with me* . . . but even as his words drifted out across the silent gathering, he wasn't sure where God had been, or whether He would have interceded between evil and innocence.

He read from Scriptures, about flesh being grass, about blessed mourners, about the inevitability of comfort, about God's policy of non-interference, about knowing the number of our days.

But where was God? God was there, he wanted to believe. Men, both good and bad, chose how they would use God's freedom. God gave life, yes, but were humans not responsible for how they lived that life? Transgressions on Earth were the stuff of man's laws and courts, and we were free to judge our fellow men's actions. Yes, God forgives, but man punishes. God said, "Thou shalt not kill." He laid the rules out clearly, didn't He?

Jack Williams was a devout man of God. He believed without conditions. Because they came from God, he avoided being haunted by other people's illness and death. Every day followed the one before, and the past had a way of slipping away, but he still believed. He had to believe. He also knew that he could forgive the killers but not forget the pain they caused. Remembering was not always a curse; it could be a blessing. God was there that day.

Don't blame God, the pastor reminded himself.

God didn't kill Amy. But He didn't save her either. He gave man the gift of choice, and sometimes bad choices—grotesque choices—were made.

Kennedy and Jenkins would be judged by other men. God would get His turn, but maybe too late for the cynics who wondered: Where was God?

Among those cynics was Becky Thomson, whose injuries prevented her from attending her little sister's funeral. Reverend Williams made a tape recording of the service and took it to her later, but she never listened to it.

Becky didn't trust God anymore. She wished two men dead. She still didn't know where God had gone that night. What God would allow a child to be flung into a dark nothingness, only to smash her fragile body on the rocks at the bottom of a horrid chasm?

Becky would wonder about God for many, many more years, and she never really forgave Him.

WHEN HIS DAUGHTER Amy was murdered, Gene T. "Jiggs" Burridge was tending bar in San Francisco's raw Tenderloin District. He had been sober a few years, divorced a few more from Amy's mother.

Almost as soon as he was born in 1928, Jiggs was nicknamed for a legendary Montana football coach, Jiggs Dahlberg. As he grew up uncontrolled and street-smart in North Casper, he compensated for his slight build with cockiness. He wrecked a car when he was twelve years old. For years, he assumed the role of bodyguard for a mentally retarded neighbor. He became a gifted brawler, quick to fight in the street and a Golden Gloves boxing champ in the ring. And he seldom lost.

The Burridge family—all fifteen of them—was uncommon, in nearly every sense of the word. Mother Alice was a justice of the peace who once sent her own teen-age son to jail for three days for drinking and minor mischief. Father G.O. was a city laborer who operated a shoeshine parlor downtown and did occasional party gigs as a ventriloquist. Brother Dean, who lived with a grandparent in Iowa, became one of the Hawkeye State's most renowned young athletes, excelling in every sport before he was ultimately drafted by the New York Yankees. Of the nine Burridge sons, eight joined the military—and the ninth tried but was refused because he'd been born with a deformed foot.

Jiggs was one of those natural athletes in whose blood and muscles was born a genius for knowing the exact arc a basketball must travel to the basket, for recognizing a fastball by its spiraling seams as it left the pitcher's hand, for sensing a gap in the offensive line before it opened. Later, as a man, he would coach town boys in all those sports.

But Jiggs also discovered booze early, a risky habit for the son of a notoriously tough judge. Liquor was the only opponent to consistently beat him, almost every time. He got in his licks, a few brief periods of sobriety, but alcohol ultimately outlasted him.

He was drafted into the U.S. Army in 1950, and after basic training, shipped directly to Korea in a combat infantry unit. He became a sergeant under fire, even though he grew up highstrung and hating guns. His frontline outfit suffered horrifying casualties, and when Staff Sergeant Jiggs Burridge finally rotated back Stateside, he never talked again about the war.

Instead, he married Toni Thomson, helped raise her two daughters from her first marriage, and had two children of their own and Amy in 1961.

He briefly served as a city councilman in Casper, but even his deep roots couldn't ultimately hold him in the small town.

Not long after Amy was born, Toni and Jiggs divorced, and Jiggs ventured out of Wyoming again. Still drinking, he took jobs as a bartender at Washington D.C.'s Watergate Hotel, and later at the elegant Top of the Mark in San Francisco. He'd been on the wagon for a few years but had come down in the world. He was nearly broke and living in mean conditions when the last wheel fell off his wagon.

On Tuesday afternoon, after Amy's body was officially identified in the hospital morgue by her mother, Jiggs' brother delivered the dreadful news by phone. Jiggs had a lifelong fear of flying, but he caught the earliest flight from San Francisco back to Wyoming, where he hadn't visited since his mother died two years before.

His younger brother, then a high school football coach, met him at the airport and took him directly to the room they'd share at the old Townsend Hotel—and where his brother could keep a close eye on Jiggs, whom he knew could be quickly enraged and, just as quickly, lured back into the saloons.

He had plenty of reason to worry. Many of Jiggs' shadier pals from the streets and the bars were ready to exact their own brutal justice on their old friend's behalf. Many made their suggestions in whispered phone calls to Jiggs' room, on the street corner, outside the funeral home. Without his brother's cooler head, Jiggs might have spiraled into an implacable and drunken rage.

His brother kept tormented Jiggs out of trouble until the funeral. A few of the Burridge brothers accompanied Jiggs and their father G.O., who'd had a crippling phobia about corpses since his mother died young, to the church. But when they tried to avoid passing Amy's open casket by slipping out a side door, one brother insisted they pay their respects.

G.O. resisted. He had seen his granddaughter Amy alive just a few days before. He'd gone to her house and as he pulled out of the driveway, she ran out of the house to show him a small trophy she'd won in a local free-throw contest. That's how he wanted to remember her, proud and smiling and unbeatable. Not dead.

But neither he nor Jiggs could escape. As they gazed down upon Amy's empty face in her casket, G.O. slumped. From that moment, he never cared if he lived another day. His wife Alice, the justice of the peace, had died in 1971, and he could no longer lean on her. And indeed, the happy-go-lucky guy who made people laugh by throwing his voice would die ten months after he gazed upon his slain grand-daughter.

Jiggs died that day, too. His spirit left him, although his blood still pumped and his flesh walked on. A few days after his child's funeral, he nervously boarded a flight back to San Francisco. During a layover in Denver, far from his brother's protective reach, he ran into some old drinking buddies. First one drink, and then another, and another . . . Jiggs Bur-ridge never drew another sober breath in his life, which ended in 1986 when he was only fifty-eight years old.

BECKY REMAINED IN the hospital for a few weeks after her rape and attempted murder. Although the shock of it had worn off and some of her lesser wounds had healed, the wound in her mind festered. Far from feeling safe, fear in-fected her and spread into her blood.

For her safety and peace of mind, doctors moved Becky to the sixth floor pediatrics ward, the topmost floor in the hospital. Her private room was at the end of the long hall-way. A guard was posted twenty-four hours a day at her door, and the locks on all the ward's doors were changed.

One night, a graveyard-shift nurse's aide, Patricia Hansen, checked on Becky briefly and then left. Halfway down the hall, she heard a blood-chilling scream. She found Becky deliriously frightened.

"They're gonna get out!" she raved hysterically. "They're gonna get out and they're gonna kill all of you nurses and me!"

Hansen tried to calm Becky, hugging her as she lay in her bed, frozen there by fear and a shattered pelvis.

"Oh, baby, they're not coming here," she said. "There's a

guard with a gun right outside your door every minute, and they're not coming here. It's okay. You're safe."

But Becky was losing control. She didn't believe she was safe, and she didn't believe there was a cop outside.

Hansen asked the deputy to come inside and prove his existence to the distraught girl.

"I can't," he said. "I can't leave this spot."

Hansen insisted, telling him Becky needed him more inside her room than outside right now.

Reluctantly, the deputy left his post and stood a few moments at the foot of Becky's bed, where she could see him, his uniform and, perhaps more importantly, his holstered revolver. He assured her he'd die before he let anyone hurt her again. She calmed down, but she never truly felt safe from Ron Kennedy and Jerry Jenkins in the hospital.

And she never truly felt safe ever again in her life.

THE CAPITAL CASE against Kennedy and Jenkins fell squarely in the lap of District Judge T.C. Daniels, a tough but venerable jurist. He wanted no reversible errors, no smudge on the case that could send two men to the gas chamber. If they were innocent, he wanted the truth to come out; if they were guilty, he wanted them to get what they deserved.

But even if he hadn't already heard rumblings that the defense would prefer the trial be moved elsewhere, he was intensely aware of the anger that had already boiled over in the community. His role would likely only be to make the initial rulings in the case before it was taken out of town.

And his first act was to find a good lawyer for Jerry Jenkins, who'd never been able to afford one on his own, even in petty crimes.

John Ackerman was a young, thirty-four-year-old lawyer born in Sundance. He had recently been appointed as Wyoming's first full-time public defender, even though he only had a relatively few years of experience. But his hands were full defending Ronald Kennedy, who had listed himself as disabled, jobless, broke and possessing nothing in this world but a Chevrolet pickup truck.

So, to forestall any accusations that neither defendant got the full attention of his lawyer, Judge Daniels decided to appoint a public defender for Jenkins, too.

He turned to Don Chapin two days after the arrest of Kennedy and Jenkins. The son of a local accountant and builder, Chapin was nearing fifty. He was the furthest thing from a criminal lawyer in the whole Natrona County Bar, maintaining his comfortable uptown legal firm drawing up land and commercial contracts. He'd represented very few criminal clients, much less accused murderers. But Chapin was solid, honest and mature, one of the most respected lawyers, and Daniels wanted his expertise and the clarity of his mind.

At first, Chapin refused Daniels' request, fearing his lack of criminal experience could only hurt. He felt he was as far outside his element as he could be. He also knew the whole town was seething, and it could only hurt his practice to be associated with Jenkins.

But Daniels was resolute, and he convinced Chapin he had a higher responsibility. The law, he said, is more important than you, your practice, or even what people will say.

Chapin took the case and reminded himself many times in the coming months, after threatening phone calls and disapproving looks from his old friends had begun, *The law is more important.*

Jenkins was no help, either. When they met, the career criminal spoke very little. He'd told the police more than he would tell his own lawyer. He had sunken into an angry pout, even suggesting Amy and Becky had been responsible themselves for ratcheting up the violence by provoking Kennedy.

But like any good defense lawyer, Chapin never asked Jenkins if he was guilty of the crimes against him. His best defense would be the law itself, forcing the prosecution to prove what he already presumed, if his client's confession were true.

The case was, indeed, moved from Casper to Cheyenne

after the preliminary hearing found sufficient evidence to try Kennedy and Jenkins. District Judge John Raper would preside, not Judge Daniels.

In a series of pre-trial hearings, the defense began to take shape. One or both of the defendants would likely plead not guilty by reason of insanity. Ackerman had also begun to raise the specter of the U.S. Supreme Court's discomfort with the death penalty. Even though Wyoming had retooled its murder laws to satisfy the court, some questions remained, and this would be Wyoming's first capital case in almost ten years.

Ackerman and Chapin knew Wyoming's first-degree murder statute was only tenuously constitutional, and they knew they must focus on the right objections and arguments to preserve the issues for any future appeal. In the months before trial, they turned to the NAACP Legal Defense Fund in New York for advice and worked closely with a young lawyer named David Kendall.[2]

BOTH MEN'S PATHOLOGIES were examined before trial. Kennedy spent thirty days in the Wyoming State Hospital, and at the defense's request, both were ordered to see a Denver psychiatrist.

Over several weeks, the psychiatrist concluded that Kennedy and Jenkins were two distinctly separate sociopaths, neither likely to commit a rape and murder on his own. But together, under the insidious influence of alcohol, they joined in a third personality that was not only capable of, but predisposed to, violent, sadistic behavior.

Nonetheless, he said, both knew right from wrong, both knew the consequences of their actions, and both were fit to stand trial.

As the case moved along, both sides also clashed over evidence photographs, particularly a large blow-up of Amy Burridge's stiffened corpse moments after she was found in the river.

The defense said the photo was purely inflammatory.

"We don't dispute that she's dead," Ackerman pleaded with Judge Raper. "And these photos don't explain how she died."

Assistant Prosecutor Dave Lewis brushed those arguments aside in a mix of blunt talk and legalese.

"Gruesome cases are made with gruesome facts," he argued. "I think that anybody who looks at a picture of a young girl whose life has been expended through the criminal agency of another is not going to be at all pleased, and this isn't why we're offering them. We are not trying to please anybody, nor are we trying to offend. . . . It is a fact in this case that there is a dead human being."

The judge allowed the photo to be used.

But the small-town defense lawyers in a highly emotional rape and murder case enjoyed a kindness that would seem unusual thirty years later.

The local daily newspaper, the *Casper Star-Tribune*, knew public sentiment had grown angry and vengeful. Kennedy and Jenkins were safely jailed, out of the reach of vigilantes and avengers of all kinds.

But John Ackerman and Don Chapin were not. Although the town most certainly knew who was defending the two accused monsters, the paper didn't wish to inflame the barely controlled rage any more than necessary.

After the first few manic days when small-town reporters and editors were simply trying to keep up with the sordid revelations, the community's fury, and fast-moving courtroom events, the *Star-Tribune* never mentioned the names of the two lawyers.

BLOOD-MEMORY RUNS COLD sometimes.

My little brother's bedroom window faced east, toward the morning sun and toward Amy's house. On chilly mornings, Lance sat on his window-sill in his underwear, soaking up the warmth.

He was Amy's age, slung between the pure blamelessness of his first ten years and the inevitable tumult of his next ten

*years. To him, life was a warm window box, lunch tickets,
sledding and snow forts, the pin-prickle of green grass on
your skin after you'd run through the sprinkler, Fat Albert
and Scooby-Doo, sleeping out in the backyard in summer.*

*Growing up was being asked to ride your bike to the
neighborhood market to buy the Saturday morning paper.
Love was knowing your older brother would always pick you
first for his sandlot team, even if you sucked. The edge of the
world was only so far as you could run in a twilight game of
kick-the-can.*

*But after Amy died, something black trembled inside,
down deep where it must have always been hiding silently
and still. Her house had changed. To Lance, it was now the
"murder house," and he couldn't bear to look at it, even
walking down the street. It scared him, scares him still. None
of us knew.*

*After his friend was murdered, he never sat on his
window-sill again. Mornings grew colder for him, even in
summer.*

*To this day, he associates the memory of Amy's death with
a feeling of cold that cannot be purged, even in sunlight.*

Blood-memory runs cold sometimes.

Part Two

*"Crime seems to change character when it crosses
a bridge or a tunnel. In the city, crime is taken as emblematic
of class and race.
In the suburbs, though, it's intimate
and psychological—resistant to generalization,
a mystery of the individual soul."*

Barbara Ehrenreich

Chapter 5

THE PROSECUTION

April 24, 1974

Seven months later, the sordid journey that began on a moonless autumn night continued when Sheriff Bill Estes himself took Ronald Kennedy to Cheyenne to stand trial for the murder of Amy Burridge and the rape of Becky Thomson.

The emotional inferno that raged over the crime had spread throughout the state in the seven months between the crimes and the trial. If vigilantes still harbored any hope of accelerating justice, Ronald Kennedy would be extremely vulnerable on the empty, one hundred-seventy-mile highway between Casper and Cheyenne.

They'd pass only five smaller towns—fewer than ten thousand people if every man, woman and child in all five towns gathered for a box social in the same place—in the three-hour drive through the wind-scraped badlands. They'd see more snow fences, pronghorn antelope and broken-down windmills than cars. They'd also pass a few trailers with old tires on their roofs, as if vulcanized rubber were a talisman (or simply a weight) against the wind. Billboards were sparse because the wind, which might blow sixty miles an hour on a casual day, would rip them out by the roots. Out there, the intermittent ranch houses, plunked down randomly in the middle of nowhere, tend to be farther apart than New York City and Poughkeepsie. And this is one of Wyoming's more populous corridors.

The middle of April is not spring in Wyoming. It is the

bitchy end of winter. The worst snowstorms blow in from the Arctic north in April, often around Easter. And when they do, this stretch of road is the first to close, mostly because it is so desolate and treacherous that a snow-blinded driver can easily disappear in a white-out and not be found until the thaw.

Civilization did the best it could against the forces of nature in this part of the world. Sometimes civilization simply went elsewhere.

The sheriff knew how uncivilized it might get out there. He used two vehicles to transport Kennedy to trial. He drove one with a shotgun rider, Kennedy in the backseat. A deputy followed, in case there was trouble.

The road from jail to trial was barren for Ronald Kennedy, and it would likely never lead him back home. He knew that many roads had intersected in his life, he'd taken many wrong turns, and the gas chamber waited at the end of one of them.

The accused killer didn't talk much on the trip, but just outside Glendo, one of those Wyoming towns barely clinging to life in the middle of nowhere, Kennedy made a request.

"My father is buried up ahead in Glendo," he said. "Could we stop and visit his grave?"

Ernest Leroy Kennedy, born in 1903 in Council Bluffs, Iowa, had seldom worked in his life. Although he'd graduated from high school in Nebraska and worked occasionally as an auto mechanic, he spent the last twenty years of his existence unemployed, crippled by arthritis and booze. He often drank up his family's welfare money, and he spent more than his share of time in the Casper drunk tank after fights, DUIs and other drunken disturbances.

He often brought his low-life friends to the little house in North Casper, where they loafed and drank for hours. When he was drunk, the little house was in turmoil, and he was almost always drunk. Almost fifty years later, in prison, Ron would allege that some of his father's drinking pals sexually molested him during their beer-soaked benders, and the abuse continued secretly for years.

Ernest's wife Hilda, who took intermittent work as a dishwasher or maid, couldn't raise her six children alone, although she tried. She literally pushed them to Mass at the Catholic church, but nothing stuck, and with only an eighth-grade education herself, she could not imbue them with any sense for the value of schooling. She wanted something better for them but simply didn't have the tools to make it happen. Most of them got in trouble with the law very young.

Ronald was the fourth eldest. He had a lengthy juvenile rap sheet before he dropped out of the eighth grade; he later finished a few more grades while locked in the boys' reformatory at Worland, Wyoming. His older brother James was imprisoned for first-degree rape. His sisters were delinquents who'd done time at the Wyoming Girls School or in the youth probation system.

A probation officer who'd known Ronald Kennedy for many years before his first major adult crime wrote to the judge before the nineteen-year-old was sentenced for breaking into an elderly woman's home and robbing her of twenty dollars in 1965: "[His parents] have never taken their parental responsibilities seriously enough ... to prevent the subject [Kennedy] from taking a headlong plunge into disaster."

Almost from the beginning, the system knew Ronald Kennedy's relationship with his father was poor, although he would tell probation investigators it was good.

Withered by alcoholism, Ernest died in Casper on December 18, 1969, of a bleeding intestinal ulcer. He was sixty-five. He was buried in Horseshoe Cemetery, a rural graveyard several miles from Glendo, a lakeside village of only two hundred souls where Ernest had lived some of the better years of his life, although none had been truly good. At the time of his father's death, Ronald Kennedy was serving a twelve- to eighteen-month sentence for burglary.

Sheriff Estes considered the danger and inconvenience of stopping at the tiny Glendo cemetery so Ronald Kennedy could visit his father's grave. He even considered that it was just another con, that the grave didn't exist. But if it did, he knew Ronald would likely never pass this way again, unless they took his body directly from the gas chamber and planted him here. Still, he wanted no opportunity for trouble.

"Not today," was all Estes said, and he sped past the graveyard.

I'M TOLD FACTS have no moral quality, only what we project upon them.

Thus, it seems to me, a criminal trial is like a cultural ink-blot test, in which society looks at a set of insensate, numb facts and projects its own history, fears, impatience, insolence, clemency, insecurities, dreams—and nightmares—upon those facts.

In theory, we are not really describing the ink blots, but something inside ourselves. And what's inside is every fairy-tale monster: A brutal ogre, a bloodthirsty werewolf, an elegant vampire, a bullying giant, a scheming devil, a predatory wolf, a sneering troll, or maybe just an abusive stepmother.

The archetypes of our fears have trickled into every heart. And when a crime captures the public's imagination before a trial, the great majority of citizens are already projecting the monsters of our collective mythology onto the suspects.

Since no courtroom in the world is expansive enough to accommodate the populace of even a small-ish town in the least populated state in America, we select twelve neighbors at random to sift and cull the truth from evidence, testimony and lawyers' speechifying. Placing our faith in randomness, we presume these twelve will reflect the psychology and conscience of the place we live, surrogates that reflect the best and worst of us. Their noble duty is to protect the public from the monsters among us. But they are charged with an equally noble trust that almost nobody else wants: to protect the monsters from the public.

A defense-lawyer I know always imagines a potential juror who receives his summons and suddenly becomes aware of the crimes he might be called to judge. He might see a story about a heinous crime in the newspaper, or hear it on

the radio or just over coffee with his buddies. Maybe he says
to himself, "Gee, I hope I don't get called for that case."

Or maybe, as my defense-lawyer friend fears, he says: "I
hope I do."

NATRONA COUNTY ATTORNEY Jack Burk rose to face his
jury on Wednesday morning, April 24. He was about to put
the biggest case of his life in the hands of twelve strangers.
Before a single word was spoken, he couldn't know whether
they would see and hear the facts as clearly as he did.

Burk was a scrapper. He was five-foot-four, but barrel-
chested and tough. His mellifluous speaking voice spilled
forth jokes and tall tales as fluidly as legal arguments, but he
always played his cards close to the vest. Everyone was acquainted with Jack Burk, but nobody really knew Jack Burk.

In ten years as a prosecutor, he not only knew Kennedy
and Jenkins, he knew their kind: lazy, shifty punks who
started with nothing and imagined society held some profound grudge against them.

Of all people, Jack Burk knew it wasn't true.

He was born in May 1927 in upstate New York to John
and Lois Burk, who were already in a wobbly marriage. Lois
gave birth to another son eighteen months later, but in the
dawning years of the Great Depression, she divorced her
husband to seek greener pastures, marooning him with two
little boys to support on the meager earnings of a traveling
tap-dance teacher.

John Burk and his two sons became nomads. They wandered the lesser highways and cemetery-gray villages of
New York and Massachusetts, landing with far-flung family
and friends, and in boarding houses while father John taught
children to tap dance. Sometimes the boys were farmed out
to willing but unfamiliar foster parents until their father
could redeem them like little pawned jewels, and then they'd
move on. They often filched both vegetables and electricity
from neighbors in the night. Between kindergarten and high
school, they attended twenty-eight different schools. They

shared a childhood without money and a full-time father, and not much more.

Their father was a soft, impassive man who had always failed to take charge of his life. Holidays often came and went without notice, although he once gave his youngest son Robert a used pocket watch for Christmas, a trifling token except it was the most meaningful gift his father ever gave him.

After high school, both boys left home for good, joined the Navy and went to war. Jack served as a signalman aboard a warship in the Pacific's Philippine campaign. After the war, he returned Stateside and attended college, but his marks were poor.

That's when a friend in a distant place made the suggestion that would change Jack's life. The friend lived in Wyoming and promised to pull a few strings to get Jack enrolled at the University of Wyoming in Laramie. Jack was happy for the chance.

He graduated from college in 1951 and moved to Casper, Wyoming. He took a job selling kitchen appliances and, at night, played music for a little extra cash.

Ten years later, he married a Wyoming girl who worked for a local lawyer. The lawyer convinced Jack he might make a fine barrister, and within a year, Jack had enrolled at the University of Denver's College of Law. When he graduated, he was an "old" man of thirty-seven and worried that he wouldn't get a chance to play in a young man's game. He thought about moving to Alaska, because he believed a new lawyer, however long in the tooth, might stand a better chance of building a practice there.

But he got his chance closer to home. He was hired as a deputy in the Natrona County Attorney's Office, a job he relished for six years. In 1970, he was elected to replace his boss.

Despite the long hours and the demands of his new prosecuting career, he kept up his music. It soothed him. He played every instrument from banjo to trombone in a local Dixieland jazz band, but he excelled at cornet. He was so good he'd joined a big-city jazz band from Denver briefly, while also playing gigs at local taverns and the city's band-shell in Washington Park.

When Kennedy and Jenkins came along, he was entering the last year of his first term, and by all accounts, would face little serious opposition for re-election—unless he failed to convict two career criminals widely presumed to have killed two innocent girls for the sheer, depraved fun of it.

For Jack Burk, it was simply being here, in this court-room, at the beginning of a great trial after starting at zero, with no money, no roots, and a family that had never truly been glued together soundly. He had overcome the model of a milquetoast father to become a robust man. He'd overcome poverty to become a lawyer.

Burk looked around the courtroom. Most of these faces had come to see justice done. It seemed he had also over-come the lack of a genuine family to become the champion of an entire town.

The gallery included relatives and friends of both the ac-cused and the victims. The accused killers' ex-wives were both there. Kennedy's and Jenkins' fathers were both dead, but their mothers had made the long journey to Cheyenne. Neither had much money, and they paid dearly for lodging and meals in a strange city.

Those closest to Amy and Becky, their families and a few dear friends, were also scattered throughout the old court-room. Courthouse workers occasionally sat in the back rows during their coffee breaks. But by far, most of the onlookers were simply the curious, the common, and the angry.

Burk approached the lectern before the jury box, drew a breath and began to argue for the death of two men.

"A couple hundred years of trials has shown there is re-ally no purely logical way in which testimony and evidence can be presented," he said. "You have to skip around a little bit. Think of it as a portrait. The portrait in this case is going to be a pretty terrible picture.

"A word of warning: Defense counsel has even admitted that parts of this case are going to be pretty shocking. You have sworn to try the facts in this case, a case that at its mildest has to be one of the greatest outrages against human beings that you have ever heard. I feel sure you are all sensitive people, but the facts in this case are seamy, they are indelicate, and they are going to tear the hearts and stomachs out of you.

"You are going to hear the story of a little girl who, by a fluke of fate, skipped death."

While a few nervous jurors looked away discreetly, most sat stoically, eyes riveted on the prosecutor asking them to pay careful attention not only to what Ronald Kennedy and Jerry Jenkins said, but what they did.

In their actions more than their words, he said, "you'll find the proof that they decided the fate of Becky and Amy before the girls ever got into their automobile.

"You will hear how the girls were beaten in the car with a sure and certain knowledge that they would never live to tell about it. You will hear how Amy was thrown from the bridge over Fremont Canyon simply to eliminate her as a witness to the rape of her older sister on this night of rape for fun. You will hear how Becky was forcibly raped by one then the other, and then thrown off the same bridge. You will hear how after that night of rape for fun was over, the defendants returned to their wives and families."

The muscles in Burk's jaw pumped as he sorted through his papers, seeking the right words. He wanted them to understand. He *needed* them to understand.

"Becky Thomson's story of abuse, escape from death, and survival is incredible. 'Incredible' means beyond belief.

"Becky is alive. She's given her thanks to God for that. I really don't think she wants your sympathy; I think she wants your attention, your understanding for the story she has to tell, for the sake of Amy. I think she would appreciate your attention to each bit of evidence, its color, its shape and where it fits into this picture."

With that, less than four minutes of opening remarks that contained only the promise of a grisly portrait to be painted, Burk gathered his papers and sat down.

Kennedy and Jenkins' defense lawyers exercised their option to deliver opening remarks after the prosecution rested its case.

The first and most crucial witness would take the stand as soon as the bailiff could escort her to the courtroom.

BECKY THOMSON WAS the state's first witness. She had waited in the county employees' break room at the old courthouse before her testimony so she didn't have to sit in the hallway with other witnesses and gawkers.

Assistant Prosecutor Dave Lewis wasted no time getting to the heart of the crime. After establishing Becky's identity for the record, his first questions cut to the night of September 24, barely seven months earlier.

She recounted going to the convenience store with half-sister Amy. She told how they drove her rattletrap Ford station wagon to buy groceries for their mother and how Amy wanted to get some candy at a nearby convenience store. Becky bought two cans of tomato paste, a cucumber and a green pepper. When they left the store and backed out of their parking spot, she noticed her back passenger-side tire was flat.

When they inched back into the parking spot beside the store, Becky said she noticed two men glide into the spot on the passenger side of her car. A dark-haired man was driving.

"Is that man in the courtroom?" Lewis asked her.

Becky pointed at Ronald Kennedy, sitting at the defense table in a blue shirt. Burk asked him to stand.

As Becky continued her story, the jury and the courtroom sat silently in rapt attention.

Kennedy asked if she needed help, and she told him she did. He introduced himself as Kenny Rogers and she shook his hand.

"I'm Becky Thomson," she said.

"What happened here?" this guy Kenny asks.

"I'm really mad," Becky huffs. "I just had my tire fixed and now it's flat, and I know my spare is flat. I don't know what to do. I guess I'll have to go to a filling station and get it fixed."

The other guy, the fat one with the greasy hair, is already opening the trunk on his dirty white Impala. "Well, maybe you can buy a tire from me or something," the fat one says, but tests the tires in his trunk. "But these are flat. We'll go to a filling station and see if one's open so you can get your tire fixed."

First, the fat guy tests his lug wrench on her tire and it doesn't fit her bolts. "So I guess we'll have to go get one of those, too," he says.

Then he takes a jack out of his car and puts it under the station wagon, but he doesn't jack it up. "We'll be right back," he says. "We're going to see if there's a filling station that's open."

"Okay, that's fine," Becky says.

"Now just wait there and make sure nobody steals it."

"Oh, sure."

When the two guys leave, Becky checks her watch. It's getting late, almost nine-thirty, past dark.

"Amy, run to the store and tell Mom that some nice men are helping us and that we'll be home as soon as we can."

Amy is only too happy to go to the little convenience store near the supermarket: A handful of spare change was burning a hole in her pocket and she wanted candy. She's off in a flash, the pink ribbons in her pigtails fluttering.

While she's gone, the two guys come back. This time the fat one who never said his name is driving and the Kenny guy is riding shotgun. They make room for her in the car, but Amy hasn't yet returned.

"Just a minute, I'm going to get Amy."

Becky goes into the Mini Mart and finds Amy. She's been secretly buying candy since she called their mom. When they come out, the two guys pull their two-door Impala near them and Kenny gets out to let them get into the back seat.

Inexplicably, even as they're voluntarily getting in, the Kenny guy presses a small knife against Becky's ribs. Amy doesn't notice, but Becky hurries her into the black-upholstered back seat. The Fat Guy is driving, Kenny in the front passenger seat. Becky is behind Kenny; Amy is behind the Fat Guy.

They leave the grocery store's lot and turn right on Melrose, assuring the girls they still intend to take them home. Then Kenny pipes up.

"We're going to go look for my house, because I have a pot roast in the oven and I think it's burning."

Frightened, Becky agrees. She's gripping her own car keys in her hand so tightly they carve sweaty grooves in her fingers and palm.

The Fat Guy looks around, appearing confused, almost comical.

"You know, it's so funny that I can find my way around real good in Los Angeles, but I can't find my way around Casper, Wyoming," Kenny laughs.

Becky tries to negotiate. "Well, why don't you take us home first and then you can go to your house."

At that moment, Becky opens her purse to put her car keys away, and Kenny erupts. He leaps up in his seat and grabs each girl by the throat, a hand on each neck, throttling them hard.

At first, Becky plays dead, thinking the sooner she ceases to be a threat, the sooner Kenny will stop choking her. She hears Amy gasping for breath, then nothing. *Oh God, she's dead!* Becky thinks and begins to fight back.

Kenny slugs them both a few times, hard. He orders them to lie down on the seat and Becky lies on top of Amy, both their heads at Amy's end of the seat. They both cry, and Kenny has what he wants: dominance.

Becky then gets an idea: She quickly reaches between the front seat and door and pulls open the door handle on Kenny's side. Shoving her feet out the open door, she hopes a curious passerby will see her feet and call the cops.

Kenny pummels her face with his fists. He tries to pry her feet off the door, but she's got a good grip. Amy is screaming, but Kenny pushes her hard a couple times. The Fat Guy yells, "Just get that door closed! Just close the door! Grab her foot!" Kenny takes her left foot and the Fat Guy holds it under his arm while Kenny closes the door.

Becky's last-ditch gambit lasts maybe fifteen or twenty seconds.

Nobody sees.

AS SHE TESTIFIED, Becky remained steadfast and composed. She seldom faltered, recounting the events of her abduction with a grave calm. At this point, she began referring to the man she'd known that night only as Kenny Rogers by his real name: Ron Kennedy.

Sometime during her ordeal, the two men had called each other by their real first names, Jerry and Ronnie—names later recognizable instantly to investigators as belonging to two well-known low-life hoods.

The two men drove slowly and aimlessly through town with the two terrified girls trapped in the backseat. They started up Casper Mountain, but Jenkins turned around when the car overheated and he remembered his tires were nearly bald. They went back through town and headed out toward Alcova Lake, a reservoir mostly deserted in autumn, more than twenty-five miles away.

"Kennedy said he had a friend who'd been hit by a car a couple days earlier," Becky continued in her testimony. The car was identical to Becky's Ford, he told them, and there was a young woman and a little girl in it. The girls, he said, left the scene, and his friend was paralyzed from the neck down. Now his friend was in a trailer out near Alcova Lake, lying low because he was in trouble, and they were going to go out to see him.

"They said if it wasn't us, then they would take us home," Becky testified. "But if it was us, we would pay for it and they would kill us."

The feisty little Amy, already certain she might be murdered by these two creeps, insisted it couldn't have been them. They'd just returned from a Mexican vacation.

"Well, we'll just go out there and see," Kennedy said.

Then the Fat Guy, Jerry, finally said something. He hadn't said anything while Kennedy was beating them, except when Becky had kicked open the door.

"Don't be mad at the service station man that fixed your tire," Jenkins said, "because I was the one that cut it."

Not satisfied with the terror he'd already inflicted, Kennedy just continued his terror tale—part fantasy and part horror story—telling them he and his buddy Jerry were Hell's Angels and were working for the Mafia peddling dope and had been living in L.A. He told them they've already had a friend take Becky's car from the grocery store lot and smash it up in a ditch. If they weren't the girls who hurt their friend, he said, they'd take them back to that smashed-up car and leave them. They were to keep their mouths shut and say they had a wreck. Kennedy also told Becky that would explain her now-bleeding nose and swollen eye.

"And if we didn't tell the wreck story," Becky told the breathless courtroom, "our lives would cease to exist."

"Anything else?" Assistant Prosecutor Lewis asked her.

"Oh, they were saying that they would just, out of the blue, give me twenty dollars to forget the whole thing. And Kennedy told me he'd buy me a new car."

"Did they say whether this man was alone out there at Alcova?"

"They said they didn't know for sure, but that some of their friends could have been out there, four or five friends or maybe just one, they weren't sure. But they would be sure and try to protect us all they could, but that's all they said."

On the way to the lake, Kennedy and Jenkins drink from a case of beer they have stowed on the seat between them, whispering back and forth, scheming out of the girls' hearing. They offer some beer to Becky, who refuses it.

Becky's mind reels. She's desperate to protect Amy and herself. She asks both Kennedy and Jenkins about their lives and families. Jenkins tells her he's thirty-nine and isn't married, but that he has an illegitimate eleven-year-old daughter, same age as Amy. Kennedy says he is twenty-nine and not married. Jenkins says he and Kennedy were in Vietnam together, and Kennedy had been shot in the head there—a warning.

"He's now more animal than man," Jenkins warns the girls. "And he'll do anything I tell him to do."

Near a little roadside store, Kennedy pulls out his knife and leaps up in his seat again.

He stabs the seat around their legs, like a deadly game of mumblety-peg. Later, investigators would remember the punctures outlining a girl's body. Then Kennedy jabs the open blade toward Becky's breasts and holds it close to her heart.

"Put your hand on the blade," he orders her. "Put your hand around the blade and feel this."

Amy starts screaming.

"Oh, please, don't make her do that!"

Kennedy jabs the knife in the seat again, but the hapless Jenkins is lost.

"Is this the right way to turn?" he asks.

Kennedy is momentarily distracted and stops terrorizing them while he gives directions to a destination Becky doesn't know. Now Amy is crying uncontrollably and trying to hold her sister's hand, but Kennedy won't let them hold hands.

"Becky, I love you so much," Amy cries.

Kennedy pushes her hands away from Becky.

"Sir, can I ask you one question?" Amy asks. "Are you going to murder us?"

"What?" Kennedy acts surprised and a little offended. "Oh no, honey, you've been watching too many detective stories on TV."

Jenkins turns off the main blacktop, onto the lower road to Pathfinder Reservoir that would cross the Fremont Canyon Bridge. Kennedy and Jenkins whisper to each other, and Becky begs them not to whisper, but Kennedy shoves her and Amy back down in the seat and slaps at their clasped hands.

Then Amy whispers to Becky.

"Becky, if we ever get through this, I'll never be greedy again."

Becky chokes. To Amy, going to the store to buy candy for herself was somehow the cause of their ordeal.

"Amy, it's not your fault at all," Becky tells her.

Suddenly, the car's headlights flash across the cold steel of a bridge.

"Is this the right way to go?" Jenkins asks.

"Yeah," Kennedy says.

Jenkins crosses the bridge slowly and parks on a narrow dirt road at the far end. From down in the seat, Becky thinks she sees the headlights paint the roof of a house of some kind—maybe where the crippled man is waiting.

"Okay, here we are," Kennedy says. "You can't go in at the same time."

The girls both beg him to let them go together.

"No."

"Oh, please, let me go in first and talk to these men," Becky pleads.

"No, I want the little one first," he insists.

Kennedy opens his door and the dome light suddenly illuminates Becky's swollen, bruised and bloody face. Amy sees it and screams, then is wracked by fearful sobs.

Unruffled, Kennedy hands Becky his open beer can. "Wanna drink?"

She sips from the can and wipes her wrist across her mouth as Kennedy tells Amy to get out of the car and come with him. Amy stops crying and steels herself.

"Okay, Becky," she says as she crawls over Becky's lap to get out Kennedy's door. "I love you."

Becky never sees Amy again.

"WHAT OCCURRED IN the car with you and Jenkins after they left, Becky?" Assistant Prosecutor Dave Lewis asked his star witness, who hadn't faltered until now.

"So many times during the night, I tried to push back in my mind that they were really going to do something to us, but I said to Jenkins, 'Are you going to kill us? Please, please tell me. Are you going to kill us? What's happening to my little sister now?' He wouldn't say anything."

She told the court how Jenkins opened his car door and spoke to nobody in particular. "Why do I always have to be the weak one? I don't want to go to jail again."

Then he called into the deep blackness of the night, "Ronnie, Ronnie." That's when Becky presumed his real name was not Kenny.

Kennedy came back. He was gone only two or three minutes.

"Your little sister is talking to a man," he told her, "and we are supposed to go up the road a bit and wait for a signal and then we will come back down and then it's your turn to talk to him."

"Okay."

Jenkins started the car and they were whispering again.

"Please don't whisper," Becky begged them. "Please tell me what you're saying. Please don't whisper."

They said nothing to her.

"And what happens next, Becky?" Lewis asked.

"We went about 150 yards to 200 yards up the road and then we stopped, and they both raped me."

THE IMPALA'S DOME light shines yellow and dull.

Kennedy quickly undresses and climbs into the back seat, where he starts undressing Becky himself. She pushes him away, deflecting his hands from touching her any more than they already have, from being more intimate than a slap or a punch to her face.

"Either you give in or you fight it," he tells her.

She stops fighting. He roughly unbuttons her jeans and yanks them off her, then tugs her red pullover sweater off like a greedy kid opening a wrapped package. Already erect and ready, he snatches off her bra and panties and climbs on top of her.

"I've never had intercourse with anyone before," she says.

"Oh, you've never been had before?" Kennedy asks as he forces himself into her and humps. "Does this hurt?"

"Yes."

He's glad it hurts. He thrusts harder.

It doesn't take long. He grunts as he comes inside her and pulls away. He crawls naked into the front seat, and starts to dress. Jenkins, who'd been sitting in the driver's seat smoking a cigarette and watching, gets out of the car, strips naked and crawls into the stained backseat with Becky.

"Touch me," he orders her.

She doesn't know what he means at first.

"My dick," he orders her. "Touch it!"

A rape isn't ever tender nor lengthy, but Kennedy can't even let Jenkins have what little time he needs to please himself and humiliate Becky even further.

"Hurry, hurry, I think I see our signal," Kennedy says, rushing Jenkins.

Jenkins mounts her clumsily. With Kennedy hectoring him, he humps faster and ejaculates, then squeezes his nude, fleshy frame out of the backseat. Becky asks if she can get dressed.

"Yes, everything but underwear," Kennedy tells her.

In the dreary glow of the dome light, as she pulls her sweater and jeans back on, she's still slimy with their lust. But she thanks them. *Thanks them.*

"Thank you so much," she says. "Thank you so much for not letting my little sister see this."

"Oh, that's okay," Kennedy says. "She's too young."

"I'm cold and the seat's wet back here."

"Did you wet your pants, baby?" Kennedy sneers.

Dressed again, Jenkins gets back in the car and starts it. He backs it down the dark dirt road to the spot where they first stopped, where Kennedy had taken Amy out of the car and disappeared for a few minutes. They park beside what Becky had thought was the dark shack where the crippled man waited. It was a weathered outhouse.

Jenkins shuts off the car and both men get out.

"We both get to take you this time," Kennedy says. "We're going to meet your sister on the bridge."

The night is impenetrably black. The sky is cold and clear, but Becky sees no moon, no clouds, and only a dusting of stars. Kennedy and Jenkins stand on either side of the car door as Becky gets out, and each takes one of her arms as they walk slowly out into the darkness, illuminated only for the first few steps by the car's interior light.

"It's dark out here," a worried Becky says, measuring her steps carefully. She knows where she is. "There's a canyon down there."

"Oh no, that's just a bunch of trees," Kennedy assures her.

"With a bridge over it?"

Kennedy says nothing.

At the bridge, not more than thirty paces from the car, Kennedy finally speaks again.

"Okay, we're going to meet Amy right . . . *here*."

At the word "here," both men grab her. Kennedy is a skinny weakling, and Jenkins is a fat weakling. They try to lift her over the guard rail, barely three feet high, but can't. This little girl has a good grip on the lower beam, stronger than both of them, and they can't heave her over. She fights like hell.

So Jenkins starts choking her.

"Make sure she's going to die," he yells. "Make sure she'll be dead."

Funny thing, the survival instinct. It sometimes does what is least expected. In less time than it takes to die, Becky's mind examines her situation and her options, and it makes a fateful choice. She could be strangled and thrown from the bridge into an infinite void, or she could take her chances at surviving the fall.

She goes limp, feigning unconsciousness. She even tips out over the rail to make it easier for them to fling her down there.

THE COURTROOM HELD its breath as Becky described her freefall in the dark, hitting a ledge, and then hitting the water.

"And so, as soon as the sense came to me that I was still alive, I thought my legs were broken, and so I just swam with my hands over to a rock and I climbed up," she testified to a rapt judge, jury and gallery.

"And as soon as I got there I heard this car go over the bridge and I saw their headlights go on the beams, then they were gone. Then after that, I looked around and there was no place I could—it was just a ledge sticking out. So I looked over and I thought I would have to find a place to stay. So I had to get back in the water and swim a ways over to this kind of sandy place, but I crawled up and I found a place that was more like a V and I went in there just for warmth because my pants had fallen off in the water, so all I had on was a wet sweater and the wind was blowing. So I leaned back against this rock and a rat jumped out, so I picked up a rock. I knew I had to use something for self-defense, and then I just covered myself up with rocks and I had my knees up to my chest and I pulled my hair over my knees and that kept me warm.

"I was just so cold that night. I knew if I fell asleep that I would most likely die, so all night long I kept awake. I don't know exactly what time I was thrown off, about one in the morning, somewhere around there, twelve-thirty. But then I heard all night long, I heard cars coming and going and I heard a dog bark. I thought, *Maybe I'm by a house; maybe I should try and climb out.* I didn't have any idea what it looked like, what I was by or anything, but I was just so bloody. There was blood on my legs, I had scratches all over, and so I waited all night long. And I thought I heard noises like people trying to scare me.

"All night long I just planned that I would crawl up, you know, and walk onto the highway. Soon dawn came and I started to get up and my legs just collapsed, and I thought my legs were broken because I have never had a broken bone in all of my life and I didn't know what it was like. I just knew I couldn't move my legs, so I cried and cried and I knew I had to get out of there.

"So I looked around and it looked like the only way out

was behind me because the rest of it was just canyon wall, and this was steep, real steep, but it was more gradual than anything around me. So I climbed up backwards with my hands like that, scooting. And I would slide back down and then I would get up again and slide some more, and I cried and cried. And then I finally realized I was hurting really bad by my right side, and I looked down and I had a great big opening in my side and I started crying worse, worse. Finally I got to the top.

"And I had never really carried my plans any further except that I was going to walk to the highway. When I got up there, I knew I couldn't walk. I just thought, 'Oh God, what do I do now?' and I started crying. I heard a car coming and I just prayed to God it wasn't a white car and it wasn't those men. It was a green car and I just waved my hand and they stopped immediately. They said, 'My God, what happened to you?' I said I was raped and thrown off the bridge and my little sister, too. They said, 'Can you walk?' and I said, 'no,' so they carried me into the car and the man put his jacket around me because I was naked except for the sweater."

After an interminably long moment, Prosecutor Lewis asked one of the hardest questions Becky would ever answer.

"When you were at the bottom of the canyon, did you have any idea where Amy might be?"

Becky paused and looked at her hands. The pain washed over her again.

"As far as I could figure, she was down there, too. I just called out her name and I looked for her, but it was dark. And in the morning, I looked for her, but you know, I had in my mind all night that she was dead. And I just think that if I would have found her, I would have died, too."

Her words hung in the air as the prosecution introduced the physical evidence that gave color and weight to Becky's testimony: Becky's panties, her torn sweater, Kennedy's knife, crime-scene photos of the bridge, the canyon wall . . . and Amy's corpse laid out on the stony shore.

One of the female jurors turned away, but others studied the grisly, oversized photos intently.

Sensing a critical moment, Kennedy's defense lawyer, John Ackerman, asked for an early break. Kennedy, who had undergone hemorrhoid surgery at taxpayer expense two weeks before, needed to see a doctor about the painful and bloody discharge oozing from his rectum. The appointment could only be scheduled this day, he said. Judge John Raper agreed, and court was recessed until after lunch so the accused killer's ass could be repaired, again, at taxpayer expense.

Chief Prosecutor John Burk wasn't amused by the irony. Becky Thomson and her family had paid for her own medical care, two and a half weeks in the hospital, physical therapy, and ongoing counseling, made necessary by the sadistic monsters who now sat across from him.

Kennedy paid nothing.

After lunch, Becky finished telling how she was rescued and rushed to the hospital and interviewed by police. How she identified her assailants. How she learned her sister had been murdered.

Then the defense's cross-examination began.

Kennedy's public defender, John Ackerman, started with an apology for Becky's pain and said he didn't wish to put her through it again.

"When Ron Kennedy turned in that car and started choking you, there was no doubt in your mind, was there, you were dealing with a monster, an insane, crazy monster?"

"Yes."

"You talked about his crazy eyes?"

"Yes."

"And his acting crazy?"

"Uh-huh."

"And that's the way he was?"

"Yes, sir, he was acting crazy."

With that, Ackerman rested.

Jenkins' court-appointed lawyer, Don Chapin, took the lectern next, also apologizing. Through his questions, he hinted at his defense: Kennedy was the leader of the two—to which Becky generally agreed.

But Becky wasn't so easily led. She pointed out that Jenkins told her he could make Kennedy do anything he pleased, even if Jenkins never seemed to be in complete control of anything.

ON RE-DIRECT, PROSECUTOR Dave Lewis looked directly into Kennedy's "crazy eyes."

"Have you seen Ronald Kennedy's eyes in these proceedings?" he asked Becky.

"Yes."

"Are they the same?"

Becky stumbled, not because she didn't know, but because she didn't want to know.

"No. Sometimes . . . well, I don't look at him very much," she said.

Under questioning, she recalled that the controlling Kennedy demanded she and Amy seek his permission before they could ask a question. Sometimes he would allow them to ask, sometimes he wouldn't. To her, Kennedy snatched control and kept it, even from Jenkins.

Lewis pressed further on the most delicate topic of all. The question needed to be asked, for evidence and for the rest of time, perhaps sensing that in the future both Kennedy and Jenkins would claim he didn't or couldn't actually consummate the rape. Yet Lewis fell short of using indelicate terms like "ejaculate" or "orgasm."

"Becky, I know you don't like this, but how did the defendants perform sexually? Were they successful?"

"Yes."

"Both of them?"

"Yes."

A SLOW, SOMETIMES gruesome parade of witnesses followed.

Dorothy Strasser, who found Becky at the canyon while on a fishing trip with her husband, described the shock of seeing a young girl naked and fantastically bloodied at the

side of a dirt road. She remembered it was thirty-four de-
grees that morning. Yet, she recalled, Becky had apologized
for her nakedness and worried more for her missing sister
and her "poor mother" than herself.

The defense had no questions for her.

Natrona County Sheriff Bill Estes testified how he'd personally gotten the call when Becky was found and how he
had rushed to the Lake. After talking with Becky briefly before the ambulance arrived, he went out to the bridge, where
he saw blood spatters at two different places on the canyon
wall, one where Becky had bounced and one where Amy had
crashed. He told how his rescue diver had retrieved the little
girl's body after being in the water less than two minutes.

The defense had no questions for him.

Rescue diver Fred Klein took the stand. He told how, as
an experienced mountain climber, he had some difficulty de-
scending and coming back up the rocky trough where the
crippled Becky escaped from Fremont Canyon. A fit man in
his forties, he used a rope and all his limbs; she was badly
injured and used only her arms. It magnified her will and her
triumph. Klein also described his haunting dive into the viscous river, where he found Amy's cold body and her loose
shoe in thirty feet of water.

The defense had no questions for him.

County Coroner Tom Bustard, in the dulcet tone of a
mortician, delivered a few macabre details about transport-
ing and autopsying the little girl's corpse.

The defense had no questions for him.

Amy and Becky's mother, Toni Case, was called to testify
about the harrowing night of the abduction and the grisly aftermath, but she couldn't be found. Court was recessed while
bailiffs tried to find her. When they did, she was in a private
courthouse anteroom, behind closed doors, comforting Becky.

They were both crying.

A CHILD'S CORPSE had brought them all together in this
place and moment. These killers, their victims, their families,

their haters, their defenders, their judges, and their jurors. But the prosecution had more.

Dr. Arnold Krause, a retired Air Force flight surgeon had long been a Casper family doctor. On the day Becky Thomson was rescued, he treated her wounds, at least the ones to her body.

On the stand, he described seeing Becky the first time in the emergency room.

"She was dirty," the doctor told the courtroom. "She was bruised very severely almost all over her body. She had some real deep abrasions, some of them that required suturing. She was alert, awake, she was cold. She felt cold; the nurses had piled on several blankets to help her warm up, but she was conscious and she was cooperative."

For the jury, he sketched some of her wounds on the blank figure of a woman's body.

The doctor scratched several long, deep scrapes across the outline of her trunk. He outlined a large gash on her left hip, so deep in real life that the underlying fat was pooching out, congealed in a bloody white mass like frayed ticking spilling from a torn mattress. He flicked his marker in short, painful strokes where the skin of her buttocks had literally been stripped away by rocks. He colored irregular blotches on her arms and legs and feet where he'd seen angry black and purple bruises.

There was more. The whites of her eyes were bleeding, staining the sclera bright red. Bruises in the shape of human fingers enveloped her throat. Her left ear was purple and the inner ear swollen.

Turning to her more intimate injuries, Dr. Krause described her genitals as bruised, sliced and scraped, particularly in and around the opening of her vagina. He swabbed a small amount of semen from inside, but the violence of her splash into the water, the loss of her pants and her swim to survival had washed too much of it away for a proper analysis.[3]

He confirms what Becky had told Ronald Kennedy as he shoved himself into her: Becky Thomson was likely a virgin before her rape.

If the pain of a living girl's nightmare wasn't enough for the jury, prosecutors turned to her dead sister to add the final brushstrokes to the grisly portrait that was emerging.

Dr. James Thorpen had examined Amy Burridge's broken little body, and in the bloodless cant of a scientist who lived among the dead, the gaunt, balding pathologist described her wounds in unemotional detail. Stripped of its esoteric, arcane technicalities, the doctor's explanation was chilling: Amy was cold and in full rigor mortis when he autopsied her. Her chest cavity was filled with dark-red and clotted blood. Her aorta had virtually exploded. Her throat was filled with a bloody froth. Her stomach still contained bits of her dinner the night before: spaghetti with a meat sauce. Shards of four ribs had punctured her lung.

But, he explained, Amy had not been raped. Her vagina contained no semen and, although it leaked river water that had seeped into her corpse, it bore no sign of any forced entry.

What killed her?

Thorpen displayed a single X-ray film. In it, Amy's spine has plunged as much as two inches into her brain.

Thorpen surmised she had crashed head-first into the rock ledge one hundred and twelve feet below the bridge, ramming her spinal column deep into her skull like a railroad spike skewering a soft-boiled egg. It was called a "ring fracture" because the spinal column had literally burst through the ring at the base of her skull and pithed her.

"Was death instantaneous in this case?" Prosecutor Jack Burk asked him.

"I don't believe death was immediate or was instantaneous," Thorpen said. "I think it followed shortly after the infliction of the injury, but I did observe evidence that at least some of the blood had been aspirated, or breathed down, into the lungs."

"How long did she live after her injuries?" Burk asked.

"A matter of seconds."

Excerpted from: Autopsy #43-C-73.
Amy Allice Anthea Burridge

Dr. James W. Thorpen, Pathologist
Natrona County Memorial Hospital, Casper,
Wyoming.

Free-falling bodies undergo constant acceleration due to the force of gravity. Speed increases by 32 feet per second every second, and the rate of increase is 32 feet per second per second. A falling body goes farther in any given second than the preceding second, thus, the falling body gains downward velocity at the above rate. The speed acquired by a free-falling body is proportional to the time of the fall, and the distance from rest is proportional to the square of time.

The kinetic energy of a moving body amounts to half of its mass times the square of its velocity. This is expressed by the formula: $KE = \frac{1}{2}m \times v^2$. Doubling the mass with the same velocity doubles the amount of energy. Doubling the velocity with the same mass quadruples the amount of energy. The retarding force of air friction increases with the speed of the falling body and may become equal to the weight of the body. The body then moves downward under balanced forces, without further acceleration at its limiting, or "terminal velocity."

A feather soon attains this. Raindrops attain it at a higher limiting velocity after falling a much greater distance. A parachutist with an open chute has a safe, low terminal velocity due to increased air friction, but if his chute does not open, the maximum speed obtained is about 200 feet per second.

So Amy fell.

One hundred twelve feet.

Two-point-four-seven seconds.

Faster than a feather. Faster than a raindrop, a snowflake, a prayer or a promise.

NEXT CAME THE cadre of small-town cops who worked the most shocking case in Wyoming's criminal history, from investigators to beat cops to deputies, each with a piece of the morbid puzzle.

Police Sgt. Ernest Johnson had visited the missing girls' home with Investigator Dave Dovala the morning after they disappeared. Later, while canvassing the neighborhood around the grocery store with Investigator Bill Barnes, they got an all-points bulletin identifying Kennedy and Jenkins as the prime suspects.

After Ron Kennedy was arrested, every cop's eye was peeled for Jenkins, his dumpier, dopier sidekick. Johnson and Barnes drew the task of finding Jenkins' white Impala, which fit Becky Thomson's description of the crime car.

Their search didn't take long in the small town. Shortly after noon, they spotted the car in north Casper and followed it for three blocks to the liquor store. But Jenkins wasn't driving. It was a woman who proved to be more observant—and more ballsy—than they expected.

Ron's wife pulled to the curb and jumped out of Jerry Jenkins' car, motioning the cops to come over to her. She asked them why they were following her. They told her that her husband had been busted. Without explaining why she was driving a car possibly used in a vicious crime less than twelve hours before, she simply said she was driving Jenkins' Impala to his Spruce Street apartment to drop it off, nothing more. So they followed her to the apartment Jenkins shared with his wife and two children. While Ron's wife went inside, they waited with the car while a search warrant was prepared.

Later, while searching the car, Johnson noticed brown flecks on the rear passenger-side and back windows. It was blood, splashed on the interior glass. It was Becky's.

Patrol officer Ohly Callies and Sheriff's Deputy Mike Johnson both told the court how they stumbled into Jenkins on his way to a north Casper liquor store a little after one in the afternoon.

In time, Investigator Dave Dovala came to the stand. He recounted how he was assigned the case, visited the girls' home, interviewed Becky at the hospital, and eventually arrested Ronald Kennedy dramatically on the main street at high noon.

Police Investigator Dick Theno, who helped search for little Amy Burridge, was the last cop to take the stand. He didn't have the smoking gun that would convict two killers. He didn't slap the cuffs on anyone. He didn't even know much of what happened until later that night. All he added was one of the most heart-rending visuals of the hunt for Amy Burridge's killers: During his three hours in the canyon where Amy's body was discovered by divers, he found two pink hair ribbons that had washed ashore sometime in the night.

The courtroom was deathly silent as the ribbons were entered into evidence.

Dr. Leo Bush, an optometrist with even less involvement in the investigation and arrests, was the last prosecution witness, but he delivered evidence that placed Becky in Jerry Jenkins' car. Without it, the defense might have easily argued it was all a case of mistaken identity.

But Dr. Bush described a single blue contact lens found on the floorboards of the Impala's backseat as identical to one he prescribed for Becky. In the violence of her beatings, it had fallen out and gone unnoticed until investigators found it the next day. Its unique mate had been painfully removed from Becky's swollen, bleeding eye the next morning at the hospital.

And on the seemingly anti-climactic note of contact lenses and hair ribbons, the state rested.

◆ ◆ ◆

THE MOST DAMNING evidence against Kennedy and Jenkins—their own words—had not been used.

A 1968 U.S. Supreme Court ruling, *Bruton v. United States*, made it impossible.

In that case, the court decided a defendant's constitutional right to confront and cross-examine witnesses is connected in some ways to the evidentiary rule that prohibits the admission of hearsay in a criminal trial. Also, co-defendants might be motivated to save themselves at their cohorts' expense, especially when faced with the prospect of the death penalty.

After *Bruton*, prosecutors were forced to choose between separate trials with admissible statements, or a single trial without the statements.

Complicating matters at the time of trial, Wyoming didn't have a general conspiracy statute on its books. Had Kennedy and Jenkins been charged with conspiracy to commit rape or murder, their statements might have been admissible.

When prosecutors elected to try the accused killers together, they were betting that they had a strong enough case without Jerry Jenkins' extraordinary confession to police on the day of his arrest, and without Ron Kennedy's creepy, almost taunting challenge to police—*How are you gonna prove it? You've got no witnesses.*

Once again, the law Kennedy and Jenkins had flouted all their lives protected them from their own worst enemies: themselves.

THE PROSECUTION'S CASE lasted only two days, and no witnesses were scheduled on Friday, but the shouting wasn't over.

In Judge John Raper's chambers, while the defense and prosecution argued over the usual motions and disputable facts, emotions boiled over. Ackerman argued the state had improperly charged Kennedy and Jenkins with trying to conceal a felony by committing murder. In fact, he said,

Amy's death hadn't been done to conceal anything, and Becky's attempted murder would have concealed her rape, but she survived.

"Your Honor, the thing that keeps surfacing in the course of the state's argument is that the state is really wishing it was Becky rather than Amy who was dead because they have a nice case there, clearly on the bridge when Jenkins is saying, 'Make sure she's dead,'" Ackerman pleaded. "Following a rape it really fits into the statute. But the court should bear in mind that Becky is not dead and it is Amy who is, in fact, dead, who obviously died before this crime of rape was even committed."

And away from the jury's hearing, the defense lawyer admitted what would have been shocking for the public to hear but what was just part of the complex role he played:

"Mr. Burk alluded to it in his argument, that they were concealing their identity by tossing Becky over the bridge. And I believe that to be the case. I believe that's what they were trying to do when they tossed Becky over the bridge. But she is alive and she's not involved in the murder aspect of this case."

It was Friday, and the court planned to take a weekend break. The judge listened raptly and took Ackerman's arguments under advisement before excusing the lawyers to go back to their hotels to prepare for the following Monday, when the defense would take center stage.

THINGS MATTER.

We write down what people say so we can read them again someday. We take pictures to remind us. We try to remember certain things we see or feel or taste or smell, as certainly as we try to forget other things. But we often invest more in saving relics of our existence, maybe just to prove we understand the value of remembering.

Maybe Becky's words hang out there in the dark and limitless vacuum of space, but the tangible mementoes of the crime against her and Amy are stored in a cardboard box, hidden away in the dusty bowels of a county building in Cheyenne, Wyoming. The haunting physical evidence, the souvenirs of a night when four lives intersected and were changed forever, was simply piled together in a box after the trial and stored away indefinitely for the inevitable appeals and posterity.

On a chilly Tuesday morning in January 2003, a county employee wheeled that box into the room where I was poring over the trial documents. He got a signature, and then left the box in a corner for me to open.

It had been years since anyone looked inside, and I simply sat for several minutes in the safe, sterile, fluorescent light of a government conference room, watching it before I broke its seal.

Thirty years after I first heard the news, ten years after I began to think someone should write it down, six months after beginning to read oral documents and listen to the fuzzy memories of anyone who recalled the crime, I was about to hold the proof in my hands.

And I was not completely prepared to release those ghosts back into the world.

I can't erase the pictures from my mind. A sad and empty Becky in her hospital bed the next morning, eye swollen shut. Various shots of the canyon walls marked with inky X's to designate the spots where Amy's and Becky's bodies bounced as they fell.

And Amy's corpse, white and cold, her face obscured, thankfully, by her hair. This is the first photograph of her I've seen in thirty years and, goddammit, it's not how I want to remember her.

I unfold a map on which Becky traced their circuitous route that night, down city streets, toward the mountains, then out toward the lake. The lake, ironically, doesn't appear on the map, as if the destination were truly some place that was not part of this world.

Here is one of Jenkins' cheap workshirts found in the backseat later, stained with Becky's blood after her beating by Kennedy.

Deeper, I find securely packaged samples of hair and blood from the girls, and microscopic slides examined by the FBI's various forensic scientists in 1973.

Inside a manila envelope, I find a pouch containing Amy's pink hair ribbons, which had been found on the opposite bank of the river before deputies found her body on the bottom.

Here are the X-ray films that show her spinal column jammed deeply into her brain, and her shattered skull.

The contact lens that placed Becky in Jenkins' car is there, too.

So are her black panties, removed for an indignity she believed would save her life, then lost in the darkness.

Investigators collected Coors and Schlitz beer cans around the spots where Kennedy and Jenkins had parked that night. They sit, some never opened, in the bottom of the box, encrusted with dirt and guilt.

The light burgundy sweater that protected Becky through the night is wrapped in a fragile plastic grocery bag that's falling apart. I unfold it across the table to see how it had been sliced off her at the hospital in one long cut straight up the front, between her breasts.

I fold it gently and put it away. I pack everything back in the box, fold its flaps tightly, and breathe deeply. My hands are black with the dirt from the beer cans, which has stained almost all the exhibits.

Everything is stained.

But I can wash my hands.

Chapter 6

THE DEFENSE

April 29, 1974

The prosecution's portrait of a crime—or at least its rough sketch—had been unveiled. On Monday morning, the defense prepared to add a few bold strokes of its own, a few dark and intricate lines.

Defense lawyer John Ackerman wasted no time. He spent less than five minutes before the well-rested jury, fresh from its sequestered weekend at a local hotel.

In fewer than one thousand words, he outlined a defense that would explore the gloomy corners of Ronald Kennedy's dark life and even darker mind, less to excuse than to explain, and perhaps to exonerate two accused rapists and killers.

"As our investigation proceeded along, I think probably the same thing happened in our minds that happened in this jury's mind last week," Ackerman said. "The big agonizing question that arose in our minds was not so much a question of what happened, but a question of why."

Don Chapin, the forty-eight-year-old soft-spoken son of an accountant whose legal practice had been confined to commercial law and contracts, was even more abrupt in his opening remarks. He saw his own client, Jerry Jenkins, as a weakling follower and dim-witted punk who probably never did anything significant on his own. He was less certain of Ronald Kennedy, who seemed more like a frighteningly unpredictable rattlesnake.

Chapin spoke only 300 words, mostly to tell the jury

he'd present no evidence on Jerry Jenkins' behalf. And he might have spoken fewer words if the mere names of Kennedy and Jenkins had not become entwined in most minds, including his own: "We intend rather, to rely on the presumption of innocence of Jerry Kennedy—or Jerry Jenkins."

Together, Kennedy and Jenkins faced possible execution for the most hideous crime ever committed in Wyoming. And now, as Chapin graciously implored the jury to keep an open mind and sat down, their fates were bound together as inextricably as their names and deeds.

THE ONLY LIFE Hilda Kennedy had ever known was hard, but to save her son's life, she was about to do the hardest thing a mother could ever do.

Born the oldest of five children in the tiny farm village of Elmwood, Nebraska, in 1913, her father was a self-anointed faith healer who barely subsisted by selling his healing touch, even in the Bible Belt. After Hilda's mother died young and poor, her three little daughters and two sons were promptly consigned to the care of Catholic nuns who ran a small orphanage in the Iowa borderlands.

In their grim, abstemious asylum from poverty, little Hilda—not yet a teenager—raised her brothers and sisters, while their father roamed Heartland back roads in search of damaged souls, and only intermittently came back to visit them.

When she was old enough to leave, she did. She had completed only the eighth grade in the nuns' school, but she left a Catholic, attending Mass almost every Sunday, even as she drifted from farm town to farm town, barely one step ahead of the Depression, taking work in greasy spoons and roadside diners, wherever she could make enough money for bus fare to the next wide spot in the road.

She met and married an Iowa mechanic named Ernest Leroy Kennedy in 1935 when she was twenty-two years old and he was ten years her senior. Ten months later, their first child, a girl, was born, and they moved to Casper, Wyoming, where the auto mechanic Ernest was certain he might find regular work. He didn't.

Without work or money, they literally landed in a heap. The rented house at 109 East J Street had two small bedrooms, a kitchen, and a front room, where a trap door led into a dank, earthen crawlspace that hid a still used by the previous owner for bootlegging whiskey. The house was heated by a small wood- and coal-burning stove, and had no running water. As more children came—five over the next sixteen years—they were bathed in a galvanized tub with water heated on the gas stove. Their bathroom was an outhouse a few yards from the back door. The fence around their mangy yard was topped by barbed wire.

Ernest never found work, which was fine by him. He dreamed of opening his own garage, but his inertia was far greater than his ambition. He preferred to stay at home and drink. About the only car he maintained at all was his black 1929 Ford Model A, which he kept running because the family simply couldn't afford a new car, and Ernest still needed a way to get to the tavern. Even though he was raised a Catholic, too, he shrugged off Hilda's church-going as nonsense.

Their union was turbulent. The typically dour Ernest was abusive and loud when he was drunk, which was most of the time. In one violent argument with Hilda, he stabbed her in the side with a butcher knife—an assault that went unreported. And they all went unreported in those days, when any day or night in the Kennedys' hovel on J Street could erupt in drunken terror for Hilda or the children.

But Hilda couldn't quit, not on Ernest, not on her family, not on herself. She took various menial jobs in local steakhouses and luncheonettes, working seven days a week and sometimes bringing home food scraps in a bucket for her growing family.

Still barely scraping by on the meager wages Hilda could earn as a dishwasher, Hilda and Ernest began drawing county welfare to feed themselves and pay their rent of twenty dollars a month. For most of the next sixty years, until she died in 1999 at age eighty-four, Hilda would draw some form of government dole.

Despite Ernest's infrequent and usually brief jobs, and Hilda's paltry bread-winning, the children kept coming. Their fourth child, a son they named Ronald Leroy Kennedy, was born on July 17, 1946. Two more would follow.

When little Ronnie was eight months old, Hilda went back to work as a dishwasher at a local restaurant. When she was working, even if Ernest was home, the baby was left in the care of his two older sisters, who were ten and six. On school days, they dropped the toddler at a neighbor's house in the morning and would pick him up in the afternoon.

In those days, Hilda took work where she could find it, local grease buckets like a well-known bootlegger joint that featured a tank full of live rainbow trout, a barbeque joint, and a drive-in. She seemed always to get the dishwasher's job, except at Bennett's, where she proudly accepted a promotion to potato- and vegetable-peeler. Sometimes she crossed the tracks and tidied houses for the uptown folks, or hired out to clean motel rooms, or swept floors—any job that didn't require more than a big heart.

Her money always paid for groceries, clothes for kids, and the ceaseless household bills, not Ernest's increasing inebriation. She hid her money from him. Sometimes, Ernest would get a job for a few days or maybe a few weeks, but he spent his paychecks on booze. At those infrequent times when he accidentally had some extra money in his pocket, he made a great show of donating it for groceries, but such generosity was rare.

He was more generous with his drinking pals. They were regulars at the house, often sloppy drunk and equally unemployed. When they were there, the children avoided the house, but short of running away to a different life, they could not entirely elude the snake pit that their home became when Ernest and his buddies were stewed to the gills.

Through it all, Hilda kept her faith in God. She attended

Mass nearly every Sunday and forced her expanding brood to go along, although none of them took to the Church as passionately as Hilda had.

Neither the usually absent Hilda nor the rummy Ernest, even when terrorizing the children, were effective disciplinarians. The children knew trouble as they knew nothing else. By adulthood, one daughter had spent five years in a girls' reformatory, another had served time in juvenile hall, and both sons had already started an impressive string of petty crimes that would keep them in and out of jail and reformatory for their teenage years. When other children were going to prom and the local soda shop, the Kennedy boys were joy-riding in their stolen cars, breaking into homes, and mugging easy marks.

At eighteen, just before Ronnie would have graduated from high school if he hadn't dropped out of school in eighth grade, he broke into an elderly woman's home, beat her up, and stole twenty dollars from her purse. It was his first adult felony arrest, but he was already a cool-headed veteran hoodlum with more than two dozen juvenile arrests. And his mother was always on his side.

They moved out of the J Street house when it was condemned by the city and leveled as a nuisance. The family moved to a new "modern" house a few blocks away and felt as if they'd come up in the world: The toilet was inside.

Ernest died a few days before Christmas in 1969 from complications of his alcoholism. He was sixty-six. Hilda remained at his side through those dark days, faithful to the end.

So Hilda single-handedly supported her family in a bleak place as she had sustained her siblings in a bleak orphanage as a child, by simply pressing on the best she could. Sometimes she worked two and three jobs simultaneously until she retired after a radical hysterectomy—ten days before her ne'er-do-well son Ronnie was arrested for abduction, rape and murder.

And now, on a late-April morning seven months later, she was about to take the witness stand in front of a crowd she knew hated her youngest son, and try to save him from the gas chamber.

The stout little woman with sad, dark eyes and graying hair took the stand on Monday morning. The simple cotton dress Hilda wore was the best she owned. She smiled wanly to her son as she slowly walked to the stand to take her oath. She was out of place in this courtroom.

Defense lawyer John Ackerman led his first witness through the perfunctory questions: Yes, she was Hilda Catherine Kennedy. Yes, she was the mother of the defendant, Ronald Kennedy. Yes, she had five other children. Yes, she had lived a hard life in Casper for most of her life, but she always tried to keep her family together and safe.

But, no, she hadn't always succeeded. Her husband Ernest was the unpredictable, foul fulcrum on which everything turned.

"Sometimes when I'd come home at night from work, the children were . . ." she testified, "well, if they weren't outside playing, they would be so scared, being as how he was drunk. They would hide under the bed until I came home. He would threaten to whip them, you know, maybe for something they didn't even do and they would just go hide until I came home, and then they would come running to me."

"He frightened them?" Ackerman asked.

"Yes, he did. But if he was sober, he was real good to the children; it was only when he was drunk."

"Which was the majority of the time?"

"Yes, sir."

"Where else would they hide from him?"

"Under the bed. Or in the coal shed."

The tumble-down coal shed was out behind the Kennedys' claustrophobic little house. Covered by a rusty tin roof, it had two windows and a door they could lock from the inside. Ernest would pound on the door and demand that they come out for their beatings, but usually they wouldn't. They'd simply cower in a far corner and wait for him to go back to his bottle. If the weather was nice, they'd spend the night in the black, dusty shed.

"Did he ever beat the kids, to your knowledge?"

"Oh, he spanked them, like most fathers would."

"I think you mentioned just a moment ago that he would spank them for no reason at all?"

"That's true. When he was drinking."

"Most fathers wouldn't do that," Ackerman said. It was not a question and there was no answer.

Hilda described Ronnie as a thin, weak, sickly boy as a child. He seemed more susceptible to illness than her other kids, and "he ate real good, but he just didn't seem to gain weight."

"Did he have any fears as a small child?" Ackerman asked.

"Yes," Hilda answered, recalling several similar incidents when her son was only five or six years old. "Him and his brother had their own bedroom. This was a small bedroom and he would be laying there with the lights off and he would just out loud scream, 'Mommy, come here!' and I would say, 'What's the matter, honey?' and he would say, 'Mommy, there's a man coming through the wall.' And I would turn on the lights and I said, 'There's nothing there.' He said, 'Mommy, you just don't see it.' "

"Anything else he would scream about?"

"Yes," Hilda spoke quietly. "In the front room of our house used to be a whiskey still and it had a handle on the door where you could raise it up, and it was all cemented up with steps. There were shelves around in there and . . ."

"Down under the house?"

"It was right in the front room. You just open a trap door and go down some steps. And his brother opened the door and said, 'Let's go down and see what's down there,' and then Ronnie saw those black widows on the door and he said, 'I'm not going down there.' And Jim told him, 'Well, I ain't afraid. I'm going down and see what's in the cellar.' Well, you couldn't get Ronnie down there. He just went hysterical over those black widow spiders. He just had a fear of them."

"Did he ever have nightmares about them?"

"Yes, he had a nightmare they were in his bed. He tore his bed up and he couldn't find anything, but he still believed they were in his mattress."

"That was still at a very young age?"

Hilda nodded.

"Very small age, uh-huh. He was awful frail."

WHERE ERNEST KENNEDY discovers mandrills, nobody knows.

Certainly, none live within 10,000 miles of Casper, Wyoming, and Ernest isn't exactly a devotee of nature magazines.

But one night, he gathers the children around him and tells them the literally fantastic story of the man-eating mandrill, an ape-like creature that had the face of a baboon, the hands and feet of a man, the horns of a devil—and the appetite of a cannibal. Mandrills, he explains in his elaborate lie, will creep into a house at night and eat children while they watch in terror as it gnaws on their living parts.

In reality, a mandrill is a baboon-like creature that lives in African rainforests and eats only spiders, snails, worms, small ground animals, grass, shoots, roots and fruit. At night it does not seek child blood, but sleeps peacefully in the highest branches, where it is safe from predators.

The children laugh nervously at Ernest's tale, but none of them sleep soundly that night. Ronnie is only six and doesn't sleep at all.

The next morning, he takes his mother aside as she prepares a simple breakfast.

"Mama, if it would come over here, would it eat me?"

Hilda hugs him and tries to reassure the frightened little boy, although she herself has no idea what a mandrill was, where it lived or what it ate—or if it existed at all.

"Well, there's no danger of it coming over here," she says. "It's probably in Africa or someplace."

That night, Ernest continues his fabulous yarn, heaping ever more dreadful lies until Ronnie is visibly agitated. The next day, as if by horrible magic, a color photograph of a mandrill, ripped from a magazine, is taped to the wall above Ronnie's bed.

When little Ronnie comes screaming from his room, Hilda is enraged. She rips the photograph off the wall and burns it in the coal stove. Then she chides Ernest for deliberately scaring the child, but he's drunk and not listening.

The next night, a new picture of a mandrill reappears.

"WHAT KIND OF child was Ron compared with your other children?" Ackerman asked Hilda, continuing her testimony.

"Well, he was . . . he was odd, very odd. I guess you would put it that way," she said, her eyes a little sadder. "He was kind of an odd little kid."

"In what way?"

"If children were to come over to play, he would be in the house. He would just stick his little head out the door and he would look out there to see if it was anybody he wanted to play with. If not, he would stay in the house. Then some days, he would go out and play."

"Was he different day to day?"

"Well, quite often," she said. "He would have streaks where he didn't want to play with any of the children."

"Did he have long-term friendships with any other children when he was young?"

"No. He might have one friend at a time, and if he got tired of him, why, maybe a week or ten days, why, he would find someone else."

"That has tended to continue up to the present day, has it not?"

"Yes."

"Did he ever tell you about it when he got hurt?"

"Oh, yes," Hilda brightened. "One incident. Around our yard we had barbed wire, you know, for the top. He took a run one day and jumped that barbed wire and he got a cut about so long on his back. But as a rule, he wouldn't say whether he hurt."

"Did you ever observe any violence of any kind between he and his father later on in life or anytime?"

"Well, yes. He and his father would argue. I guess they just couldn't see things alike, and Ron does have kind of a hot temper and they got into arguments where, oh, he has slapped his dad open-handed. Shall I tell about the spaghetti?"

"Sure."

"I was cooking spaghetti on the stove and he picked up a plate and filled it full of spaghetti and threw that in his dad's face so his dad wouldn't say any more to him, I guess."

"Hot spaghetti?"

"Hot spaghetti."

Ackerman was pressing for every detail of Ronald Kennedy's life that might illustrate a scrambled mind, but so far he'd only elicited a mother's anecdotes about nightmares, childish fears of spiders and night-intruders, and a father–son spat that had merely ended in a mess of tomato sauce and wet noodles. He knew it wasn't enough to convince a jury—or perhaps even a common man on the street who'd probably had similar childhood fears and conflicts with his parents—that Ronald Kennedy was truly insane.

He pressed ahead with Hilda.

"Now you talked about the fears of people coming, a man coming through the wall, spiders and things like that. Since Ron has grown up, has he had any of those?"

Hilda nodded.

"He had an awful fear of lightning. If there was a storm coming up, he would cover all the windows or pull the shades."

More common childhood fears, not insanity. Ackerman was losing the jury and the gallery by holding up a kid's ordinary phobias as evidence of serious mental illness. What child hasn't quailed at the rumble of distant thunder, or covered his eyes at the flash of lightning?

"In the last year, has anything like that occurred with lightning?"

"Yes," Hilda said. "He was home one day and he says, 'Mama, there's a storm coming up. It is lightning real bad.

Why don't you pull all the shades?' And I said, 'What for?' and he said, 'Well, Mama, pull the shades. I'll feel better.' So he pulled the shades, then he went in the bedroom and shut the door. He put the blanket or the bedspread over his head, and he was scared."

"Did he put anything over the windows other than pulling the shades?" Ackerman asked.

"Oh, yes," Hilda said. "He covered them with either blankets or towels, bath towels, to make sure it was dark."

"Can you remember another time?"

"It was out to my girlfriend's house. . . . a storm come up, she lived eleven miles out of town and the lightning was real bad and he went in and said, 'Aunt Elsie, will you cover the windows?' She said, 'What for?' He said, 'I just don't like lightning. I just have an awful fear of it. Have you got a blanket?' She said, 'Why? Are you cold?' He said, 'No, I just want to cover my head.' "

But this time, in both cases, Hilda Kennedy wasn't talking about familiar childhood fears.

The Ronald Kennedy who frantically covered windows with towels so lightning couldn't flare in his eyes and thunder wouldn't fill his brain was no longer a little child. He was twenty-six years old.

SOME DEFENSE WITNESSES did not appear gladly. In fact, only a few were there to help Ronald Kennedy and Jerry Jenkins avoid the gas chamber.

One was Ray Sternberg, a rancher who tended bar at the Sage Club, a scruffy little roadhouse where Kennedy and Jenkins had spent much of the day of the crime. He knew both defendants well.

Sternberg was tending bar that day when Ron Kennedy came in around 1:00 p.m. He was cash poor, tapped out, and asked to charge a six-dollar case of beer. Ray turned him down, saying he didn't have the authority to approve a charge. So Kennedy used the bar phone to sweet-talk the owner into letting him have beer on credit.

Sternberg's shift ended around 4:00 p.m., but he stuck around to play pool and have a few beers with some of his barfly buddies. Around six or seven, Kennedy was back with Jerry Jenkins and begging to charge another case of beer. While Sternberg called and asked the owner if it was okay, Kennedy and Jenkins huddled quietly at the end of the bar, whispering. Sternberg said his boss had okayed the earlier charge, so Kennedy was allowed to charge another case of Coors beer and a pint of Canadian Lord Calvert whiskey. He signed a credit slip for $9.60 and thanked the bartender for vouching for him, then left.

Even though he'd apparently helped guzzle a case of beer in the past four or five hours, Kennedy didn't appear drunk to the veteran barkeep.

Dr. Nelson Frissell, a former MASH unit doctor in Vietnam who became a family doctor in Casper, followed. He'd seen Kennedy three times for a variety of complaints, none life-threatening: hives, dizziness, and a feeling he described as "half-awake, half-asleep." Kennedy had enumerated pains behind his ears, in his neck, and radiating down to his arms. He also told Frissell he'd recently lost twenty-five pounds, but when the doctor weighed him, Kennedy was actually five pounds heavier than a visit two years before.

Dr. Frissell suspected stress and further asked if Kennedy was depressed, but Kennedy said he wasn't. He complained that he'd just returned from jail on a minor beef in Billings, where he'd undergone $2,000 in tests, but got no answers.

Frissell ordered some tests and X-rays, and he scheduled a physical exam a couple weeks later. When Kennedy arrived for the next visit, he said he'd suffered more hives, but that they only came out at night and disappeared if he did a full day's work. He also said that when he went outside, he had the sensation of being lifted off the ground, and it bothered him to think about it.

Kennedy went on to say he hated when people touched him because it would blanch his skin. And then, apropos of nothing, he remarked he'd just bought a car and trailer and was having trouble paying for them.

But Frissell only found a chronic case of hemorrhoids and chronic sighing common to people who are anxious and nervous, but no organic disease. Kennedy's thyroid, urine and blood were all normal. The doctor prescribed a tranquilizer.

Kennedy was told to return five days later, but he didn't. And he never paid his bill.

Kennedy's brother-in-law was next. He'd known Ron for seven years, since he'd married Ron's older sister. A taxi driver in a town where taxis were few and peculiar, he and his wife lived just a few blocks from Ron in north Casper.

Ron's older sister had left home when she was thirteen and Ron was only eight. She'd glimpsed his odd behavior and believed he needed professional help, so she told him to see a shrink, but he always smiled and told her he wasn't crazy.

Frank described for the jury a fishing trip, just a few months before the crime. Ron had come to his house that morning, already drunk. On the way to the Lake, they bought more beer, and each drank four cans on the half-hour trip. After only an hour at the Lake, Ron blacked out. His eyes got big, and he fell on the ground. His brother-in-law carried him to the car and rushed back toward town.

But before they arrived, Ron came around and, clear-headed as he could be after drinking at least eight beers in two hours, asked: "Hey, do you want to go fishing?"

"Some other time," he said.

Later, while Ron's sister and brother-in-law were watching a late movie on TV, Ron burst into their home, extremely agitated.

He'd been walking from his mom's house about six blocks away when he heard a buzzing over his head. The invisible swarm hovered over him and followed him down the street and onto his sister's porch. It terrified him.

The brother-in-law told the court Ron's eyes were bugging out of his head, and he was "kind of crazy looking." He believed something—not someone—was pursuing him. His skin was icy to the touch. He ran into the little house and started closing all the blinds. He went outside and wandered around, but heard nothing except the sounds of a spring night. Still, it took almost two hours for Ron to calm down.

And a third incident was described a few weeks later. While drinking together for a few hours at a club which was a favorite hangout for the tough crowd, a party of strangers sat nearby. When they asked to borrow an empty chair, Ron growled, "I wish you guys would quit bugging me." A gut feeling prompted the brother-in-law to grab his arm and say, "Let's go."

Halfway home, Ron turned and said calmly, "I think I'm going to beat you up."

Surprised, but tough enough to defend himself against his scrawny kin, Ron's brother-in-law warned him: "You better knock it off or there's going to be trouble."

With that, Ron started crying and never stopped until after the other man dropped him at home.

After that, he told the court, he feared Ronald Kennedy when he'd been drinking.

Kennedy's third wife took the stand next, another in a long line of witnesses intended to show how crazy he really was. They had known each other for nine years, she said, but had been married for only nine months—wedding him only a month before the crime.

She nurtured a simmering hatred for Becky Thomson, believing (as Ron had told her) that Becky was fabricating the whole story against her husband. Several police escorts were assigned to Becky during the trial and spent part of every morning and afternoon inspecting her car for bombs or other devices.

But now she was one of the bit players in the drama, and she brought her husband's jailhouse letters, in which he professed his love for her in dreamy, delusional terms—and more.

One of the letters, written less than a month before the trial, referred to their two stillborn children from past pregnancies. Oddly, he doesn't refer to a third child who died *in utero* shortly after he was jailed for the rape and murder of Amy Burridge and Becky Thomson.

The Kennedys had wanted proper rites for them, so they

were both buried in Casper, one in Highland Cemetery and one in Memorial Gardens.

March 31, 1974

My Darling wife:

I just received your letter and other things. I've wanted to write you. But when they brought us back from lander they kept our things out front till the jailer could check through them. Last night i got my things. But i couldn't get a pencil to write with until today. My darling i will never be mad at you for visiting our babies Robert and Candy. I just wish to god i would have went with you. I know you're grieved over them. But i have also grieved over them too. Honey we both loved them very very much.

Honey i want you to pick some grass or dirt from Roberts and Candys graves and bring it to daddy.

I pray every night for our children that god called away from us. I also pray every night that the lord will let our baby to be live. The names you are going to give our child make me so happy. My wife i love you with all my heart and soul. I just couldn't live in this world without you. My Darling ive been such a big fool. It hurts me so deeply to know the pain ive caused you. Please my darling forgive me for hiding my feelings to you. Every night i dream that were together and ive built us a beautiful home with lotts of trees and green grass for our baby to play in. Also where the sky is blue. Where we can walk together and be together the three of us forever. I promise you my Darling if theres every away that ill be with you again and i am not to old to get around All build you that home with my own bare hands and make you very happy my wife & child. I love you and i will till the day my life ends and then behond that forever.

I will write again tomorry until then may god watch over you and baby.

Love you very much forever your husband
Ron Kennedy

After the letter was read in open court, Kennedy was clearly unnerved. Ackerman asked for and received five minutes while his client tried to regain his self-control.

When court resumed, Ackerman tried to introduce another letter, in which Kennedy appears to say he believes he can receive messages through his stomach. But Judge Raper denied it as immaterial, saying Kennedy only writes in the letter that he has a belly ache.

KENNEDY'S FIRST OF three known wives, Jane Green, testified that her ex-husband had stalked her, one time shooting at the car in which she sat with her date. She also recounted how he had virtually abducted her after she filed for a divorce, forcing her to have sex in a trailer behind his mother's house because, he claimed, having sex during a separation rendered any divorce action moot.

She also testified under cross-examination that he occasionally visited their young son, "who was always happy to see his father. What disappointed him was that Ron had promised him things and would come back again and not have these things. He's seven years old now, and at that time he was six and he was old enough to know when he had been lied to."

When police first interviewed Jane about Ron's suspected role in the crimes at Fremont Canyon, she told them, "it would take a sick person to do something like this."

Lorine Mullen, a bartender who'd known Ron Kennedy for years and whose children called him "Uncle Ronnie," told the jury how she, her husband and Kennedy went to a local roadhouse a few months before the crime.

Kennedy was already liquored up when he asked them to go out with him. After a few hours of more heavy drinking, just as Mullen and her husband were encouraging Kennedy to look for steady work, he lapsed into a trance. She said his eyes were wild ("like he was in another world") and in the middle of a sentence, he started mumbling about a variety of subjects, all different. Nothing made sense. The incoherent babble had gone on for almost an hour when the woman decided to call Kennedy's sister for help, but her husband objected.

As they began to bicker about what to do, Kennedy erupted angrily.

"If you don't stop talking to her like that," he growled at Mullen's husband, "then I'm going to knock you down!"

She yelled back at Kennedy and he laid his head on the table, apologizing. For two or three minutes, he kept his head down, not talking. When he sat up again, the conversation resumed where it had left off.

Mullen asked if he knew what had happened. He said, "Nothing." She told him and he called her a liar.

It happened again a few weeks later when Kennedy came to the Mullens' house, drunk again. This time, they wouldn't go out with him, but they shared a few drinks at the house. Once again, Kennedy soon grew unintelligible and confused, his eyes widening to fearful proportions. He didn't even recognize his old friends as he demanded the annoying stereo be turned off, then the television. Finally, he plopped on the floor, where he mumbled strange names for an hour.

THE LAST DEFENSE witness was Dr. Fritz Cubin, who testified he had seen Kennedy in his office after he complained of shallow breath, insomnia, fatigue and chest pains. On December 19, 1972—less than a year before the crime—Kennedy came to Cubin for the first time and filled out the Cornell Medical Index, a common questionnaire containing about 195 questions designed to help a doctor diagnose his patients.

Kennedy's answers generally suggested he was healthy, in mind and body. The only item he answered "yes" (and three "yes" answers were required to red-flag some infirmity) was to the question "Are you a nervous person?"

Cubin's diagnosis: Kennedy suffered from paroxysmal atrial tachycardia, a condition in which the heart rate skyrockets to anywhere from 140 to 220 beats per minute, as opposed to his normal 82. He prescribed Inderal, a new drug at the time, and told Kennedy to take it three times a day.

Other attacks ensued, and the usually unemployed Kennedy always went to the hospital's emergency room. After a few more episodes, Cubin told Kennedy that his nervousness might be the main cause of his problem and sent him to see a psychiatrist. Kennedy went to his first appointment but skipped the rest.

Neither doctor ever saw Kennedy again.

Under cross-examination, Prosecutor Jack Burk asked Cubin what emotional problems he believed Kennedy suffered.

"I felt that he was quite an anxious person, very nervous and very concerned about the symptoms of shortness of breath, which I feel were justified."

"I get the feeling this questionnaire is, let's say, where you screen out and find if you have a person with severe mental problems on your hands?" Burk asked.

"Yes," the doctor replied. "In a way, it's a rough guide to whether or not a patient has emotional problems."

"And he showed up completely clean on it?"

Cubin didn't hesitate. He wasn't a shrink, but he had no doubts about Kennedy's sanity.

"Yes."

RONALD KENNEDY'S DEFENSE was almost done. Only one possible witness remained.

In the privacy of Room 308 at the City-County Building, just down the hall from the courtroom, Kennedy met with his lawyer, John Ackerman, and a court reporter who would record this pivotal moment in his own defense: Should he testify?

Ackerman spelled it out.

"All right, Ron, the reason we are here is I now have to advise you again for purposes of the record only of your right to testify in a case in which you are a defendant, and of the fact that it is a decision which you alone can make. I can only advise you as to my feelings regarding that decision. My advice to you is that you not take the stand. I think it would be disastrous to your defense for you to take the stand, but I want you to know it is your decision and I want you to tell me now what your decision is."

Kennedy shrugged. Different from his unemotional, almost gentle, demeanor in court, now he was petulant and mean.

"Just 'no comment,'" he said, side-stepping his lawyer's advice.

"Well, that puts me in a position where I don't know whether to call you as a witness or not," Ackerman said. "Do you want me to call you?"

"You are neatly advising me that it is best that I do not take the stand?"

"That's right. But I'm also advising you that it is a decision you have to make. It is not one I can."

The ensuing pause is so long that even the court reporter noted it.

"Counsel knows best."

"So then it is your decision that you will go along with the recommendation that I have made?" Ackerman pressed.

"The burden lies on your shoulders."

Ackerman is openly frustrated.

"Yes or no? You will go along with my recommendation?"

Kennedy eyed him disdainfully. Early on in the case, Kennedy had voiced his mistrust of Ackerman, whom he believed to be a pawn of his prosecutors, of the town and of all his enemies in the world. His suspicions hadn't subsided.

"I will go along with your recommendation."

At the same time, Jerry Jenkins was meeting with his own defense lawyer, Don Chapin. In contrast, Jenkins listened carefully to his lawyer's advice and responded clearly, almost eagerly.

This case hadn't been easy for Chapin. Criminal defense wasn't his strength, but he'd taken the case out of respect for the process of law. Still, it had taken its toll on him and his practice. Telephone threats and subtle shunning in town were bad enough, but some nights when he'd get home late from the office and sit down to warmed-over

dinners alone, the blood would spontaneously trickle from
his nose.

In the face of overwhelming evidence—including Jenkins' own words in a police interrogation—his strategy was
simple: Say nothing, and hope the prosecution stumbled.

Chapin cut to the meat of Jenkins' legal and material
dilemma. He'd already made a detailed confession, and with
a police record longer than his memory, he was simply not a
sympathetic character. He might have stuffed his short,
greasy, corpulent body into a blue suit for the trial, but all the
miserable reality of him would spill out on the courtroom
floor if he opened his mouth.

"Mr. Jenkins, although I represented to the court that we
would have no witnesses on your behalf, I did want to afford
you an opportunity to testify in your own behalf, should you
so choose. We have previously discussed it. It is my recommendation that you not take the stand because it exposes you
to cross-examination by the state and to the admission of
certain statements you made during your incarceration. It is,
however, your decision and I want you to tell the court reporter what your disposition about testifying on your own
behalf is."

"No, I don't want to testify," Jenkins responded quickly.

THE DEFENSE HAD been brief in the face of incendiary evidence. That was a good thing in one respect: Kennedy and
Jenkins smelled so rancid that Ackerman had been forced to
complain to the bailiff about the stink, demanding the two
defendants be bathed before the next day.

For all intents and purposes, Kennedy and Jenkins had
said all they wanted to say. Their defense rested, and the final round—the prosecution's chance to rebut the defense's
claims, which had been a jealously guarded secret to this
point—began.

Prosecutor Burk called Dr. Lincoln Clark, a court-
appointed psychiatrist, to the stand.

A graduate of Harvard Medical School, Dr. Clark had

Today, very little has changed at the Fremont Canyon Bridge, which spans the North Platte River, some thirty-five miles south-west of Casper, Wyoming. In 1973, Becky Thomson and Amy Burridge were thrown from a spot near the end of the bridge.

Little Amy Burridge was the sparkplug for her grade-school volleyball team and they all looked to her for inspiration.

ABOVE: Becky's Kelly Walsh High School yearbook photo.

RIGHT: Amy's school photo, which appears on a memorial plaque in her school.

Photograph of plaque by the author

ABOVE: Becky, photographed here at a friend's birthday party, seldom showed any outward sign of the demons that haunted her after the crime.

RIGHT: When Becky's stepfather couldn't be at her wedding to give her away, the next most important male figure in her life—Police Officer Dave Dovala—stepped in.

Ronald Kennedy (left) and Jerry Jenkins, the morning after the crime.

A young Ronnie (right), with his father Ernest and brother James.

CLOCKWISE FROM TOP LEFT: Jerry Jenkins at Christmas 1972, almost a year before the crime; Ronald Kennedy as a baby in diapers; Ronald and James Kennedy in an undated photograph; a childhood photo of Jenkins.

Photographs courtesy of Ronald Kennedy

Although once condemned to die, Ronald Kennedy has enjoyed some surprising freedoms in prison. He was allowed to marry while serving his time, enjoying prison dances (top) and monthly conjugal visits until his divorce about ten years later.

ABOVE: Staff illustrator Greg Kearney eulogized Becky Thomson a few days after her death in 1992 in the Casper, Wyoming, *Star-Tribune*.

LEFT: Becky's ashes were buried atop her sister Amy's casket in Casper's Highland Cemetery.

Artwork used by permission from the Casper Star-Tribune
Grave photograph by Ashley Franscell

A few days after Becky Thomson died after plunging off the Fremont Canyon Bridge for the second time, artist Michael Carr was moved to paint his "urban petroglyph" on the canyon wall under the bridge: two falling girls holding hands, with the poem he wrote.

been a widely published psychiatrist for nineteen years, working as a professor of psychiatry at the University of Utah and a forensic consultant to the Wyoming State Hospital, a mental asylum.

Dr. Clark first met Ronald Kennedy four months after the crime at Fremont Canyon. He examined him four times at the state hospital's forensic ward, a locked ward on the top floor of one patient dormitory, where Kennedy had been sent for thirty days of observation when he entered his plea of innocent by reason of insanity. All told, his examinations lasted about three hours, the only time for the entire thirty days Kennedy was allowed to leave his locked cell at the end of the unit.

His diagnosis: Ronald Kennedy had an anti-social personality, a general term for many patterns of disturbed behavior. In this case, Clark described Kennedy as living "a disordered lifestyle or pattern of life which involves repeated anti-social acts, failure to conform to social and legal expectations and so forth."

"Was any psychosis found?" Burk asked him.

"No."

Judge Raper had allowed Dr. Clark the unusual privilege of remaining in the courtroom to hear the witnesses before him—and to evaluate what they said. What he learned from Kennedy's mother, sisters and friends didn't surprise him.

"This fits much with behavior that one sees in an individual with this form of personality disorder, this expression of poor social judgment and vindictiveness, getting back at people in this inappropriate fashion, the poor emotional control, the temper," he said.

"Do you attach any significance to the childhood fears that were testified to?" Burk asked.

Dr. Clark didn't skip a beat.

"No, only that childhood fears like this are very common. Many children experience fears like this. And understandably Ron was raised under conditions where there are a good many things to be feared. And to translate them to nocturnal terrors would not be surprising. And if you take the history of the childhood of many people, you would find similar memories."

Dr. Clark, who was also a medical doctor, described Kennedy's heart syndrome as unrelated to his mental state, "an incidental condition . . . relatively benign and relatively harmless."

Burk had only two more questions for the doctor—the crucial questions that would draw a definitive line between common craziness and legal insanity.

"Did Ronald Kennedy know the difference between right and wrong on the night of the crime?"

"Yes."

"Did he know the consequences of his actions?"

"Yes."

To those who listened, there seemed little doubt Ronald Kennedy was, by common standards, a crazy man. He'd killed a little girl and raped her sister who, by luck, had dodged death. Sane men don't do those things. But the law had higher standards for judging how a man's mind and heart worked.

Defense lawyer John Ackerman started by asking Dr. Clark to explain the difference between neurosis and psychosis. Clark responded that neurosis is "a partial disturbance of functioning and emotional life." The patient functions relatively well, leads a productive and socially acceptable life, etc. But he has a specific fear, obsession or compulsion. It's so common, he explains, that "a considerable number" of regular people are clinically neurotic.

But psychosis is far more intense, a "very severe disturbance of functioning that affects almost all aspects of a person's life." It's usually associated with a loss of accurate perception of reality, distortion of reality, abnormal thinking, delusions that are misinterpretations of reality, inability to think straight, logically or to perceive accurately.

Ackerman hammered at semantics.

"Is anti-social personality a 'mental disorder'?"

"Yes," Dr. Clark admitted.

"Is it a treatable mental disorder?"

"No, not satisfactorily treatable. No."

Ackerman referred to a report by a Denver psychiatrist who also examined Kennedy and Jenkins before the trial. Among his conclusions: Kennedy was a classic sociopath exhibiting an extraordinary number of the symptoms associated with anti-social personalities. Kennedy's condition reminded him of pseudo-neurotic schizophrenia, a condition of a person with multiple neurotic symptoms presented as phobias, pathological fears. They have obsessive, inappropriate compulsions, depression, hypochondria, suicidal ideas and paranoid tendencies.

"The overall picture is one of a very borderline personality for which controls, including medication, are very much indicated," the doctor wrote to the court.

Yet it frustrated Ackerman that Ronald Kennedy might still not fit the court's model of insanity. He wanted somebody, anybody, to simply admit his client was mentally ill.

"All right, then at this point, I take it, we could agree that Ronald Kennedy is suffering from a mental disorder which requires controls and medication of some sort?" Ackerman asked Dr. Clark on the stand.

"No, I would not treat him with medications at this time."

"Then you don't agree with the other psychiatrist?"

"I don't know what condition he was in at the time he saw him. What I have seen of Mr. Kennedy is he's been relatively composed, not acting in a disturbed or violent fashion."

Throughout his questioning, Ackerman used the word "schizophrenia," but now he asked Dr. Clark to define it for the jury.

"Schizophrenia is a form of serious mental illness," Dr. Clark said directly to jurors. "It is the type of mental illness that the lay person would call insanity. And these people are generally obviously seriously impaired in their thinking. They often tend to not make sense when you talk to them; they express wrong ideas or delusions; they may believe they are God, have special powers or that they are under control of other people. They may behave in bizarre fashions and adopt strange postures. They communicate very poorly and relate very poorly generally to other people."

Ackerman wanted more.

"Now in trying to arrive at a diagnosis in this area, would you agree that family background, the family transactional background, is of significance? If you take, for instance, a small child exposed to a particular family environment, the likelihood of his developing schizophrenia may be greater than in, say, another family environment, is it an important consideration?"

But Dr. Clark wasn't so easily led by the young lawyer.

"No, studies suggest the genetics are more important than rearing. Nature more than nurture."

Ackerman hammered that a brutal, alcoholic father and absent mother must have created a prime environment for schizophrenia.

"If we look at this environmental situation and we assume a small child in a situation where he is the victim of repeated aggressive acts by an alcoholic, brutal father, would you agree that in this background one will often find a repression and a denial by the child in order to preserve the dependent parent–child relationship?"

Dr. Clark resisted the young lawyer's facile—and self-interested—suggestion.

"If you put it another way, a boy with an abusive father will still try to relate to him in hopes that he would get some love and some good relationship, even if his father is very mean to him. Now if you wish to say that he is denying or not fully recognizing how mean his father is to him, that I would agree with. But in behavioral terms, I would say they can struggle and continue to seek a good relationship from a very mean person."

Ackerman went back to the roots of schizophrenia.

"One of the first things that will happen is that the patient will become aware of increasing tension?"

"Yes."

"One might find blocks or breaks in his conversation?"

"Yes."

"He might not speak or respond appropriately to his companions?"

"Yes."

"He may look fixedly away or appear to stare off into space?"

"Yes."

"And during this period, would you agree that some patients express undue worry over their physical condition?"

Dr. Clark shrugged.

"Worry about one's physical condition is common in a variety of situations, yes, and in normal people."

Ackerman tried to drag him back.

"Would you agree this is especially suggestive of an approaching schizophrenia when the complaints are unusual or unlikely?"

"Not necessarily."

Ackerman quoted what Kennedy told his doctor: " 'When I walk outside I feel like I'm being lifted off the ground.' Is that bizarre? Isn't that unusual?"

"Not that bizarre," Clark said. "The feeling, 'I have a pain because rats are gnawing the lining of my stomach,' that's bizarre. Or 'whether my breath smells bad because my sperm is rotting in my body and it's being exhaled through my breath,' those would be schizophrenic types of . . ."

Ackerman interrupted the shrink's ghastly but colorful hypotheticals.

"Well, the feeling of being lifted off the ground is not a complaint that one would frequently hear in medical practice from a patient, is it?"

"Well, people talk as if they are walking on air, it's not an unusual expression . . ."

"Or that 'half of my body is asleep and half awake.' That's not really common . . ."

"No."

Ackerman turned to Dr. Clark's own examination of Kennedy.

"Is it possible for a schizophrenic to be clear-headed, know where he is, orient past and present, be able to calculate, remember, and for him to have a satisfactory mental evaluation?"

Dr. Clark explained "sensorium," the adequacy of one's sight, smell, hearing, taste and touch. Schizophrenics, he said, often have a clear "sensorium" and can function quite well in a specific, controlled setting.

Ackerman turned to the physical aspects of schizophrenia, pointing out that schizophrenics often lose weight as the disease begins to blossom, and pointed out that the slender Kennedy lost twenty-five pounds in a few weeks before he went to his doctor. Clark admitted it was true but retorted that Kennedy gained sixteen pounds in the state mental hospital.

"What is the effect of alcohol on someone who is suffering from a mental disorder?" Ackerman asked. "Would it tend to be a catalyst in the release of this aggression?"

"It may, yes," Clark said. "It may, in my language, decrease impulse control."

"Sure, and this is probably especially true of a schizophrenic who has very poor ability to repress the impulse in the first place?"

"No, not necessarily schizophrenics. It is the individual personality disorders which are more likely to be in trouble from drinking. Schizophrenics tend to be withdrawn people who are generally not bar fighters. That's not their thing, as a rule."

Ackerman was running out of questions, but more importantly, he had run out of strategies to paint Kennedy's insanity decisively for the jury. He pursued his examination a little further, but his questions had dissipated into the arcane. Finally, he rested.

Prosecutor Burk rose to hammer the last nails in Kennedy and Jenkins' coffins before closing arguments.

"Doctor, for a total of 70 minutes during your cross-examination you were asked questions about schizophrenia. Have any of these three examinations ever disclosed any symptoms of schizophrenia?"

"No."

"Do you have any feeling there is schizophrenia involved?"

"No."

It was done. Both sides would have only one last chance to make their cases. The next day, after a long, sleepless night, they would stand before the twelve jurors and make a wish. The jury's choice would be clear.

Acquittal or death.

JOHN ACKERMAN STOOD before the jury a few minutes past four o'clock in the afternoon on Tuesday, April 30. One could almost hear his heart pounding inside him, a desperate drumbeat as his case came down to the last few words he'd have the chance to speak to the men and women who would decide Ronald Kennedy's fate. He admitted his fear that he had not saved his client's life.

He never apologized for Kennedy, never denied his role in the rape and murder of two young sisters, and never excused the crime. He briefly suggested there might be other explanations . . . *might Amy have plunged off the Fremont Canyon cliffs while running away from her captors in the dark?* . . . But his defense was simple and straightforward: Ronald Kennedy was crazy and couldn't be held responsible, *couldn't be guilty*, because his mind had been scrambled by abuse and rage.

"His life started out in a shack, a small shack with an outdoor toilet, and in the presence of a domineering, brutal, aggressive and alcoholic father and an absent mother. . . . He had more infectious diseases than the other children in the family . . . As he grew older, when he was four or five, his alcoholic father started using him as a toy to play with."

He pointed at Kennedy, a lanky and blank young man at the defense table. The man who'd flipped off the world at his arraignment sat forlorn and quiet now.

"This was a small boy. You can imagine the tension, the anguish that was building in that small mind against his father . . . You can almost feel the smoldering rage against his father building within, even as a small boy."

The rage fastened itself to Kennedy's heart and mind like an evil tumor, becoming an organic lump of him, Ackerman

suggested. It showed up in a series of illnesses and medical
complaints. It showed up in episodes of odd behavior, from
drunken mumblings and mysterious buzzing hordes that
chased him down city streets, to a mysterious being that spoke
to him through his stomach. To sadism. To monstrosity.

The burden of proving Kennedy's sanity on the moonless
night of September 24, 1973, was the state's. Ackerman reminded the jury it was not Kennedy's obligation to prove his
own insanity. Even Becky Thomson had described Kennedy
as a "crazy-eyed, insane monster."

John Ackerman expressed little doubt.

"He's an insane animal," he told the jury, "an insane
creature."

Don Chapin, Jerry Jenkins' lawyer, was less complex in
his brief closing argument: He blamed Kennedy for everything. Kennedy dominated the girls and dominated Jenkins,
too.

Whatever happened, he said, "Amy Burridge certainly
did not come to her death at the hands of Jerry Jenkins."

Jenkins was not part of a deliberate scheme, Chapin reit-
erated, but he was caught up in the undertow of a drunken,
extemporaneous spree, a joy-ride at knifepoint that rico-
cheted out of his control. Kennedy drove the hideous events,
and Jenkins merely drove the car.

He recounted Jenkins' rueful comment that he was "always the weak one" as evidence of his lack of commitment
to the evil acts he had been compelled—by Kennedy—to do.

"It seems apparent to me that Jerry Jenkins simply lacked
the courage, lacked the good judgment to say, 'No more.
This is it; this has transgressed what we started out to do.
Now I want no more of it,' " Chapin told the jurors. "But he
is not charged with cowardice or ignorance . . . . He was
fearful of Kennedy. And I think he simply lacked the intent,
the will, to perpetrate these alleged acts."

Jack Burk rose to rebut the defense's closing arguments
and angrily scoffed at them.

"You have skillfully, by one of the best trial lawyers in
the state, been smoke-screened on the sanity issue," he said.

"Ronald Kennedy knew what he was doing well enough to consummate a rape. He knew what he was doing well enough to throw a little girl off a bridge to get rid of her. He was beating them into submission, hard enough to blow blood against the back window."

Was Kennedy crazy? Not in the law's eyes, he said.

"Becky said Kennedy was a wild-eyed, insane monster. Here's an eighteen-year-old virgin having the hell beat out of her. How would you describe the man who was doing it?"

IF RONALD KENNEDY were, in fact, insane because of poverty and a terrifying childhood, then Jerry Jenkins might have had an equally good insanity defense.

Jenkins' childhood was as impoverished and empty as Kennedy's. His father and mother co-existed unhappily, the family was in constant trouble and turmoil, and they were thrown together in a rootless existence, moving from rented house to rented house all over town.

But there were even darker elements in Jerry's life.

Jerry told friends his mother had been raped by her father when she was very young and had given birth to a son. For years, Jerry was told the half-brother who lived in another state was his uncle, but the real relationship was revealed only when he and his siblings were older.

His father brooked no nonsense and was brutal in his punishment. He was an alcoholic, and family fights often erupted. Occasionally, the police took someone to jail.

Jerry also told friends that while his father was away—as he often was—his mother whored openly. Jerry maintained that, as the oldest, it was his job to cover for his promiscuous mother. His mother, Dorothy, who didn't drink or smoke but certainly wasn't religious, occasionally worked as a maid, but mostly did nothing beyond drink and bang other men when her husband was away.

When Jerry was fourteen, his mother brought home a drunken lover, who stayed the night and then left in the new car Edgar had bought for her. He crashed it.

When Edgar got home and saw the wrecked car, Jerry took the fall. He said he'd taken it joy-riding. Later, Jerry would say he got the worst beating of his life for his lie but never ratted out his mom.

Other horror stories surfaced.

Jerry's younger sister Margaret was once raped by one of his mother's paramours, he claimed. And after a while, the kids just vanished when strange men came over.

At the time of his rape and murder trial, Jerry was the blackest sheep in his family. A few years later, his sister would be convicted on federal drug and white slavery charges, serving time briefly as newspaper heiress-turned-insurgent Patty Hearst's cellmate in federal prison. A hopeless drug addict, Margaret shot herself to death in 1987 rather than go back to prison for violating her parole by carrying a gun.

Jerry's youngest brother David was convicted of two brutal, unrelated killings—one in Wyoming and one in South Dakota—in the late 1970s, both involving possible homosexual rape. He is still serving his life sentence in a Pierre, South Dakota, prison.

Kennedy and Jenkins lived separate, discordant lives.

The dysfunctional Kennedy family produced two rapists wholly independent of each other, something rarely seen by forensic psychiatrists.

Oddly, the dysfunctional Jenkins family also produced two rapists, again wholly independent of each other and again, an occurrence rarely seen by criminal psychologists.

And then, these rare families crossed paths, like two poisonous meteors colliding.

The result was horrifying, sadistic and violent.

But the roots of their deviance were likely different. Both had inadequate or absent fathers, trapping the boys in intensified relationships with their mothers and rattling their masculine identities. And both were likely verbally and physically abused by their parents, inspiring aggression and—for the child repeatedly called a faggot, pansy, queer, pinhead, asshole or other humiliating names—retarding self-esteem and sexual adjustment.

To them, power was the ability to control their own environment, and violence was the extreme expression of that power. In their separate careers, both had violent criminal scrapes, such as assault and rape, but neither was a full-time bully. They picked their fights and their victims carefully, and they seldom engaged in face-to-face conflicts unless their weapons or their numbers were unquestionably superior.

In psychiatric terms, Jenkins was likely an opportunistic rapist, an impulsive sociopath who surrendered to his worst urges on at least two occasions. If his memories of an adulterous mother are true, her promiscuity might have sexually aroused and frustrated him simultaneously. His mother's betrayal also might have provoked intense anger against and mistrust of women.

Nonetheless, while he participated in rapes fully and without hesitation, he was a follower who needed a leader. He revealed as much when he said in front of Becky Thomson before her rape, "Why do I always have to be the weak one?" In the 1968 rape, James Kennedy was his leader; in 1973, James' younger brother, Ron, was his leader.

Ron Kennedy could be classified as a power-asserting rapist, a habitual criminal and a rootless abuser whose victim wanders into the wrong place at the wrong time. His weapon of choice was subterfuge rather than a gun or knife. He beat her with his hands, made only a shallow attempt to hide his identity from her, and raped in the evening before 1:00 a.m. In Kennedy's case, murder was just a casual, sadistic twist.

No evidence suggests his mother was either as seductive or promiscuous as Jerry Jenkins' mother had been. If Kennedy is telling the truth—and the gaps in his honesty are absurdly prodigious—his unreported and prolonged molestation by his father's drunkard friends might have been a more powerful factor.

But in the end, despite Kennedy's insanity plea, neither

of them wanted to be seen as insane. Kennedy believed their own lawyers were part of a grander conspiracy to railroad them.

Neither Kennedy nor Jenkins could understand how they could be crazy.

BEFORE SHE DIED, Hilda Kennedy's faith had been tested by life. Even if her father's faith-healing powers had been genetic, even if she'd absorbed all the supernatural strength of the convent-school, she might not have been able to heal all the broken, poisoned hearts around her.

Nor her own.

But every night, she kneeled beside her bed and prayed to Mary and the saints to comfort the souls of her children, especially the tainted ones.

And, after September 24, 1973, she always put in a special word for the souls of Amy Burridge and Becky Thomson.

Chapter 7

THE VERDICT

April 30, 1974

The jury's deliberations were short.

On Tuesday night, the nine men and three women retired for their dinner break and ate their last supper together.

They entered the cramped jury room. On the enhanced murder charge, Wyoming's law mandated the death penalty, so each juror knew the consequences of a guilty verdict. They could choose no lesser penalty. But only one expressed any hesitation about putting a man to death. After some tearful, sympathetic discussion with the other jurors, she assented. Ronald Leroy Kennedy and Jerry Lee Jenkins' guilt was never the question, only whether the jurors could consci... ably walk away with the killers' blood on their hands.

Somebody mentioned how unmoved Kennedy and Jenkins appeared throughout the trial, even when a large photo of Amy's corpse was displayed. To them, it seemed disrespectful at best, inhuman at worst.

They returned to court with their decision only four and a half hours later, just before 10:00 p.m.

In a deathly silent courtroom, the jury foreman, a retired lieutenant colonel in the Air Force who drove a Volkswagen and collected rocks, read the verdicts against Kennedy and Jenkins, who stood emotionless at the defense table as he read.

They were guilty on all counts.

Guilty of the assault and battery on Becky Thomson.

Guilty of her rape.

Guilty of murdering Amy Burridge.

The defense asked the judge to poll the jury.

"Do you concur with the findings?" District Judge John Raper asked each of them in turn.

"Yes," said the young housewife and mother.

"Yes," said the Wyoming Air National Guardsman whose sister was about the same age as Becky Thomson.

"Yes," said the Catholic wife of an insurance examiner who volunteered at the local animal shelter.

"Yes," said the postal worker who coached Little League and whose brother was a cop.

"Yes," said the young city worker with a three-year-old son at home.

"Yes," said the young father and Army veteran who ran the credit union for state highway workers.

"Yes," said the newlywed who worked at the phone company and whose husband was a teacher.

"Yes," said the electrical engineer and World War II veteran who lived in a wind-blown farm town just this side of the Nebraska state line.

"Yes," said the state government worker with a college degree in child psychology who collected bottles and swam in the city pool for exercise.

"Yes," said the childless postal worker who now spent his free time bowling or at the Elks Lodge.

"Yes," said the former Air Force officer who had an eleven-year-old daughter.

There were no cheers in the courtroom, no nervous murmurs. Just silence.

Relief flooded Don Chapin, Jenkins' lawyer. Not because he wanted his client to go to prison, but because the case that had consumed him, that had made his blood pulse so robustly that his nose bled over dinner, that had forced him to choose between flesh-and-blood friends and an abstract legal principle, was over. He'd given his best effort, as the law prescribed, to defend a man who was a rapist and a killer, but he knew, deep down, that if the man had been acquitted, he'd have lost some respect for the law.

Now, it seemed like he was attending a modern hanging, where citizens come to see justice meted out not in the town square but in a late twentieth century courtroom.

John Ackerman never contemplated, much less expected, a "not guilty" verdict. He never believed it could happen. His only goal was to save Ron Kennedy's life. He believed the death penalty was barbaric, beyond the pale in an advanced society. Ackerman simply didn't want to think about how he'd feel if the jury had absolved Ron Kennedy.

The next day, as Judge John Raper prepared to impose his sentences, he asked Kennedy and Jenkins if they had anything to say for themselves.

Jenkins had nothing to say, but Kennedy spoke.

"Up until yesterday, I've always believed in law and justice," said Kennedy, whose first of over two dozen arrests was for assault at the age of fourteen, "but the last several days, going through what I went through and seeing what I've seen happen, is, as far as I'm concerned, a miscarriage of justice."

Without any special acknowledgment, Raper sentenced both to not less than thirteen years for the assault with intent to murder Becky Thomson, and both to at least thirty-five years for her rape. He paused to point out that, according to accepted mortality figures, both men could expect to live only another thirty-five years anyway.

Another breath later, Raper became the first Wyoming judge to deliver a death sentence in nine years. Ronald Leroy Kennedy and Jerry Lee Jenkins were to be executed in the Wyoming gas chamber just before dawn on September 25, 1974, exactly one year after Becky Thomson escaped Fremont Canyon, and Amy Burridge's body was found under the deep, green water.

His death sentence ended with a final command to the executioners: "Herein fail not."

WYOMING'S DEATH HOUSE was a prison within a prison.

The block building tucked safely within the high concrete

walls of the stately Romanesque prison built at the turn of the last century had only two purposes: to execute Wyoming's condemned prisoners and to heal the rest. Ironically, Death Row sat directly above the prison's infirmary.

Only one door at the top of a long, metal stairway led into Death Row. And before 1981, when a new prison was built, inmates rarely walked back down.

The killing floor consisted of six cramped cells, the gas chamber and the old gallows, which weren't used after 1933. Prisoners spent nearly every hour of every day in six-by-seven-foot cells, furnished with a steel cot, bare and cold concrete floors, a polished metal mirror, a toilet and a sink. An average-sized man could easily touch both steel-plate walls with outstretched arms.

Occasionally, they were allowed inside the "bull pen," a narrow caged space outside their cells, but except for weekly showers under a nozzle beside the gallows in one corner of the room, they were confined to their kennel-like cubicles under constant watch.

The first prisoner to die here was Joseph Seng, a killer hanged in 1912 for murdering a cowboy. His last throttled breath was drawn on the same state-of-the-art Julien gallows where the infamous cattle detective Tom Horn had been hanged in Cheyenne in 1903. After Horn, the gallows—which were triggered by the condemned man's own weight, technically executing himself—were moved to the new state prison, where they were used nine more times, starting with Seng.[4]

In 1937, murderer Perry Carroll became Wyoming's first condemned man to die from lethal hydrocyanic-acid gas in a controversial new chamber designed by a metal-worker from Denver. To be sure it worked, the warden gassed a pig in it just before Carroll. In time, four more men—and pigs—followed Carroll and his pig into that claustrophobic closet, ending with child-butcher Andrew Pixley in 1965.

Nine years later, Kennedy and Jenkins were next.

They literally faced death every morning. Their cells were seven paces from the gas chamber and the gallows platform.

Like most condemned prisoners before them, their first moments, days, weeks and months were spent in the cells closest to the death-devices, as if to punctuate where their sentences would end. Later, they'd be moved to cells that faced away, and as their death-date approached, they'd be moved back to face the machines.

So for their first couple months on Death Row, Ron Kennedy and Jerry Jenkins awoke every morning to see the exact spot where they would die.

GUARDS LOCKED RONALD Leroy Kennedy and Jerry Lee Jenkins in their cells on Death Row in the Wyoming State Penitentiary in Rawlins on a Friday morning, May 3, 1974—two days after being sentenced to die.

Their cells had been unoccupied for nine years since the 1965 execution of killer Andrew Pixley. Now, they would sleep only a few steps from the gas chamber where the state and most of its citizens expected they would die.

But they wouldn't.

Their fate—a fate of life, not death—was sealed by a U.S. Supreme Court decision handed down a year before their crime.

In the 1972 case of *Furman v. Georgia*, a divided U.S. Supreme Court had already struck down most federal and state death penalty laws, declaring them "arbitrary and capricious." Existing death-penalty laws, the court said in its landmark decision, violated the "cruel and unusual punishment" definition of the Eighth Amendment and the due-process protections of the Fourteenth Amendment.

Furman actually consolidated appeals from three convicted murderers then on Death Row in two states. The main case involved William Henry Furman, a twenty-six-year-old black burglar in Georgia who had been surprised by his victim during a break-in. Although he was carrying a revolver, Furman fled.

But during his escape, Furman said, he "dropped his gun, which discharged and killed the homeowner." Furman was arrested, tried, and convicted of murder. His jury could choose life in prison or death. It chose death.

The other two cases involved black men in Georgia and Texas who had been condemned for rape.

In a 5-4 ruling that effectively outlawed executions in the forty death-penalty states, the Supreme Court said a death sentence must not be imposed unless the judge or jury finds at least one legally defined aggravating factor and then weighs it against any mitigating factors the defendant claims.

To impose death, the court said, the judge and jury must consider the circumstances of the crime and the character of the defendant.

The Supreme Court didn't rule the death penalty itself to be unconstitutional, only the specific laws by which it was applied. Justice Potter Stewart also criticized the capricious imposition of the death penalty, saying it was used disproportionately against minorities and the poor.

Public support for the death penalty reached its lowest point in 1966, when a Gallup poll showed only forty-two percent of Americans approved of the practice. And at the time of *Furman*, nobody had been executed since 1967 as states observed an unofficial voluntary moratorium on executions while the Supreme Court grappled with the issue.

So *Furman* flung Death Row's doors open across the United States. More than 600 condemned killers sentenced between 1967 and 1972 had their death sentences lifted.

But the law is a living, breathing creature, evolving to suit its environment.

After the Supreme Court had finally articulated its constitutional qualms, states began writing new laws to satisfy the court's uneasiness. Statutes in Georgia, Florida and Texas became the new model, giving courts wider discretion in applying the death penalty for specific crimes, and providing for the current "bifurcated" trial system, in which guilt or innocence is determined in a first trial, then punishment in a second.

But Wyoming legislators, believing they were complying

with *Furman*, drafted tough new first-degree murder laws making death *mandatory* if a killing involved certain heinous circumstances, such as killing someone to hide another crime, or to obscure the criminal's identity.

It was a fatal assumption.

Wyoming embodied every Wild West myth, even if the reality was something less wild, more civilized. Yes, Wyoming's frontier history was stained with harsh justice, from hanging trees to ruthless ranch regulators who summarily killed squatters and rustlers and simply left their corpses to the coyotes.

But in the eighty-four years between statehood and 1974, only eighteen men were legally executed in Wyoming—thirteen were hanged and five were gassed.

Among them was Tom Horn, the legendary scout, Pinkerton agent and range detective hanged in 1903 for murdering the teenage son of a rancher disliked by Horn's employers. In the Cheyenne jail, Horn braided the gallows rope that would ultimately snap his neck. His last words to his executioner were, "Hurry it up. I got nothing more to say."

In 1965, Andrew Pixley, a drifter who had raped, murdered and dismembered two girls in a Jackson hotel the year before, became the last Wyoming inmate to be executed before the *Furman* decision. For him, the gas chamber was a tender mercy after narrowly escaping a lynch mob in the small town where he had slaughtered his victims.

One finds more evidence of mercy and restraint than vengeance and blood-lust in Wyoming's Death Row history.

Charlie Starkweather, one of America's coldest spree-killers, was captured in a high-speed chase just outside Douglas, Wyoming, on January 29, 1958, after killing eleven people on a bloody month-long murder binge across Nebraska and Wyoming. When he was caught, the nineteen-year-old thug's tee-shirt was still stained with the blood of a traveling salesman he'd killed moments before.

After a large meal and a good night's rest, Starkweather confessed to the brutal murders, including his girlfriend's family back in Lincoln. When reporters were led into the jailhouse, he retold the story again and again, brazenly and without remorse.

Within twenty-four hours of his capture, Wyoming Governor Milward Simpson—father of future United States Senator Alan Simpson—made a startling announcement: He opposed the death penalty and, if Starkweather were convicted of murder in Wyoming, he promised to commute the killer's sentence to life. But Simpson also told reporters he'd sign Starkweather's extradition back to Nebraska "in a jiffy."

Starkweather was sent back to Nebraska within days and was quickly convicted of murder. His father raised money for his appeal by selling locks of his hair, but death was more certain for Charlie Starkweather than anything ever had been in his short, miserable life.

On the eve of his execution, he was asked to donate his eyes but he refused. "Why should I?" he asked. "Nobody ever gave me anything."

Nebraska gave him what Wyoming wouldn't: the electric chair, less than six months after his capture in Wyoming.

RONALD KENNEDY AND Jerry Jenkins appealed their death sentences within days of their conviction in 1974. The state law on first-degree murder, they argued, was clearly unconstitutional by the definitions set forth in *Furman*.

Among the defense lawyers who contributed to their appeal was Gerry Spence, a Wyoming lawyer beginning to establish himself as one of Wyoming's brightest young advocates—and one of the most colorful.

But the lead lawyer remained John Ackerman, the public defender who had become a dean of the National College for Criminal Defense at the University of Houston's law school shortly after Kennedy and Jenkins were convicted.

Five of Wyoming's nine justices eventually agreed, but not without angst.

"We will not repeat the unpleasant and revolting factual situation from which these charges arose," Wyoming's Chief

Justice Rodney Guthrie wrote for the majority. "[But] no amount of discussion or analysis can alter, change or modify the requirements of the United States Constitution by which we are bound."

On January 27, 1977, relying heavily on *Furman* for guidance, the Wyoming Supreme Court reversed Kennedy and Jenkins' death sentences. The justices upheld the murder convictions but sent the two killers back to state district court to be re-sentenced.

Among the court's new options: making the life sentences *consecutive*—that is, running end-to-end, rather than simultaneously—with the rape and assault sentences. Under that scenario, Kennedy and Jenkins would be forced to serve their time on the "lesser" crimes before starting their life sentences for the murder.

They'd both done the math. Even with good time, it would be almost thirty years before they'd start their life sentences, if they lived that long.

At their re-sentencing, both killers spoke from where they stood, in the shadow of death.

Jenkins, the follower, addressed the judge first. He was, as always, playing a veteran con's game:

"I have sat here for four years and I ain't saying I'm guilty or not guilty. The State said I'm guilty, so I got to go along with it. But I've always thought the laws were not only to punish people but to rehabilitate people. And sitting on Death Row for thirty-five months and thinking about this, and going over it in my mind every day, seven days a week, twenty-four hours a day, I just don't feel it's going to do any good if I got to pull the rest of my life in a penitentiary.

"I was all set, ready to die, and I sat for three years waiting to die, because the law said I had to die. Now they say, you know, 'You don't have to die, but yet you've got to spend the rest of your life in a penitentiary.' I don't think the law was made for that. And I know it's not right to break a law, but I just don't think the law was made for that. I think it was made to protect the innocent but it was also made to rehabilitate the guilty, not just shut 'em away and say, 'We don't like you no more so we want you out of sight. We are going to lock you up for the rest of your life.' I don't think the law was made that way. That's all."

Then Kennedy stood and delivered a condemned man's sermon on fairness and constitutionality:

"My feelings are kind of the same as Mr. Jenkins' in a lot of respects. That I spent three years of my life preparing myself to die because I didn't have the faintest idea that this law was going to be found unconstitutional, whatsoever. And now that it has been found unconstitutional, and I find out there is a chance that I have to spend the rest of my life in a penitentiary for crimes that I don't feel was necessarily really proved beyond a reasonable doubt, I just don't feel that it would be fair to receive a sentence running consecutively with the other two sentences. I don't feel it would be constitutional to impose that kind of sentence."

District Judge Alan Johnson, who later became a federal judge, wasn't swayed.

"The court is aware of the sentences that were delivered by Judge Raper following the conclusion of your trial," he told Kennedy and Jenkins. "It is evident that the concept behind those sentences was to protect the public from you. Of course, there is no step more drastic in retribution and removal from the public than a death sentence."

Judge Johnson re-sentenced them, according to the high court's wishes, to "no less than your natural lives." As they feared, he tacked their life sentences onto the end of their rape and assault sentences.

Ironically, other states were already digging graves for convicted killers. On January 17, 1977, less than a year after the U.S. Supreme Court effectively reinstated the death penalty—and only ten days before Kennedy and Jenkins' death sentences were overturned by the Wyoming Supreme Court—convicted murderer Gary Gilmore told his Utah firing squad, "Let's do it," and became the first man executed under the new laws.

But for Kennedy and Jenkins, the reprieve was permanent. Their sentences were commuted to life in prison, an act of mercy demanded by the same laws they had flouted all their lives. And a life sentence offered the two killers something else: Hope.

It meant they would someday be eligible for parole, even if they would both be elderly men when the chance came.

WHEN THEY LEFT Death Row and returned to the main line—the general prison population—Kennedy and Jenkins felt right at home. They were thirty and thirty-three, respectively, and had already spent most of their adult lives in the steely embrace of prisons and reformatories. The rhythms of incarceration were, at worst, familiar, and at best, comforting. They might have preferred life outside, but they were at ease inside, too.

Besides, time was finally on their side: Going back to territorial days, murderers only served an average eight years and four months in Wyoming's prison. Every killer—even the most inhuman—had a feeling, at one time or another, he would be free. Sooner rather than later.

Kennedy and Jenkins were lifer-loners who deliberately avoided notice. They kept to the edges of prison life, usually alone. They were not always in the same cell blocks, but even when they had the chance, they seldom hung around together.

One reason: They were baby-rapers, the lowest social caste in prison society. Although they hadn't literally raped a child, they had murdered one, and crimes against innocent children sentenced a man to a harsher punishment in the joint than any other.

In those early days, Kennedy and Jenkins most certainly suffered some "exploitation"—a gentle, bureaucratic term for a wide variety of inmate-meted humiliations, from slavery to sodomy. It was partly because they were baby-rapers, partly because they were both easy pickings for the more exploitive inmates, the other violent sociopaths and the young gangsters who sharked around the yard. And the prison's perverse internal protocols simply demanded it.

Some baby-rapers and "chesters"—child molesters—are clever and socially skillful enough to maneuver around the stigma, but most can't. Kennedy and Jenkins weren't, but neither did they become perpetual toys for other inmates.

Jenkins was older, more streetwise, and was slightly better equipped to overcome the hierarchy. He was also more of a loner, focusing on hobby work and generally avoiding the attentions of the predators. Eventually, he ran the prison's low-power radio station, a tiny studio where he was usually locked for as many hours as he could be out of his cell. In there, he'd turn off all the lights, working only by the dim lights of the control panel. In or out of the shadows, he tended to brood.

A lover of the blues, Jenkins had a song for every person in his life. It got to the point that every song reminded him of someone, or maybe a time when they were together. Every song was the story of someone. He and Darci had played a game when songs came on the radio. "Who does that remind you of?" they'd ask each other. When he heard "Midnight Train to Georgia," he thought of Darci; when she heard "Tears of a Clown," she thought of him.

Perhaps still dreaming of becoming a Christian missionary in South America—or just wanting to assume the role of a man who might mean something to someone—Jenkins became an ordained minister in prison.

He had a few visitors. Among them was his half-brother's wife, with whom Jerry had once fathered a child whom he reportedly loved dearly. She often begged him to marry her, even though he was in prison, to get the official relationship they never had. Another visitor was his first wife.

His oldest daughter Chera also came to see her father. She had re-connected with him secretly, and sometimes she visited him in Rawlins without her mother's knowledge. She shared the details with her little sister who also kept her secret but never cared to meet her father. When Chera came to the visitors' room or wrote clandestine letters to him, she talked about her life, about her family and about her happiness to be able to talk to him again.

Jerry seldom attended his own parole hearings and never wrote any pleading letters to judges or lawyers. His guards came to see him as a pathetic creature, with low self-esteem and a frustrated desire to be accepted by anyone who came within his orbit. But they didn't feel sorry for him; they just thought he was weak.

Kennedy was more outgoing and verbal, and eventually became more astute in "prison ways." He learned to talk his way out of most pinches.

Oddly, even though they were technically baby-rapers, they got extra points in the social system for having been on Death Row for almost three years. No other inmate in the general population had been on Death Row. In the warped pecking order of prison, they were slime, but slime that had ventured to a mythical place no others had gone. In a way, they were odious heroes.

Their occasional parole hearings were more show than substance, more to satisfy the policies of the parole board than to seriously consider shortening their sentences or freeing them. Before 2002, Kennedy and Jenkins appeared before the parole board only on their assault and rape convictions—their consecutive life sentences hadn't even begun.

They both had more enemies than friends, but they outlasted the grim days before prisons became more segregated, safer and watchful. When they first went to prison in the 1960s and early '70s, a hundred inmates—from checkkiters to serial rapists—might shower together unsupervised. By the time Kennedy and Jenkins emerged from the ironic safety of Death Row, the prison was evolving into a more controlled environment.

They had unfettered access to a law library, where Kennedy became a prolific jailhouse lawyer. He filed a flurry of appeals, complaints and motions, often using a faux Ciceronian vernacular as he pled his case for a new trial or outright freedom. His arguments were usually based on flimsy, sometimes specious, interpretations of the law and clearly "re-imagined" evidence.

Besides his constant letters to judges and lawyers, Kennedy continued for several years a disrespectful, angry correspondence with the public defender who argued his original case, John Ackerman. He often tried to raise minor factual inconsistencies to the level of serious appeal material—*if Ron Kennedy was sitting on the front seat when Becky Thomson and Amy Burridge were forced into the car, how could he have pushed the seat forward for them to get in?*—but his "facts" were generally irrelevant to his case.

Ackerman's polite responses were generally patient explanations of the law and gentle corrections of Kennedy's distorted facts.

Kennedy was fed up with what he saw as Ackerman's unhelpful views.

"I have been more patient with you the last year than I feel I should," Kennedy told Ackerman in one letter. "However my patience have [sic] grown thin over the perturbing injustice that seemed to occur quite frequent [sic] in this case. It is quite upsetting to know that some lawyers would much rather prosecute there [sic] client, than defend him. . . . I will tell you this much. That for six months I have carefully prepared with the utmost of care a legal action to file against you, and I guarantee will not take much to set it off."

Ackerman always responded in dignified, sympathetic—but firm—tones.

"I know it is quite easy for someone sitting in prison to develop the feeling that their attorney isn't doing anything about their case," Ackerman responded to one of Kennedy's fuming letters during the appeal of his death sentence. "I suppose if I were to write to you every day and tell you that I . . . had trouble sleeping at night from worry about your case or how I have spent literally hours going over and over in my head the testimony in the case and the argument I will make in the Wyoming Supreme Court, you would feel more at ease about my dedication to your case.

"(But) I will not, however, be moved by your express and implied threats to take a ridiculous approach to this matter. It is very clear from reading your letters that you have been listening to some of the marvelous legal minds who inhabit the Wyoming State Penitentiary. If I were in your position, I might wonder why those people with all their legal genius were in prison.

"I think it is very important for you to understand that, regardless of how you may feel and regardless of what you may know to be the truth concerning your case, the evidence against you was substantial and in many cases, overwhelming. I believe it is unrealistic for you to expect any court is going to determine that you were innocent of the charges against you. If I can somehow legally prevent the State of Wyoming from executing you in the gas chamber, I will feel that I have done you a great service."

Far from grateful, Kennedy promptly asked for a new—and taxpayer-provided—attorney.

And he got one.

It might have disappointed the many law-abiding people living outside prison walls who were hoping other inmates could exact a kind of justice the law couldn't. If society couldn't avenge the crimes against Amy Burridge and Becky Thomson in the gas chamber, society hoped months or years of prison rape would ease the pain.

It didn't.

PRISON WASN'T HELL for Jerry Jenkins. It almost felt like home.

One night, a few months before the crime and the trial, Jerry and his wife Darci were driving aimlessly through the town, with no inclination or money to be more entertained. Darci had just turned eighteen and was four months pregnant with their second child. They talked about life and futures and, more importantly, pasts.

Jerry got quiet. Darci asked him why.

"I gotta tell you something, before you hear it from somebody else," he told her.

He turned down a side street, and then looked around. He turned left, then right, as if he were looking for something.

On a downtown back street, Jerry pulled to a stop in front of a squat office building whose façade was a monolith of mirrored glass.

"What is it, Jerry?" she asked.

Timidly at first, he told her he'd been in jail before he met her. Not once or twice. At least four times, he claimed—but in reality, that wasn't the half of it.

Darci was seventeen and pregnant when they were married by a justice of the peace in the next county less than a year before. Jerry was twenty-eight and already a three-time loser who'd spent the last half of his life in and out of reformatories, jails and prisons. Darci never knew.

Quick to anger, his wife peppered him with tough questions about his crimes. He answered them all sheepishly, but Darci thought he was being honest.

Then he told her about the worst crime he'd committed, but for which he'd never gone to jail. On a summer night in 1968, he'd joined in the gang rape of a woman he knew. In fact, he tricked her with his friendship. With Ron Kennedy's older brother, Jim, and another buddy, he'd convinced an old girlfriend to come for a ride, maybe to get a soda. She knew Jerry, but not the other two. *Just like old times, you know?* She went along because Jerry asked.

Instead, the three drunken men drove her to a remote spot far from town, out beyond the little airport, and parked beside a deep irrigation canal. They told her if she didn't fuck them all, they'd tie her up and throw her in the water. She struggled at first, but they pinned her to the dirt behind the car, where first Jim Kennedy and then Jerry raped her. The third guy got his in the backseat on the ride back to town.

Bruised and barely clothed, they dumped her in the alley behind her apartment and told her they'd kill her if she told anybody. But she reported the crime, and the cops soon arrested her three assailants.

In the first of three separate trials, Jim Kennedy was convicted of first-degree rape a few months later, but at a severe cost to the victim. She was savaged by Kennedy's defense lawyer as a divorced, loose woman who willingly and happily had sex with three men.

By the time Jerry Lee Jenkins was to be tried for his role in the same rape, the victim refused to be verbally raped again on the witness stand, and charges were dropped. Jerry Jenkins knew now he had dodged a legal bullet that should have buried him in the prison system for most of the rest of his life.

Darci was stunned. Jerry's other crimes—burglary, forgery, prison escape and more—paled by comparison to a rape. A rape he admitted now, but for which he had never truly paid a price. But there was more.

"I heard she was pregnant at the time and I hear she lost the kid," he told her, not looking up. "I'm sorry for you and it's the thing I'm most sorry about."

That was too much. Darci, still a young girl herself and carrying a child inside her, exploded.

"Why? Because I'm pregnant now?" she fumed. "Can't you see what would happen if that happened to me right now? What would happen to you and to me?"

Jerry just hung his head and stopped talking, stopped answering her questions altogether. They sat for a long time in silence, until he spoke. His wife cried for all of them.

"Do you know what a 'habitual criminal' is?" he asked his young wife.

Darci shook her head. She didn't.

He explained it to her how some men couldn't stay out of trouble, how it could be a crime to be a repeat offender without ever beating, killing or ripping anybody off, how the cops and the courts gave up on such men after two or three major convictions. And how maybe these guys gave up on themselves, too.

"You really believe there's such a thing?" Darci asked. "That a man can't go straight no matter how hard he tries?"

Jerry shrugged.

"You see that plate glass window on this building?" he asked her. "I knew a guy in prison that had been out for a couple of months, went out, got drunk, came right here to this spot and threw a brick through that glass and waited with his bottle of beer for the police to pick him up. He did it on purpose just to go back to prison."

Darci couldn't imagine a life in prison—in any prison for any man for any length of time—being preferable to life on the outside.

Jerry could.

"Everything is so easy," he said. "You don't have to think, worry or do anything. You're fed, clothed, given a bed, even told where to pee. When you're inside, it sometimes scares the shit out of you to think about coming out. It's like you get the shakes and can't stop, but it's all on the inside. To get a job is hard but to hold it is harder, so you start shakin' again. And the first thing you want is a beer or a drink to calm you down, but sometimes that doesn't help. There's no one who can tell you how to make it stop, and there's no books in prison that tell you how to love the right way, or work the right way, or even how to fuck the right way. There's lots of different opinions but not one will show or guide you and all of a sudden you're supposed to have the brains to figure it all out which way is right. Believe me, I can tell you how many of the wrong ways aren't right."

Darci said nothing for a long time. She just studied the light reflecting off the glass windows of that office building.

"You ever think about throwing a brick through that glass?" she asked him.

He looked up at the fragile, gleaming barrier that stood between him and going back to the joint, and he smiled.

"Yeah," he said. "Lots of times. But not so much since I met you."

FOR A ONCE-CONDEMNED man who literally lived three years within whispering distance of the gas chamber, a life in prison seemed downright comfortable for Ronald Kennedy, too.

Within a few years of his release from Death Row, he was

deemed dependable enough to be a "trusty," an inmate granted special privileges and access denied to most other prisoners.

During his trusty period, Ronald Kennedy roamed the prison a little more freely and was even allowed to keep pets in his prison cell, including a puppy named Bandee. He lifted weights regularly, sometimes with the warden himself. He had helped Kennedy through some family difficulties and saw him not as a typical violent, sadistic, predatory killer, but rather an accidental criminal who couldn't control his baser impulses.

He was also allowed to marry a woman.

In 1983, ten years after the crimes at Fremont Canyon Bridge, Ron Kennedy and an old friend wed in a small prison ceremony. His last wife had divorced Ron in 1975 while he was on Death Row, and his new bride was a childhood friend from Casper who'd long carried a torch for him. "She was always in love with me ever since she was a little girl, and when I ended up in prison, she was finally able to catch me," he joked years later.

For the next nine years, they shared a strange union, going to prison dances and spending one weekend a month together in one of the prison's "pecker palaces," state-owned mobile homes where married prisoners were allowed to have sex with their wives.

In 1985, Ron's youngest sister Lynnette died in Casper at the age of thirty-three. A single guard was assigned to take Ron, unshackled, to the brief funeral in his hometown. He didn't wear a prison uniform, but simple black slacks and a black short-sleeved shirt.

After the service, he mingled with family and friends at a wake at his sister's house, where he posed for pictures with his mother, wife and other relatives, even played with children in the front yard—all under the most casual watch of his keeper.

At the time, Becky Thomson was still living in Casper, deathly afraid Kennedy and Jenkins would someday be paroled and stalk her, hoping to finish the job they once botched. The radio station where she worked was even organizing a petition drive that would send about 15,000 signatures to the Wyoming parole board, urging that the two killers never again breathe free air.

But here was Ron Kennedy, probably not more than a mile from Becky Thomson at that moment, enjoying a measure of freedom she would not have imagined in her worst nightmares.

Free to visit with his family outside of prison.

Free to keep pets in his prison cell.

Free to play with children in a quiet neighborhood.

Free to dance on New Year's Eve with a woman he married while ostensibly being punished for tearing other families apart.

Free to have state-sponsored sex, even to father children if he pleased.

Luckily for Becky, she never learned any of those things.

RON KENNEDY WASN'T a model prisoner, but he wasn't a troublemaker, either.

He lost his precious trusty status when a shakedown found marijuana in his cell. Later, prison authorities suspected the pot had been planted by a guard who typically resorted to dirty tricks to bring down both inmates and fellow prison workers, and they cleared Kennedy of the charges.

Nonetheless, Kennedy was busted back to medium-security status and lost most of his special privileges. But even today, he continues to file a wide variety of legal motions, appeals and complaints.

In 2001, he filed a federal complaint in which he alleged he was stripped naked by two female guards, ogled and searched. "Nice package," he claimed one of them cooed after he disrobed. After he confided the incident to a guard, he alleged he was forced to take a rigged lie-detector test, which the prison said he failed. After that, he said, he was locked naked in solitary confinement with no furniture but a small towel.

The Wyoming Department of Corrections, which had

once trusted the rapist and killer Ron Kennedy with extraordinary freedom, claimed a strip search of a male inmate by female guards was not, in itself, a violation of his civil rights. Further, a forcible polygraph test is completely within the rules, the prison answered, and Kennedy's stay in The Hole was neither cruel nor unusual because he was not deprived of essential human needs like food and water. Beyond that, the prison had no comment on Kennedy's allegations.

In the end, it was moot. A federal judge tossed out the case for the simple reason that Kennedy had not followed proper administrative procedures when he filed his complaint.

KENNEDY SAID HIS "best friend" in the joint was another once-condemned killer named Julian Turner—whose similar crimes give Kennedy hope he'll someday be free.

On a snowy winter night in December 1973—just three months after Kennedy and Jenkins killed Amy Burridge and raped Becky Thomson—Turner and Billy James Cloman, two black, teenage drug dealers from Portland, stabbed two Cheyenne-area ranchers to death, dumped their bodies in a snow drift and stole their pickup truck.

A few days later, Turner and Cloman were stopped by Chicago police in the stolen truck, where cops found blood stains and a large amount of heroin. Later, defense lawyers challenged one of the traffic cops for having no reasonable cause to stop the truck. He replied, "Two black guys driving a Wyoming pickup in downtown Chicago is reasonable cause."

Turner, then twenty, and Cloman, eighteen, were convicted of first-degree murder in late 1974 and sentenced to death. They briefly joined Kennedy and Jenkins on Death Row, but all four got a reprieve when the Wyoming Supreme Court overturned their death penalties a few years later. Turner and Cloman each received two consecutive life sentences.

Turner saw the "friendship" with Kennedy a little differently. They were friendly and talked on occasion, sometimes exercised together, but they "were not close," in Turner's words. Their conversations might have been weekly, but not daily, he said, even though they lived in the same unit. Nonetheless, to Ron Kennedy, Turner was his "best friend," perhaps illustrating his low esteem among other inmates more than the intimacy of his relationship with Turner.

Turner was paroled in November 2001, rekindling Ron Kennedy's hope of someday going free. Prison authorities declared Turner was dying and mercifully allowed him to spend "his final days" among family in New York.[5]

But everyone makes mistakes.

Yes, Julian Turner suffered from a heart condition, and indeed, he went back to New York City to live with his sister. But soon after he got "home," the sister moved away, and he moved into the back room of a storefront church in Jamaica, Queens, where he did minor janitorial chores and got by on the kindness of the flock.

When I first talked with him in 2003 and again around Christmas 2005—more than four years after he was expected to die—Julian Turner was very much alive. He was still living on the frayed margins of society, but he was *living*. In 2005, he was fifty-two years old, collecting disability, resting after a recent heart-related hospital stay, and living in a private home for the longest period since he was a child. While he wasn't vigorous and strong, he certainly was not on his deathbed either.

Kennedy technically began his consecutive life sentence for Amy Burridge's first-degree murder in 2002, when he was fifty-six years old. His sentences for assault and rape are finished. He now will appear before the Wyoming parole board every five years, starting in 2007. But what governor would set him free and commit political suicide? So the likelihood of Wyoming's best-known killer walking out of prison as a free man is low.

But it's possible, as Julian Turner proved.

Whether Turner was a good friend or not, he remains a beacon of hope to Ron Kennedy.

✦ ✦ ✦

JERRY LEE JENKINS died a little before 11 p.m. on Oct. 29, 1998, still an inmate at the Wyoming State Penitentiary in Rawlins. His life sentence was abruptly commuted by a grossly clogged and weak heart. He was fifty-four.

Earlier in the evening, he had complained to a guard about pain that emanated from his chest and coursed down his left arm. It had been building all day. The overweight Jenkins had long suffered from high blood pressure and had at least one earlier heart attack, made worse by a chronic case of hepatitis and kidney disease. The prison doctor sent him to the community hospital in town, where, within a couple hours, his heart simply and painfully clenched, and Jenkins was dead.

When word of his death reached the prison, several guards reportedly cheered and high-fived. "He's burning in Hell right at this moment," one said, beaming.

A couple months before he died, Darci talked to Jerry on the phone for the last time. She'd long ago remarried happily, but she wanted to tell him that his beloved daughter Chera had died. He thanked her and said she had been the only person in his life who ever saw the good in him. After they hung up, Darci was saddened to think a man could look back on a life of fifty-five years and, for better or worse, find only one person who believed in him.

The killer's body had been autopsied and reduced to ash by the time a local reporter called Dave Dovala, then the Natrona County sheriff, for a comment on Jenkins' death.

"It pleases me," was all he said.

The prison called Roy Jenkins to pick up his brother's personal effects: a TV and a box of letters, legal papers and photographs. He brought it all home and put the crap in a closet, but after a couple years, he just took it all to the county dump.

Jenkins' ashes were buried on a sunny, strangely windless Friday, November 6, at two in the afternoon in the Garden of Christus at Memorial Gardens, a family-owned cemetery on the western brink of Casper, well beyond the truck stops, roadhouses, trailer parks and machine shops. And far across town from the cemetery where Amy Burridge was buried.

His ashes—never removed from the crematory's cheap plastic shipping container—were to be placed at the foot of his father Edgar's grave, only about two and a half feet below the lawn. His father's grave site was getting crowded: his sister Margaret had also been buried there after her 1987 suicide.

Roy, who'd visited his killer-brother in prison only once, arranged a quick, quiet burial. His elderly mother, Dorothy, had asked for as little flourish as possible, fearing Jerry's grave would be desecrated. She knew what her son was, and how hot the town's hatred still boiled even in 1998. She worried that if anyone knew where her son was buried, some people might even want nearby graves to be moved a safe distance from that spot—the spot where she, too, would eventually be buried.

Because there was no wind, the cemetery erected its green canvas privacy tent for mourners. But only two came. Jenkins' mother and brother. Nobody else. They lingered briefly, then left, less than five minutes to say goodbye to a brother, a son, a rapist and a killer.

So there was no pastor, no prayer, no memorial and no marker. The owner of the cemetery was so moved by Dorothy's grief and shame that she had waived the $435 in burial costs. Jerry Lee Jenkins was buried as he had lived most of his life: at someone else's expense.

The gravedigger, barely twenty, threw dirt over Jenkins' trifling plastic box after the mourners left. Although he hadn't been born at the time of the crime, he knew the story. He knew who was going into the ground.

When I visited the cemetery on a subfreezing day in February 2003, the cemetery worker scraped a crust of frozen snow away from Edgar Jenkins' brass marker with his boot, then brushed away snow down to the dormant grass. He paced off the length of a man's body and stood at the foot of the grave.

"He's right here," the gravedigger said.

Part Three

"Believe those who are seeking truth.
Doubt those who find it."

Andre Gide

Chapter 8

THE NEXT LIFE

Becky Thomson lived two lives.

One was the essentially happy life of a little girl in a family of girls, growing up to begin eagerly finding her way and her place in the world, dreaming of places she'd never been, boys, and her own children. The life she hadn't yet begun.

Her first life ended at the exact moment her second life began, on Fremont Canyon Bridge.

Like false dawn, the life she expected was not the life she would live. Her second life was the life of a dead girl who simply hadn't stopped breathing. One represented the blossoming of a girl into a young woman, and the other represented a woman in decay.

Her life after the crime was not just a long string of disappointments. At times, Becky was truly happy, absorbed in moments of extraordinary joy when she forgot completely about that night, flashes of light that drowned out the dark.

BECKY'S PHYSICAL RECOVERY from her injuries took months. Her pelvis healed slowly, and her other flesh wounds healed, although some scars never faded.

Her emotional wounds were far deeper.

A few weeks after the crime and Amy's funeral, Toni took Becky and her sister back down to Mexico, where Jack was working. They returned to Wyoming for occasional court appearances, but Mexico was supposed to be Becky's sanctuary, where she could rest and feel safe again, away from the putrefying evil, the whispered rumors and the silent pity. But her days were often spent crying with her mother and sister, looking at photographs of the family they'd been.

Spending a year in Mexico after the crime, Becky took a job teaching at a private school in the American enclave where they lived outside Monterrey. She loved the children, and in a small way, she always felt they reconnected her to humanity, from which she had been detached.

But while she was there, she started drinking.

Mexico didn't heal her. When she came home to Casper for good, the crime and the trial were months behind her, but she wasn't yet whole.

In Casper she drifted into other jobs, seldom for very long. The crime and its aftermath had thwarted her plans to go to college. Over the next few years, she worked as a city meter maid, briefly sold advertising for the local newspaper, then a little rock 'n' roll radio station. She was good at selling, because she was a genuinely warm woman, and pretty. It allowed her to be creative and meet new people, which took extraordinary courage for her. But her clients in the small town also knew who she was and what she had endured. To many of them, they were not only buying advertising, but helping Becky get her feet back on the ground.

But even if Becky loved selling advertisements, the rest of her life deteriorated. She'd begun smoking pot and taking antidepressants, along with a growing dependence on booze. At one point, she checked herself into a local rehabilitation clinic when her addictions outgrew her ability to control them, and the clinic's counselors suggested her substance abuse might be related to unresolved issues from her rape and attempted murder about ten years before. She was referred to a local psychiatrist.

The psychiatrist told her she was blocking out many of her memories of the crime and he thought she would do better if she could remember everything that had happened. He scheduled a session in a private office at the hospital, where she later told friends he made her breathe a gaseous truth serum that would help unlock memories she had pushed beyond her conscious grasp.

The doctor told her to let him know when she started feeling the slightest bit unusual, but because she was an addict and because the gas's first soothing effects flushed her with a kind of euphoria, she didn't say anything. As she breathed deeper, she only wanted more. It made her feel good, and she believed that it might even help her.

Instead, she woke up three days later and couldn't remember anything.

She had a vague recollection, however, of some sexual encounter while she hovered in a dream state, half-awake, half-dormant. When she told her friends, most passed it off as a drug-induced hallucination. And when she told her disbelieving group therapists about it, they asked the psychiatrist to answer any questions she might have in front of her fellow addicts and other staffers.

Becky was humiliated and backed down. She knew how it sounded. It not only disgraced her even further, but she felt she was risking the whole medical community turning against her, and she wanted to be liked more than she wanted to tell a story that might only have been a dream.

In 1985, Becky visited a local family physician, Dr. Joe Murphy, for an unspecified illness. Two years before, two of Murphy's college-age daughters had been killed in a dreadful car crash, and perhaps his own grief drew her. Since it was her first time in his office, she was asked to fill out a form for new patients. On a line that asked why she was seeking treatment, she simply wrote: *I want to be normal again.*

She took a series of other jobs, including one as a night clerk for a local convenience store and gas station, where she met the man she eventually would marry. But after a Christmas Eve armed robbery there in 1986, she begged the general manager of KVOC Radio, the local country station, for work.

He rescued Becky. About the time she started selling ads

for KVOC, her mother and stepfather moved to California, but she fell into a whole new family, literally and figuratively. At the radio station, she made fast friends, especially with Lisa Pearce, one of the broadcasters who also helped sell advertising on a small staff where almost everyone did double-duty.

Far from surrendering to incipient glumness, Becky became a sparkplug among her co-workers. She left happy greeting cards on their desks for almost every occasion and played girlish practical jokes. At lunches with her friends, she often yearned more for dessert than the main course, preferring amaretto cheesecake to just about any entrée on the menu. On birthdays, she was the top kick and lead singer who gathered everyone together to sing "Happy Birthday." She even kept a goofy pair of sunglasses—complete with battery-powered windshield wipers—in her desk for special moments. She was more likely to hug somebody than to wish them a good morning.

Becky was also a good saleswoman, consistently among the top sellers every month. She poured herself into her work.

She was suddenly among a small, new family. When her friend Lisa Pearce got married a year after Becky first met her at KVOC, Becky was her matron of honor. She was becoming more integral to more people.

Kennedy and Jenkins still haunted her, but she now had new supporters. Soon after she joined the KVOC sales staff, the two killers were scheduled for a routine parole hearing. It so rattled Becky, Ray Ebert offered to mount a statewide petition drive urging the Wyoming Parole Board to refuse any clemency for Kennedy and Jenkins. In only a few weeks, the radio station gathered more than 15,000 signatures, which were delivered to the parole board in an impressive stack. Although it was unlikely the two would have received any reduction in their sentences—they had served only fifteen years on a minimum thirty-five-year sentence for Becky's rape and hadn't even yet begun their life terms—the petition buoyed Becky's spirits.

Becky seemed to be making progress in her life. On a

bright June morning in 1987, thirty-two-year-old Becky married Russ Brown, a gas-truck driver who delivered fuel at the convenience store where she worked briefly. After dating a while, Becky had gotten pregnant, but miscarried. In the hospital, Russ proposed.

Because her oil-rigger stepfather Jack Case couldn't get away from a drilling job, Becky turned to the next most important man in her life to give her away at her wedding: Dave Dovala, the police detective who had arrested her would-be killer, comforted her mother, been her bodyguard at the trial, and had become a friend who ardently wished her life would somehow turn out better than it seemed. Theirs was a father–daughter relationship, no more physical than a hug when they saw each other, but for Becky, who hadn't really known her real father and who had suffered at the hands of many of the other men whose paths she crossed, it was priceless.

After the crime, Dovala had become attached to the young victim. He interviewed her several times, and sometimes the interviews were simply a cup of coffee and few kind words. Long after the trial, he pulled some strings to get her a job as a meter-maid for the police department. Everyone in the cop shop was rooting for her.

In those first years after the crime, Dovala came to know her and her family, and even helped retrieve Becky's younger sister when she ran away from home once. They often bumped into each other on the street and small-talked for a while.

He knew she had an alcohol problem, but he didn't know that it had taken her over. She simply didn't talk about her addiction.

They never talked about the crime, either. Becky kept things to herself, and she never really asked for advice or help. As such, she never seemed to him to be depressed or haunted, so he never suggested counseling, like he might for any other crime victim.

But he was among the first she told when she was to be married.

Now, she was the happiest he'd ever seen her. Dovala thought she positively glowed in her wedding dress as they posed for photos; her dark eyes finally reflecting some inner light he'd seldom if ever seen.

Maybe she had turned the corner.

NEWLY MARRIED, MAKING new friends at work and discovering sympathy she hadn't known existed, she suddenly felt vindicated and loved.

Her real family had also seen Becky's wedding as the beginning of her new life. They liked Russ, and they believed he was good for Becky. They respected him for loving her.

But the marriage wasn't a perfect match. It wasn't abusive, but it was lonely. The clean-cut, quiet Russ quit his job as a truck driver to have back surgery, and then took some college computer classes. When he wasn't in school, he seemed to be hunting and fishing with one of his buddies, leaving Becky home alone much of the time. Friends who visited Becky to keep her company during that time rarely remember seeing Russ, and Becky told some friends she thought her husband spent more time with his outdoor buddies than he did with her.

Maybe Russ wasn't ready for married life, or maybe Becky wasn't. God knows Becky had every reason to never trust a man again, to be truly intimate. Until she married Russ, she'd floated through several boyfriends like a night wind, not really caring where it went. She'd even gone through a promiscuous period, trying to be what she mistakenly believed men expected of her. And given her significant encounters with men, starting on the night of the crime, who could blame her for having a perverse misconception?

But getting married seemed to change everything, even for Becky, who yearned for an ordinary life that had eluded her.

Russ and Becky's newlywed difficulties simmered unresolved until 1990, when Becky gave birth to a baby girl. The birth was difficult, because of Becky's once-shattered pelvis. The pain, for once, was worth it.

Years later, her mother saw the baby as Becky's gift to

the family, a kind of replacement for Amy, the little girl taken from them. Becky wanted her daughter to live the life Amy never got the chance to live. She poured her life into her. She stayed home with the baby as long as she could afford time from work. The child became her whole world, especially as her marriage continued to decline.

The next Christmas, just six months after she was born, Russ told her he wanted a divorce. Rather than seek to repair the marriage, Becky abruptly ended it. She simply didn't have the strength to be humiliated by begging Russ to stay. Within a few months, she was suddenly an officially single mother, trying to make ends meet on sales commissions for a tiny radio station that offered no health insurance or hope of future riches.

Her mother pleaded with Becky to move to California, where she'd have help exorcising her ghosts far from the scene of her addictions and the many crimes against her, but Becky felt an attachment to Casper, even if her life there was disintegrating before her eyes.

In 1991, before the baby was even a year old, Becky tearfully gave two weeks' notice at KVOC and moved to the biggest radio station in town, where she was promised better sales, higher commissions and health insurance for herself and her daughter. It was like another divorce, maybe even more painful because she truly loved KVOC and they loved her, but she had to think of her daughter.

Rather than restart her life, though, it seemed to throw up another hurdle. Her new co-workers were young, robust, pressured salespeople who were staking their careers on their personalities. Rejection wasn't just business, it was sometimes personal. The urge to seek release, reassurance and renewal—including drinking—was just a subcultural reality. After years of hiding her drug and alcohol abuse, and trying to shake it, Becky could now hide it in plain sight.

STARS HAD CAST the only light during Becky Thomson's nightmare in Fremont Canyon so many years before. Although Orion was the only constellation she recognized among them, they were her only comfort in the black void at the bottom of the gorge.

So perhaps it was understandable when, fifteen years later, she searched the stars for answers. If the mothers, mental health professionals, cops, teachers, lawyers and preachers couldn't explain what happened—why Amy died, why her killers were allowed to live when society promised they would die, why Becky felt she should have died, too— then maybe the stars knew.

If it was written in the stars, she believed, perhaps it was destiny's fault—not Becky's—that Amy died and Becky lived.

In 1989, Becky enrolled in a community college class on cosmobiology, an astrological technique that purports to forecast psychological, physical and sociological life events. Becky believed that if she knew more about how time, space and human life intersect, she'd know why it all happened.

At a workshop for her class, a renowned German-born cosmobiologist used Amy and Becky's astrological data to show how her methods could chart a personality and identify trouble spots in life. The workshop was videotaped at Becky's request.

She first explored Amy's stars. Her charts indicated the eleven-year-old was popular with boys, but more as a teammate than a girlfriend; she was intuitive, magnetic and powerful, but sensitive; she was trusting but vulnerable to exploitation.

Amy's astrology also showed her to be vulnerable to addictions. Given that her three older sisters had each fallen into various substance abuses, it was either a facile or a haunting prediction.

Her stars also said she was destined for fame, but the cosmobiologist rushed to point out that perhaps as the victim of a grotesque crime that shocked an entire state, she had achieved exactly what the stars predicted.

And violence was prominent in Amy's heavens. It was likely, the astrologist suggested, that Amy's darker stars aligned with Ronald Kennedy's darker stars, but at her birth, Amy lived beneath a forecast of brutal victimization. Pointing to a chart based on the hours of the crime, she believed all the forces of life—astrologically—were in a maelstrom at the moment of Amy's death.

Amy's intuition might not have saved her life, but it might have made her death easier, the cosmobiologist surmised, by letting her accept fate and go gently into that terrible night.

But turning to Becky, the woman was direct: "You were simply not destined to die yet."

Flashing Becky's star-chart on a wall-sized screen, she showed how Becky's stars were classically aligned for violence and rape, how her magnetism also attracted the wrong kind of attention, and how she was prone to more accidents than most. She predicted Becky would likely experience strange, incomprehensible dreams.

In her most ominous—even hopeful—prediction of the day, the cosmobiologist told Becky her stars showed a "complete transformation" of her life in the next few years.

True to the prophecy of the cosmos, Becky was indeed changed three years after the workshop. But as the woman herself warned when she began, some indicators are not what they seem.

In the same way Amy had to die to become inadvertently famous, Becky had to go back to the Fremont Canyon Bridge to be transformed.

IF THE STARS hadn't offered any clear answers to Becky, neither did life on Earth.

But while visiting a local shelter for abused women, Becky heard murmurs about the psychiatrist whom she still suspected of molesting her in some way: Other women were talking about similar encounters with him. The murmurs eventually became whispers, then quiet coffee talk, then open discussions.

Several women at the shelter began to share stories that

they, too, had been assaulted by the same doctor. The rumors and complaints grew so thick that one of the shelter's counselors invited a local woman whose alleged encounters with the doctor were an open secret to speak to the women—including Becky.

The meeting aroused many of the women to consider lawsuits or criminal complaints, but Becky remained timid. She said flatly she wouldn't testify against him because she feared no one would believe her. She abandoned the idea for herself, although some remained angry and obsessed with seeking justice.

Several years later, Becky ran into the young woman who'd spoken to the group, and they slipped away to a small coffee shop. Amy's killers—Becky's rapists—were seeking a new trial, and she admitted to another woman in her group a crushing fear they might someday be free again. The woman tried to reassure her they were unlikely to be released from prison, now or later, but that perhaps counseling might help her vanquish her fears.

"I can't afford it," she said. While Wyoming had enacted new victims' rights laws in the wake of Becky's case, she couldn't benefit from them. No governmental assistance was available to her; even her extensive medical bills after the crime had been paid out-of-pocket and by her stepfather's health insurance. She desperately wanted counseling to exorcise all the demons summoned by the crime against her.

The woman mentioned that several of the psychiatrist's former patients had recently filed civil suits against him, and one had already won a large settlement.

Becky was intrigued. If she could hold it together, if she could prove what seemed like a dream to her, she might finally get enough money to repair herself properly. The nightmare of the crime, of the one-night stands, the drugs, booze and fear might all be finally purged.

She said she wanted to do something, so the woman gave her the name of a lawyer who had handled some of the other cases. As they finished their coffee and went on their way, Becky felt a new hope bubble up inside her.

◆ ◆ ◆

ON A WATERCOLORED spring night in 1992, in a violent thunderstorm, Lynn Sedar drove Becky to an Alcoholics Anonymous meeting. Rain fell so hard against Lynn's car that the stuffy air inside seemed to churn. The windshield wipers flicked incessantly, but rills of cool rain spilled down around them, to the street, to the river, to the sea. Nothing was settled.

At a stoplight on the way, Lynn casually asked how Becky's struggle against addiction was going.

"It's hard," Becky said. "It should have been me that night. I struggle with it every single day. It should have been my life that was taken, not Amy's."

Lynn was stunned. Becky had never talked about the crime to her, and she certainly had never suggested it wormed deep in her heart like an antagonistic cancer that she tried in vain to drown with drugs and alcohol.

Survivor guilt is a tricky thing. A volatile fusion of self-blame and grief, it causes survivors of traumatic events to question their own survival when others died. If they helped themselves to survive, the anguish can be especially bitter, forcing them to focus what they *didn't* do to prevent the crime in the first place.

On this dark, weeping night, broken and battered Becky, her guilt over Amy's death and her own survival unsalved for years, was still struggling in vain to make sense out of the great mystery of our existence. The obsession weighted her down like a stone around her neck: Why is Death not fair?

Becky began to cry. Lynn reached across the seat and squeezed her hand, then began to cry, too. They cried together across a few rainy miles, until they reached the meeting house.

Lynn had known Becky for many years, but only after the crime. They'd met at parties, where Becky was looking for acceptance, freely flowing booze, maybe some pills, maybe a one-night romance. In the late 1970s, the parties that middle-class Casper kids like Lynn and Becky attended featured mostly beer and cheap wine, marijuana, some cocaine and heroin, cross-tops, hash, quaaludes, peyote, and mushrooms. Sometimes, they happened in the darkened basements of private homes, sometimes empty warehouses, sometimes around a bonfire out beyond the well-known beats of rural deputies.

Becky felt comfortable among drunks, where the alcoholic haze enveloped all of them, and the din of their collective doubts was drowned. The party-girl routine took its toll on both Becky and Lynn.

They went separate ways for a while, but when they ran into each other on the street in 1992, their friendship picked up as if it had never been interrupted. Lynn was now sober, and she knew from friends that Becky was rehabbing, too. But as they talked on the sidewalk in front of a downtown café, Lynn sensed sadness in Becky.

After some small talk, Lynn slipped into the code of recovering addicts.

"You doing okay?" she asked.

"Oh yeah," Becky said, looking away. "Having a little trouble with the pills."

In fact, Becky's life was a wild, up-and-down carousel of depression, drugs and booze. She took an anti-depressant for a long time, but one day just stopped taking it. She had gotten hooked on prescription medication, an addictive anti-panic and anti-anxiety drug that slows the nervous system by deadening the part of the brain that controls emotions. Another doctor tried to wean her from it with an anti-seizure medicine that could produce depression and dizziness, and that reacted acutely with booze. And booze was a constant in Becky's life.

She was an addict, and she knew it. Some days, she wasn't sure what pills to take, some days she took none of them, and some days she took too many. Friends once found Becky sobbing in her car after lunch. The reason has been lost to time and memory, but Becky admitted she had already taken eight alprazolam pills and the day was only half over.

So Lynn suggested they attend some AA meetings together. They exchanged numbers, and Lynn called in a few days and made a date with Becky. Their first meeting together was the rainy spring night.

Becky had submitted to AA meetings, psychologists, rehab, drugs that were intended to help, and cold-turkey schemes, but nothing ever stuck. She'd quit for intermittent periods, and knew with all her heart that she wanted to be clean and sober, but eventually her cravings were always bigger than her heart.

Her depression sucked her down like a whirlpool over a storm drain. No matter how much she longed to escape, the pull of it confined her in a subterranean darkness where light shone irregularly and always just beyond her grasp.

By its very nature, AA tries to shift dependence from substances to people, to faith. And for it to work, its members must depend on others—and be depended upon. Because Becky never completely transcended her dependence on drugs, as much as she desired to be free of them, she never became anyone else's savior. She couldn't save herself.

She thought the drugs helped. They numbed her. She knew in her head they were bad, but in her heart, she also knew they deadened her guilt, memories and pain. The booze and pills were weapons that might kill the gnawing evil inside her, but not without killing her, too.

That night, damp with rain and tears, Becky shared her struggle with a handful of other addicts, each with their own demons. They understood her struggle with chemicals. But she didn't really talk about her other demons, about the crime itself, about her fears. They were with her, deep inside, consuming her from the inside out.

Waiting.

A LITTLE BEFORE noon on Wednesday, July 29, 1992, Becky met her friend Lisa Pearce Icenogle for lunch at one of their favorite downtown eateries. Becky wore a summer dress—she never wore slacks to work—and they sat across from each other at a table near the front of the restaurant, where the lunch crowd flowed closely past. Lisa thought about getting another table toward the back, where it would be quieter and more private, but it really didn't matter enough at the moment to cause a stink.

As always at this place, they ordered sandwiches and a loaf of fresh baked bread, which they slathered with butter. Becky had just turned thirty-seven and butter—lots of it—was a guilty pleasure. One of the many reasons she and Lisa enjoyed each other's company was that neither nagged or tattled about the calories on which they inevitably (and cheerfully) feasted.

And today, Becky needed such a friend. She was feeling punky, wracked with a stomach bug, a water-borne intestinal parasite called giardia, which nauseated her whenever she ate. A doctor had given her some medicine, but she wasn't taking it.

"You gotta take it," Lisa told her. She'd had giardia, too, and knew too well how uncomfortable and debilitating the cramps, vomiting and diarrhea could be.

"I can't," Becky told her. She paused. "It reacts with alcohol. My doctor says not to take the medicine until I stop drinking. It would make me even sicker."

Lisa was perturbed. She knew Becky wanted to be sober, but she also knew how difficult it had been for Becky to kick the habit.

"Then you gotta stop," she warned. "You gotta get off the booze, Becky."

"I know, I know," Becky held her hands up in surrender. "I'm working on it."

Lunch arrived. The waitress put their sandwiches in front of them, then took away the plate of crumbs left from the loaf of bread they virtually inhaled.

Lisa always prayed before a meal, so she reached across the table toward Becky, who rested her hand on top of Lisa's. After the quiet blessing and thankful "amen," Becky tightened her fingers around Lisa's.

"And thank you, Jesus," she said, perhaps for the first

time she ever spoke during one of their mealtime prayers, "for my special friend Lisa."

They prepared to eat, but Lisa wasn't easily put off.

"So how? How are you working on it?"

Becky shrugged as she hovered over her lunch.

"Well, for one, I'm gonna break up with my boyfriend. Tonight. Tomorrow. I dunno."

Becky's sister had introduced her to an itinerant worker who wasn't polished and lived in a shabby motel. Lisa knew him, and she didn't like him. At thirty-three, she thought he was as rough as a cob, poorly groomed and not very smart, not worthy of Becky. She'd been around him when he was drinking and, to her, he was not well educated or refined. Although oil and construction workers made good wages in those days, Becky paid for almost everything, including the booze they shared, and she could hardly afford it with a child at home. Getting rid of that guy was a good idea for a lot of reasons, Lisa thought.

"It's just not working out," Becky continued, sensing Lisa's unspoken approval of the impending breakup. "He's just dragging me down. And maybe if he's not around, I can quit."

Becky's pager beeped. She checked the number: It was her boss.

"Dammit," she said. "She checks up on me all the time. I just hate it! She probably saw my car and is checking up on me to make sure that I am working and not taking a long lunch or something."

"Does she do this a lot?" Lisa asked.

"Yeah," Becky fumed. "She does it a lot."

In fact, Becky's boss kept her on a tight leash, calling throughout the day, pushing her to make more sales calls, pump up her numbers. No mystery about it: Becky simply wasn't making her sales quotas, and she knew it.

But since Becky had left KVOC, she and Lisa didn't talk much about their work anymore. They were now competitors, so neither spoke much about how much they were selling or how much they weren't. They occasionally dished about certain clients they both knew, or about the scuttlebutt at their stations, but mostly they talked about husbands, boyfriends, vacations, food, mutual friends and more personal stuff. And Becky rarely talked about her deeper, darker secrets.

Just a few days before, Becky had rented a videotape of the film *Ode to Billy Joe*, about a star-crossed first love shared by two rural Mississippi kids—but with a sexual twist that drives Billy Joe McAllister to jump off the Talla-hatchie Bridge. After the dewy-eyed Billy Joe dies—hardly a swimming-pool high dive compared to the Fremont Canyon Bridge—his bereaved girlfriend laments, "It takes a lot to become a legend. And sometimes, it just takes a lot." The overly sentimental movie about a troubled teen who falls from a bridge was Becky's favorite, and not just because of the bridge's symbolic lethality: The cast, like the lyrics of the 1967 Bobbie Gentry hit that inspired the film, also featured a character named Becky Thompson.

Becky had watched the film four times that weekend, always crying.

"I just had to see that movie," Becky told her boyfriend after the last viewing. "It reminds me."

"Why?" he asked, believing it was a memory she'd rather forget.

"Because I like to cry," she told him.

They ordered dessert—Lisa had the spumoni, Becky her beloved amaretto cheesecake—but Becky was still troubled. Even though Becky's spirituality consisted mainly of a lack of trust between her and God, the two women talked about faith briefly, and then let it drop. Lisa sensed that Becky wanted to talk about something more, but Becky was just struggling to keep it together. And because they were sitting in full view of the lunch crowd, it was even more important to her to appear that she had put it all back together again, with no missing parts.

They finished lunch a little early. Becky wanted to get back to the street, where her boss expected her to be. They made vague plans to get together again for lunch soon.

"If there's anything I can do for you," Lisa offered, "just call."

Becky hugged her and they went their separate ways, but Lisa was unsettled. She sensed Becky wanted to say something, but just didn't. Or couldn't.

Becky's downward spiral was accelerating.

Lisa didn't know that Becky was considering declaring bankruptcy to shed some crushing debts she couldn't possibly pay. Becky also hadn't told very many people that she'd already visited a lawyer to prepare a civil lawsuit against the psychiatrist she believed had raped her while she was in a drug-induced fog. Nonetheless, all things known and unknown, spoken and unspoken, weighed heavily on her. The darkness of her depression and fear was seeping in around the edges, like a television screen going bad fast.

Her mood swings had grown more frequent and pronounced. One moment, she could be laughing and energetic, the next angry or despondent. Her heavy drinking didn't help, and neither did her infrequent dalliances with counseling.

Becky had already tried to commit suicide a few times, though the results were more tragi-comic than lethal.

She'd purposely swallowed an overdose of aspirin and booze more than once, failing each time to take enough to even be taken to a hospital. She begged her sister not to tell anyone.

Another time, she called her sister, intending to shoot herself while on the phone. But the handgun—a gift from her ex-husband for her protection, not her demise—fell apart in her hands as she talked. Frustrated, she flung the parts on the floor.

"Well, I couldn't do this right," she huffed before she hung up. "I'm going to bed."

Worst of all, she believed her own sadness was toxic and would infect her child, the last true purpose in her life.

As if from some distant universe, the one ray of light that would have brightened her entire universe had shined, but it hadn't yet reached Becky.

Unknown to Becky as she finished her long lunch with Lisa Icenogle that afternoon, the Wyoming Supreme Court was preparing to announce it had just denied Ronald Leroy Kennedy and Jerry Lee Jenkins new trials. For two years the two lifers, who had already been luckier than their stars, had been clamoring for even more, claiming John Ackerman and Don Chapin were ineffective defenders in their capital case and that they should have had separate trials—not realizing that a joint trial had probably protected them from each other.

THE NEXT MORNING, Becky called Lisa on her cell phone. She hadn't broken up with her boyfriend the night before. The struggle against her addictions was failing. She wasn't keeping up with work. She felt like she was losing control.

"I need your strength, Lisa," she said. "I need your strength."

"You've got it and you know that," Lisa promised. "Whatever you need me to do."

Becky calmed down a little bit and started to cry. Lisa said she'd pray for her—which Becky liked to hear—and that she was going to be fine.

"I'm here," Lisa said. "Just call. I'll do whatever I can and you can always lean on me, Becky. You know that, right?"

Becky knew. She composed herself and they hung up.

Never one to miss a birthday, Becky bought a birthday card for her mother that day, signed it with love and kisses, and mailed it.

Becky also called Lynn Sedar that day, but only left a message on Lynn's machine in a shaky voice: "Lynn, this is Becky. Give me a call. I'd really like to talk to you. I'll try your ex."

Lynn's ex-husband was an old friend and also struggling with his own dependencies. Becky wanted to get together, for support, for conversation, maybe even for an evening with a man she respected. They made a date for later that night, but he never showed up. Instead, he went to an AA meeting.

Earlier that afternoon, Lisa Icenogle had been driving across town and passed Becky's car on a highway overpass. Becky's boyfriend was riding shotgun. Lisa's eyes met Becky's as they passed, and Becky appeared sorely embarrassed.

BECKY LEFT A phone message for Lisa early on Friday morning, July 31. When Lisa picked up the message, she called back, but got no answer. Throughout the day, she called Becky's work, home and mobile numbers to no avail. She even tried their old code—two rings, hang up, and call back immediately—but Becky never answered.

That same day, on an end-of-the-month Friday afternoon, a Supreme Court clerk called to tell former Assistant Prosecutor Dave Lewis, now in private practice in Casper, that Kennedy and Jenkins would not be granted new trials. Only one person on Earth could be more pleased than Lewis about the decision: Becky Thomson.

He searched for Becky's telephone number so he could pass on the good news, but he couldn't find it. Typical of a Friday afternoon in a law firm, deadlines loomed and other matters were more pressing at the moment, so he put off his call to Becky until Monday.

After almost twenty years, a couple more days won't hurt, he thought.

Becky was out anyway. She bought herself a new dress at the local mall and had a late lunch at a local Chinese place. She knocked off work early, about 3:00 p.m.. She went directly to her boyfriend's room at a cheap flophouse-cum-motor court that catered to oilfield and construction workers for whom even an apartment was too much of a commitment.

They shared a couple shots of schnapps, and tried to make love. But for whatever reason, they just couldn't consummate, and Becky got mad. She wanted out, of the motel and the relationship, but she could do neither cleanly. She dressed hastily in her pink pullover top and blue jeans and, together, they left the motel in Becky's car.

They stopped at an automated teller where Becky withdrew thirty dollars, then picked up her daughter from the babysitter. But she didn't go home. She just wanted to drive around for a while and try to shake the pernicious depression that was coming over her.

They stopped at a roadhouse where Becky wrote a five-dollar check for a six-pack of Miller Genuine Draft, which they drank as they drove aimlessly around town with her two-year-old in the backseat. A sullen Becky was depressed, angry, frustrated and, soon enough, drunk. She was utterly lost in the most familiar place in her world. If she'd had a destination in mind, it was someplace beyond her grasp, now and forever, and she'd never been so wretchedly sad. She had no place to go, and no good way to turn.

The bridge.

She abruptly announced to her boyfriend she knew where they were going. Fremont Canyon Bridge. Thirty-five miles away.

"I don't think that's a good idea," he protested.

"I've been there before," she said. "It's okay. I've been there before."

Yes, she had. She convinced a friend to take her once a few years after the crime, and they drank two bottles of wine to fortify themselves for the journey. Another time, she told her friend Lisa, her husband Russ had unwittingly driven her across it on their way to a fishing hole. The man's thoughtlessness enraged Lisa, but she said nothing for fear of damaging the already fragile equilibrium in Becky's marriage. Besides, it was entirely possible—maybe likely—that Becky had visited Fremont Canyon Bridge alone, too, on secret outings that nobody knew about.

Earlier Becky and her boyfriend had some alcohol. The idea of visiting the bridge made him uneasy, but at that moment, it seemed bigger than him. It propelled them faster and faster toward it.

"I just don't think . . ." he stammered.

"I have to go," she snapped back.

The more he protested, the faster she went. By the time they crossed the city limits, passing the happy, twinkling carnival lights at the county fair, she was going over seventy miles an hour. He shut up.

Less than a month before, he and Becky had gone to a parking-lot carnival in town on a summer night. There, they had bumped into Becky's older sister, who had just left the midway's five-dollar-a-leap bungee-jumping attraction, a tall crane rigged to drop thrill-seekers several stories toward the pavement before plucking them back in the nick of time. She was thrilled, the adrenaline still gushing through her.

"Oh, I want to go!" Becky bubbled.

Her sister was surprised, but said nothing. It was, after all, only a carnival ride, wasn't it?

Becky and her boyfriend both paid their money and took the breathtaking drop, and never said anything more about it. Although the thought of Becky taking another long plunge horrified her mother when she heard about it, Becky apparently only saw it as a carnival thrill. She was only a young, vibrant woman seeking excitement, not a moth drawn to a flame.

Becky, her boyfriend and her daughter now sped through the sunset-washed hills and scrub cedar badlands, virtually flying over the rises in the twisting country road. The night was clear and mild, but the low spots in the ancient landscape were already filling with darkness. Long shadows were getting longer.

Becky slowed when she reached the sixty-foot steel span, which rose into view unexpectedly as they rounded a curve in the road. She drove across and parked in a graveled turnout at the north end of the bridge—the exact spot where Kennedy and Jenkins had first stopped on a tragic night nineteen years earlier.

With her boyfriend and daugher in tow, Becky walked onto the bridge. She stopped at a waist-high railing and looked down into the slow-moving green water below.

"Here," she said. "Here is where they threw Amy. And me."

Becky's boyfriend stood beside her and looked down. His head swam with the loftiness and his intoxication. Becky continued, pointing farther down the graded county road where they had parked.

"They raped me up there. Then they threw me over the bridge right here. See that little outcropping there? That's where I hit the wall, then fell in the water. They found blood there on that little ledge."

She choked up.

"Amy hit farther below, down there. See that ledge right at the water? They found blood there, too."

Becky pointed to the shrubby crevice where she hid all night, freezing and scared, half-naked and gravely injured, comforted only by stars and darkness. From that spot near the water, she traced her impossible escape route, a couple hundred feet up the talus slope to where she dragged her useless legs across the dirt to the spot where her car was now parked.

She started to cry, but it upset her daugher. So she turned away and sat down, her legs dangling over the edge through the railing. Becky's boyfriend sat down beside her, and held the two-year-old's hand to shield her from the dizzying edge.

"I told them I'd do anything," Becky said. "I begged them. They took her. They took her here. You know the last thing she said? She said, 'I love you, Becky.'"

Becky broke down completely, sobbing aloud.

Her boyfriend hugged her, and Becky's daughter began to cry, too.

"The baby shouldn't see you cry," he said. He stood and took the child's hand. "C'mon, with me, sweetie. You going to be okay, Becky?"

Becky nodded, wiping her eyes. He walked back to the car with the little girl, leaving Becky to compose herself. He opened the car door for Becky's daughter, who crawled into the seat while he walked around to the other side of the car to urinate.

Suddenly, he heard an explosive splash echo up the steep canyon walls.

Gathering the baby in his arms, Becky's boyfriend ran back to the bridge where Becky had been sitting. She was gone.

His heart pounding, he looked into the water, but it was already turning dark and he saw nothing.

"Rebecca! Rebecca!" he screamed. "Answer me!"

Nothing.

He shouted again, then started to cry. The baby began to wail, too. He ran up and down the bridge trying desperately to see through his tears and the pitch blackness.

Nothing.

She was gone.

IN THE NINETEEN years since he'd arrested Ron Kennedy on the town's main street, Dave Dovala had gotten himself elected sheriff of Natrona County. And by all accounts, he was a good one, too. A genial cop with a dry-as-velvet sense of humor, he liked people, and they liked him. On nights like this, he was more likely to be out at the county fair chewing the fat with folks than home watching TV.

And that's exactly what he was doing—wandering the fair's carnival midway—when a call came from his dispatcher.

"Dave, they need you out at Fremont Canyon Bridge," she said. "It's the same girl . . . well, you know."

He knew.

His vector lights flashing, Dovala rushed out to the bridge, praying out loud it wasn't Becky. He was going so fast, he passed a fire truck speeding to the scene. When he got there, a helicopter life-flight team had already come and gone, their services unnecessary. Some deputies and paramedics stood around with an unfamiliar young guy and Becky's little girl, whom he recognized immediately.

He shined his powerful light down into the water, where he saw a body floating face down in the turbid water. A storm was blowing in, and the swirling wind at the river's surface had pushed Becky's body below the southern end of the bridge.

The corpse's dark hair splayed around her head like a silken web, but even if he hadn't immediately recognized her hair, he knew Becky's shape at a glance.

It was her.

A night that began calm ended in violence. The wind shifted twice while he waited on the bridge that night. A thunderstorm rolled over the top of them, and lightning illuminated the haunted chasm where Becky floated.

He didn't go down to the water's edge, and he didn't look at her when they fished her out later that night. He'd seen dead people before, and he especially didn't want to see this one.

BECKY'S MEMORIAL SERVICE was five days later, on a sweltering August afternoon in the same sanctuary where Amy had lain in her casket almost nineteen years earlier. More than five hundred people, some of whom never knew Becky, squeezed into the church to say goodbye.

Unlike Amy's murder nineteen years before, the ripples from Becky's plunge into Fremont Canyon radiated around the Earth. Wire services picked up the story, and major metropolitan newspapers like *The Washington Post* sent reporters to tell the story of the girl who died twice.

Dr. Joseph Murphy, who had counseled Becky as a doctor and a friend in the years before she died, officiated. He recalled what she said about wanting to be normal.

"Becky, you were normal," he said to her spirit. "Who of us here today could live through her awful experiences and not bend, not break?"

Her friend Lisa Pearce Icenogle and Becky's ex-husband Russ Brown also spoke fondly, recalling memories of the girl who had died twice and tried valiantly to live just once.

Becky had fallen almost one hundred twenty feet, crashing into a rock ledge just three feet under water. Her neck was broken and because there was no water in her lungs, death was presumed to be instantaneous. The violence of her impact was so great that the autopsy noted the woven imprint of her clothing on her skin in some spots.

After interviewing Becky's boyfriend and Becky's family, deputies ruled out foul play. Evidence of past suicide attempts, her anguished mental state and the mere location of her death suggested she was not murdered.

Without ruling it a suicide, the coroner had listed the cause of Becky's death in clinical terms: "Total body trauma with skull, cervical spine and multiple rib fractures with C-2 cord crush, due to a fall from height."

But no death certificate has a blank that would have allowed him, even if scientific proof existed for such things, to write a different truth: "She died of sadness. She died because she always thought she should be dead and her sister should be alive. She was suffocated by the prospect of her tormentors' freedom. She died because she had already been murdered many years before. She fell from such a height that it took nineteen years to hit the bottom. She was crushed beneath something bigger than she was."

Becky's ashes were buried atop Amy's coffin in Highland Cemetery, and a new stone that bore both of their names— together in death, at last—was later placed on the grave.

She was only thirty-seven when she died the second time. She had lived the last nineteen years of her life in the shadow of that bridge, that crime.

The program for her somber memorial service bore the color photo of an idyllic mountain lake, surrounded by a forest, blue sky and white clouds. Inside was a funeral verse by an unknown poet: *Do not stand at my grave and weep, I am not there . . . I am the thousand winds that blow . . . I am the gentle autumn rain . . .*

As the mourners left the stifling church, a thunderstorm boiled up. The services had begun in sunlight, but now a petulant wind scoured the town and when fat raindrops began to fall, the hot and unsettled afternoon seemed to weep.

• • •

DID BECKY THOMSON jump from the Fremont Canyon Bridge, or did she simply lean too far over the dizzying edge? Was she intent on dying, or muddled by alcohol, betrayal, pills and depression? Was she tempting fate, facing her fears, when a sinister wind nudged her over the side?

Only she knows.

In many ways, the last nineteen years of her life had been a freefall. It was not entirely bad; in fact, Becky enjoyed moments of great joy. But as time passed, her plunge gained momentum. By 1992, she'd reached a kind of terminal velocity.

For a long time, her family clung—at least publicly—to the theory that Becky was distraught and drunk, too close to the edge of sanity and the bridge's meager guardrail on a night of shifting winds. Anyone who has peered over the brink of the bridge to the green water far below feels a kind of magnetic, acrophobic tug, as if a hellish gravity itself might reach up and suck one down.

Her family doesn't believe Becky would have taken her little girl to that place for the simple purpose of attending her death. She had bought a beautiful new dress the day she died and was excited about new job prospects at the radio station. But at unguarded times, when they talk about Becky's last night on Earth, they inadvertently say things like "when she killed herself" or how survivor's guilt claimed her, not a misstep on a steel bridge that had become as much a part of her as her bones.

When the coroner contacted Becky's two surviving sisters, while investigating her death, both were saddened but not surprised.

Almost nobody else, including Becky's closest friends, believes her death was accidental. She had lost all confidence in the order of her universe. She had reportedly botched suicide attempts before, and she was grasping for any handhold against the storm her life had become.

But her official death certificate left the question open, noting specifically that it could not be determined whether Becky's fall was accidental or suicidal.

• • •

WHAT MAKES A SURVIVOR?

The first ingredient is calamity. After a dark night of the spirit, survival is genuine dawn, where we can begin to trust in an orderly and predictable universe again.

Some never survive until dawn, and others survive but never see it.

True survivors of extreme adversity—war, a life-threatening disease, rape, murder, childhood abuse and terrorism, to name a few—are able to repair themselves. The rest die physically, emotionally or both.

Bernard Kempler was born to Jewish parents in Poland in 1936. As a mere child, he endured life in ghettoes and concentration camps, a barbed-wire escape, a clandestine and penniless existence on the run, in which he dressed as a girl and hid in crawl spaces in burned-out buildings. After the war, he emigrated to the United States and became an eminent Jungian psychologist.

He credits his survival to his flexible psyche as a child, not taking the horrors personally, a sense of spiritual protection, his temperament, and his ability to dissociate from the terror at hand.

When psychiatrist Dr. Robert Lifton studied survivors of Hiroshima and the Holocaust, he also found that truly resilient people have many adaptive mechanisms. His conclusions: They are able to integrate seemingly incongruous ideas and actions, seek consistency and ordinariness, remain connected to human events, and search for spiritual meaning.

Becky tried. For almost nineteen years, she struggled to wriggle free from her demons, waiting for the first light to break so she could scratch her way up an insurmountable canyon wall, just as she had on her horrific night in Fremont Canyon.

But in the end, the dawn was false.

It never really came. The story of that one single night didn't end at daybreak; for Becky, it never ended. The memory of it stayed too big to go away, too alive.

There's something else, it seems to me: The bridge.

Bridges are part of our mythology, furniture in our folklore. They represent unnatural paths to new places, transitions in spirit as well as geography. On a bridge, we are suspended between what lies ahead and what we left behind. We have taken the first step out of our comfortable world into something new, but we have not yet crossed the threshold. Offering no safe escape while suspended in the air between two pieces of terra firma, bridges are symbolic of change, risk, transformation and, in the case of a mythical hero's death, a place of resurrection.

We associate bridges with death, partly because of their metaphoric value to our literature, film and art, but there is likely a more instinctive dread. Did the ancients fear they were defying the gods by bypassing their natural, impassable rivers and gorges? Do we fear our own vertigo will carry us too close to the edge, perhaps over it? Why do we awake startled when, in our dreams, we fall? Even now, in the days of jumbo jets and space shuttles, a journey that takes us over empty space or water can be unnerving.

Very simply, we fear falling.

In the days and weeks after the World Trade Center towers fell, we widely embraced the symbol of the collapsing buildings, knowing thousands of lives were vaporized and crushed inside as they crumbled.

But the images that made us turn the page quickly were of desperate people who leapt from the towers. Even today, years later, those gut-twisting images of soon-to-be corpses hurtling toward infinity only appear on Web sites where the viewer is forewarned against what he is about to see.

In Tarot—where Becky briefly sought answers, also without satisfaction—a disaster is foretold by Card XVI, a lightning-shattered medieval tower from which bodies are plunging.

We fear falling.

The bridge is symbolic of something in Becky's story, too, not just a wrinkle, not just a happenstance. I don't believe in wrinkle theories. It's there for a purpose. Something, somewhere was waiting for the bridge, the opportunity, the har-

monic convergence of cohorts, a moonless night . . . I don't know. But it was not an accidental prop.

When I heard the news of Becky's death, I was the editor of a small daily newspaper in northeastern Wyoming. Grief comes out in different ways for different people. A storyteller and a friend, I wrote a column that same weekend, although I'm not sure whose story I was telling, mine or hers:

It isn't ironic that she died at that spot. Only tragic.

So on that night long ago, we lost innocence and gained fear. We were just children, raped by wickedness. After that night, the days are not so bright in my memory, and the nights are terribly darker. Evil that we never imagined now can never be forgotten.

And as the years have passed, I have thought often about Becky in her bright summer dresses and about Amy standing alone in the outfield, waiting for the long ball that never came.

Maybe Becky went back, but we can't. The days may be brighter ahead.

I wanted to believe that Becky had finally taken control. She had decided in 1973 to survive a harrowing ordeal that would kill almost anyone else. And she decided in 1992 that her survival had served its purpose—to punish Amy's killers, to bear a child, to laugh again even when it hurt—and she was ready for her end.

She didn't choose how her first life, the life before the bridge, turned out. But she chose how the second would end.

I don't want to contemplate the possibility it was an accident. If she merely slipped and fell at that particular haunted spot, it would be a tragedy of cosmic proportions. I don't want to think that Becky, in the end, was just another victim of circumstance, in the wrong place at the wrong moment. I don't want to believe she had come to exorcise a ghost, but was devoured by it.

So I don't. But it's an admitted supposition, a hypothesis of my heart. Neither more right nor wrong than any other presumption.

The only thing we know for certain is that Becky died.

On the last day of July 1992, she shattered her neck falling twelve stories from the Fremont Canyon Bridge, where she already died once nineteen years before.

The rest of the truth, whatever it was, was swept away on the wind.

Chapter 9

UNTOLD DESTINY

Ronald Kennedy had been in prison more than fifteen years for the rape of Becky Thomson and the murder of Amy Burridge when he began to rewrite his personal history.

At first with a pencil and legal pad, then on a prison typewriter, he committed the first half of his life to paper in a 468-page, typewritten memoir he titled *Untold Destiny*. Part *Huckleberry Finn* and part "*Penthouse* Forum," Kennedy's chronicle explores his youth frame by frame, from birth to his near-death in the gas chamber.

His younger sister brought the plastic-wrapped manuscript to a late-night interview with me at a Casper pancake house in March 2003, hiding it on the seat beside her until it was time to go. For a couple hours, she answered my questions—mostly about family history and her relationship with Ron—but she remained a little detached, measuring her responses carefully. Later, I realized I was being sized up, and my motives were being measured. My questions were her answers.

A blizzard had begun as we talked. When it came time to leave, we pulled on coats and gloves for the cold sprint across the slick parking lot—and that's when she handed me a package I hadn't seen. It was her brother Ron's typewritten life story, a couple inches thick.

Written more than ten years before, nobody outside the Kennedy family had ever seen this manuscript, nor even knew it existed. A secret manuscript by the convicted rapist and killer who was the linchpin in a horrific crime that had never been explained adequately hefted thick and momentous in the hand. Would the last survivor of that night finally explain his life, his crimes, and his heart? Reveal some subtle details he'd never spoken to police or lawyers? Apologize?

His first page promises Dickensian twists, perversions and depravity, without the filter of eloquence or gentility:

> During my lifetime, I have experienced many downfalls, and by far more than any human being should ever have to experience. I have experienced physical hurt the likes of which nobody should have to endure, and I don't have any idea why. The readers of this book will find the journeys of a little boy, to becoming a grown man that was more interested in helping his poverty-stricken family than anything else . . . The hurt in my life has been devastating and heart shattering . . .
>
> The conversations in this book ring true to my ear and my heart, but it must be understood that they have been reconstructed from my memories. The events that I am writing about meant so much to me, however, and I have lived them over to myself during so many long nights, years, that I think my story is as close to reality as if it were only last night that my life first began . . .
>
> A special dedication to my deceased wife Sally, who was my first love and the light of my life.
>
> To Sally . . .
> I've told it,
> Not the way they think it is,
> Or the way they heard it was,
> Or the way they wish it was,
> But the way it really was,
> The only way you'd want it told.

***

Sally was Sally Springs.

In his words, Ronald Kennedy met her on the last day of seventh grade in 1959. She was a student aide in the library at Dean Morgan Junior High School. For him, the pretty young blond girl with green eyes seemed to appear from nowhere, but he'd soon learn she'd apparently had her eye on him a lot longer.

He was ready for school to be done. By his accounting, the year had been Hell on Earth: His usually above-average schoolwork had been sabotaged by intolerant teachers who hated him. His adversaries lurked among secretaries, teachers, rich kids and librarians—although a wise black janitor became his mentor.

All because he was a kid born into a poor family on the "wrong" side of the tracks, he says. And he stood up for what was right against the implacable, dark motives of a System that wouldn't share its advantages.

But the world wouldn't beat Ronnie Kennedy, no sir. By the end of his seventh-grade year, all the kids in school felt safer because Ronnie was around. And Ronnie himself counted his blessings, which included the love of a good dog that followed him everywhere, and a devotion to everything that was good and right, despite the odds in an unfair world. He was the hero of his own story.

And Sally Springs was his Dulcinea.

"That is quite a load of books," Sally told the skinny kid who was cleaning out his locker on the last day of school.

"Yes, it is," he said, confident and suave.

"My name is Sally, and I already know what your name is."

"You do?"

"Yes, it's Ronnie."

"That's right."

"How did you do on your final grades of the semester?" she asked him.

"Well, three out of four classes I earned A's. In the easiest class, I was given a D. However, I'm on my way to get that corrected right now."

"What do you mean?"

"Well, Sally, take a look at my final term paper in this class, then you tell me."

Sally scanned it.

"Mistakes like that just don't happen by accident," she said.

"You're right," Ron agreed, feeling tougher by the moment.

"You have made yourself quite a reputation in this school, but not a bad one. Everyone is grateful to you for what you have done, including me."

"That's good to know," he said, smiling in his dashing, sexy way.

"You have some pretty powerful friends to be able to run the principal out of the school."

"You don't say."

"C'mon, quit teasing me!" she giggled.

"Sally, I would rather not think of them as just important friends. If you know what I mean."

Sally's eyes must have brightened; her heart must have skipped a little beat.

"Oh, yes, I do," she said, flirting. "What are you going to do on summer vacation?"

"I work at the pool hall, I like to go swimming, I like to go walking in the forest across the river from where I live. There's lots of ways for me to spend the summer."

"Are you coming back to this school next year?" she asked, a little hope in her voice. "It would be nice if you would."

"Well, Sally, I don't see why not. I have to keep my reputation intact, don't I?"

Sally asked if girls were allowed down at the pool hall.

"It depends on who they are," he told her.

"Me!"

"In that case, exceptions can be made."

"For me?"

"For you."

And with that fateful exchange between an adoring little girl and her newest hero in a small-town school library, an improbable love story begins—and the tortuous path of Ronald Leroy Kennedy's doomed life is diverted momentarily. After Sally, nothing will be the same.

At least, that's the way he tells it.

RONALD LEROY KENNEDY is reborn on the first page of his autobiography: A child of a poor but loving family in a remote place he describes as one of the intermediate circles of Hell, pleasant enough for wistful memories but ultimately a kind of punishment.

> I was born in Casper, Wyoming, in the year 1946 to Mr. and Mrs. Ernest L. Kennedy. I was give [sic] the birth name Ronald Leroy Kennedy. He who is born in Casper never quite gets over it. . . . As a child I can only remember growing up as a loner, with the exception of my four sisters and one brother . . .
>
> I can credit our families [sic] closeness to the poverty that we suffered from. My family was extremely poor, and it wasn't by design. We lived in a neighborhood on the north side of town, simply called North Casper. It was completely segregated from the rest of the town. North Casper was my home for most of my life, and the poorest neighborhood in town. There were a few families in my neighborhood that I can say were not poor, nor friendly either, when compared to my family. . . . However, the biggest majority of the families in North Casper were extremely poor like us.
>
> Not to mention that my neighborhood was the roughest and the most dangerous place to live in the whole town. Transients from all walks of life, places, were always passing through North Casper. It was not unusual to find a dead body laying [sic] down by the river, or shoved underneath the river bridge. It was just the way of life in the part of town that I lived in.

He describes the genesis of his father's alcoholism as a

tragic accident. He recalls a sheriff's deputy coming to his house on a cold winter morning to deliver bad news. While working as a night watchman, Ernest Kennedy fell eight stories through a hole in the floor, shattering his skull and breaking his neck, back, arms and legs.

> As time passed by, I watched my father become a stranger to me. He had become an alcoholic of the worse [sic] kind. Being just a child the hurt I felt from my father's accident, and the change in his life, only increased the hurt I already felt inside for my family. I started to draw away from my family as a child living in my own little world, so I would not have to see or feel the hurt I knew all my family was going through, because of the unconditional love that I had for each and every one of them in my own beautiful ways.
>
> I use to set [sic] and wait out in the backyard by the garbage cans waiting for my father to come driving home from work. I could hear his 1929 Model A Ford coming a block away. . . . I waited anxiously for him to step out, then call for me. My father's hair was as black as the dark of the night, the same as mine is now. His cheek bones were high on his face. His cheeks were slender, and his eyes were the color of the sky on a clear blue summer day. My father was a very handsome man. Soon as he got out of the car I always knew that he would turn around, and say, "come here, boy." It made my little heart beat fast, and fill with love, especially when he would pick me up and hold me in his arms with what I knew was a special kind of love between us that I never wanted to end.

At age six, little Ronnie had no friends. His mother worked; his father seldom spoke to him. His most faithful companion was a half-Husky, half-Lab dog named Snooks. One of their favorite haunts was a local park where all manner of low-lifes loitered, doing drugs, gambling and sometimes slicing and stabbing each other—"a natural part of life" to the kid.

> Sometimes I would earn as much as fifty cents from the

dice-shooters in the park by standing at the end of the park road with a whistle. I was told if I seen [sic] a cop car coming to blow the heck out of the whistle, which would give them all time to get everything hid that was going on illegal. I didn't realize I was doing anything wrong. . . .

I kept saving every cent that I made, and put it in this box, then hid it across the river. Soon I had six or seven dollars saved up which seemed like forever to do. I wanted to buy my mother, father, sisters and brother something nice that would make them happy. I took the money home and gave it to my mother and father. I told them what I had done to earn it, but with a tiny lie.

His mother accepted the lie, even if his suspicious father punished him without ever knowing the truth. Exceptionally precocious, Ronnie knew his father's heart was freighted by his failure to provide a good life for his family—a task that fell to his long-suffering mother, Hilda.

I never heard my mother complain. I can remember my mother getting odd jobs of all kinds, such as cleaning rich people's houses and washing clothes, and many other things just to keep food in our mouths and a roof over our heads. It didn't matter how rough the going got for my mother to take care of us. . . . (She) was a very gentle woman, with a heart as big as the sky. Her spirits were always pleasant to be around. As a child I can remember how beautiful my mother was. Her eyes were soft brown that seemed to capture your attention and your heart with a love as sweet as the heavens in the sky. Her cheek bones were fairly high, her cheeks were slender, her body was trim and slender as a warm summer breeze. Her love for her children was without end.

By age seven, Ronnie excelled in school, but remained a loner—until he met a couple older boys who taught him how to steal bags of candy from the corner market. He got very good at it, so good his mother grew curious about where a desperately poor second-grader would get pockets full of sweets.

So for the first time in my life I had to lie to my mother, and tell her that one of the boys at school gave me the candy. Mother thought it was very nice. My mother never questioned me other than just asking me about things, because up until I took the candy from the store I had never lied to my mother or father because I never had a reason to, they never had a reason not to believe me. I gave most of the candy to my mother to give to my little sisters. It made me feel real proud that I could give them something that our family rarely ever had to give us.

Stealing candy proved so easy, Ronnie got bolder. He started pilfering from other nearby stores until he had a regular larcenous trapline. Convinced he could steal something while the owner watched him, he got downright cocky about his budding criminality.

My father was an extremely intelligent person, so I guess I inherited his genetic makeup in many ways. . . . Because of being so bright, it allowed me to go anywhere. . . . In my own way, I was an innocent child, unfamiliar with what grown-ups would call during my generation "the sins of the world." For the first time in my life, I was introduced to the art of stealing, but I did not view it in my mind as something bad. I kept going into the same store, taking items that my sister and I needed for school. The more I took, the easier it started to become for me. . . . It made me happy inside knowing my mother could use her hard-earned money on other things that our family needed badly. At last I began to feel some of the hurt I felt inside of me subside to a degree, knowing that I was helping my poor family by helping myself.

Shoplifting provided a sense of accomplishment, but it wasn't really putting food on the table. Oh, he'd long been pinching kitchen staples like flour and sugar, which he added to his mom's cupboard canisters bit by bit so she wouldn't notice, but he aspired to more and better. So Ronnie hatched a new plan: a late-night burglary at a local chicken house, where he snatched live chickens and still-warm eggs, which he sold to another unsuspecting shop-keeper for cash. And that winter, when the Kennedys were too poor to buy or even chop a Christmas tree, he stole one from a local lot.

Ronnie was seven years old and, in his mind, his net worth was blossoming. He was contributing to his family in regular but mysterious ways. He had accomplished the daunting athletic task of swimming across the treacherous North Platte River. And his extraordinary intellect was re-warded when his school let him skip from second grade to fourth, where by sheer dint of genius he was again superior to his older classmates.

But he still felt compelled to help his struggling family in any way he could. At eight, he went seeking real employment.

I went to each place telling them how important it was that I be given a job. Some of the places I went to just laughed at me, some were nice about it, but said I was too young for them to hire me for any reason.

One of the stores I went to was mean to me. The owner told me to get my ass out of his store, that I was just a little bum, that he would kick my ass all the way out the door I came in. The hurt I felt from this was like a burning rage in-side of me. It created an anger that no child should ever have to experience. This was the beginning of changes to come in my life.

I knew there was only one way that I could help my fam-ily now, and keep all of us from starving to death. That was to take what I wanted at any cost. The very first place I was going to start taking from was the place that threatened to hurt me.

On a sub-zero night, with no winter clothes, little Ronnie crept from his bed and sneaked down snowy alleys to the store. He pried open a back window, crawled in and unlocked the front door. Pulling a child's wagon behind him, he loaded up with food and left. Parking the wagon on his back porch, he curled up beside the coal stove to warm himself and his nearly frostbitten feet, and fell asleep.

The next morning, his mother found the food on her routine winter sprint to the outhouse and presumed it was a gift from well-meaning neighbors.

> It gave me a warm feeling in my heart to know that our family would have food to eat at least for a while. I knew then that my family would never have to go without food anymore, not if I had anything to do about it, and I did.

RONNIE WOULD BE many things in his heart and mind, but sturdy wasn't among them.

In fifth grade, he was gangly, slight and skinny—an easy target for bullies. One day, three bigger kids ganged up on him, kicking and punching him into unconsciousness. He awoke two hours after the beating in a vacant lot, when the faithful Snooks found him, licked his face and provided support for him on the long walk home.

The next day, he sought out the two older boys who'd taught him to steal candy, and he asked another favor: Revenge. So one early morning, the two boys bushwhacked Ronnie's assailants, who never again hectored the frail Ronnie Kennedy. Feeling the noble urge to repay a debt, Ronnie helped the two older boys break into a laundromat and rifle all the machines of $120 in quarters, a rich payday for a poor kid in 1955.

But after a bit, the loner in him took charge again.

> I decided to take on the laundry mats [sic] myself. It seemed real easy for me to do. I didn't realize what I was doing would lead to other things. For the moment, I was content because I was making money to help my family. To me that was the most important thing in my life, otherwise there

was no need for me to do such things, nor would I have even tried to do such things, because I wasn't a thief.

But he was a kid without real friends. He writes that he preferred the company of fawns, sparrows, squirrels and other wild things to people. He recalls being much loved by the neighborhood adults, since he was a hard worker, a bright child, and a kind spirit, but he simply couldn't make young friends. In the whole chronicle of his youth, he mentions only two close friends—Gene, who introduced him to marijuana, and Jack, who introduced him to a whole spectrum of other reckless boyhood thrills.

> I was also a very shy boy, even at the age of ten. Perhaps it was due to my being a loner. There was no kids to play with when I was growing up. That could account for some of it. Although I preferred to be by myself in my own world, free from hurt from bad past experiences. It continued to follow me. Our neighborhood, poverty didn't allow me to fit in with many kids my age. It affected me in many ways. At age six, terrible hate started setting inside my heart, mind, that no child should ever have to experience, especially at such a young, tender age. Children at age six cannot understand such things, or how they are going to affect him, or her, in later life. This was all brought on because of poverty.

Until he was in sixth grade, he'd never been out of north Casper. When he finally crossed the magical threshold of the train tracks, he entered an alien world, Oliver Twist in Our Town. In a single day, he wondered about the interior design of a movie theater, saw the shops where rich people shopped, and watched rough men and their painted women drink, smoke and brawl in several saloons—he even watched one drunkard gouge another with a broken beer bottle. And the pool halls, my God, the pool halls.

He was fascinated by the commotion in those Center Street parlors where gambling, drinking and billiards entangled the musk of man-sweat, cigars and stale beer. He ventured into one, like an explorer in his new world. Down the steps, below street level, into a smoky space divided by a drape. On one side were pool tables, but hidden behind the drape were gambling tables, beneath dim bulbs.

This was no place for kids, but Ronnie felt at home for some odd reason—until the bouncer wrapped him in a bear-hug and slung him toward the door. Ronnie yelled for Snooks, who came bounding down from the street and clamped onto the bouncer's meaty leg.

The proprietor, a short, swarthy man who wore a fedora and chomped an unlit cigar, suddenly appeared. He wasn't mad that his bouncer had just been mauled by an interloper-kid's mutt. In fact, he was intrigued by the spunky child and impressed by his dog's loyalty. So naturally, the perceptive boss, who introduces himself as John the Hatter, offered the kid a summer job.

School ended and eleven-year-old Ronnie went to work at the pool hall, swabbing the floors, wiping counters, waiting on gamblers, and fetching dollar-a-bottle beers from the cooler. But every working man needs a good pair of shoes, and so one afternoon, Ronnie went shopping. Many of the stores tossed him out, apparently for the obvious reason that he was a poor child from the wrong side of the tracks.

> I kept thinking of how I could get me a pair of new shoes. The only thing that came to mind was to steal a pair. I didn't really think there was anything wrong with that, especially since we were so very poor. I just had to figure out how to do it. . . .
>
> When I went into the store, I looked around . . . I picked the first pair of shoes that had the size on them that would fit me. I pulled the box off the shelf. I placed it under my arm. . . . Just as I was about to the door, I heard a man shouting towards me, "Hey, you with the shoes under your arm, where do you think you're going?" . . . I dropped the shoes and ran out the door.

The angry store detective chased Ronnie, threatening to kill him if he caught him. Ronnie ran toward the river, still more than a mile away. At a bridge, he leaped into the water as shots rang out. Ronnie felt a stinging hot stab in his side. He'd been shot.

A friendly doctor patched him up and promised to tell Ronnie's mom he just got a superficial scratch. And in the next few days, John the Hatter—who confessed to shady roots in Chicago, and who hosted an endless stream of smartly dressed out-of-town wiseguys in his pool hall— presented Ronnie with a new pair of shiny leather brogans— the same ones he tried to steal. He also told him the trigger-happy store owner would no longer be a problem.

Summer ended, but Ronnie's pool-hall job didn't. He started junior high school with new shoes and a new, surrogate father in John the Hatter. By his own account, the eleven-year-old was already a skilled thief, a pothead, a precocious delinquent, a cat burglar, a lookout for gamblers and drug addicts, and a budding sociopath, but his exploits in seventh grade made him look like a naïve choirboy up to that point.

On the first day he called the principal's secretary a liar and an ugly bitch. The principal, Mr. T, labeled him a "natural born trouble-maker," because of his address in north Casper, and meted out an after-school punishment just for being born across the tracks. And when he arrived late for a class because his locker was deliberately placed farthest from his classrooms, the teacher scolded him, and little Ronnie called him an "ass."

> I knew from that point on that I was not welcome in the school, nor welcome before I ever got there. I didn't do anything to these people, but yet they treated me badly, only because I came from the poor part of town. I didn't even want to return back to the same school because I knew I was in for some of the worst times of my life.

He was right. Hectored by a prepubescent kid named Bulldog and his gang—all sent by Mr. T, whom Kennedy's

autobiography portrays as half-godfather, half-warlord—
little Ronnie finally took his fate in his own hands when he
caught Bulldog alone in the boys' bathroom one day.

> I looked around. We were the only two people in there.
> That was good. Then I reached down in the back of my
> pants and pulled out this blackjack. I said, "Hey you sack of
> shit, you like hurting people for no reason. Well, that's
> come to an end." I cracked him across the knee . . . then I
> cracked him across the lower part of his back. I took the end
> of the blackjack stick and smacked him right between the
> legs. . . . I felt this sorry bastard needed just one more good
> tap to really learn him a lesson, that is if he was capable of
> such a thing. I grabbed him by the hair, bent him back-
> wards, and smacked him across his midsection. That let all
> the air out of him, including whatever he had for lunch. I
> bent over him, then said, "The next time you and your
> friends even look like you're going to mess with this north
> Casper guy, I'm coming for you. When I catch you, I swear
> I'll break every bone in your rotten body."

Violence is just another force of nature in Kennedy's life
story, as natural as the wind. One day, he watched a black
woman empty her handgun into her knife-wielding husband
after a high-stakes craps game on a spring day in the park.

> It wasn't something I was soon to forget. The taking of a hu-
> man life was taught to me as a very bad thing, and some-
> thing that should never be done. They never filed any
> charges against her. They said it was self-defense, I believe
> that it was. I was in shock for several days after the killing
> before I finally came out of it. . . . We knew that it was
> morally wrong to take the life of another human being.

But back at school, Mr. T remained a more frightful en-
emy. In a final storm of vengeance against Ronnie, Mr. T
beat him unconscious and dumped him on the schoolhouse
steps, where the heroic black janitor, Mr. Black, scooped

him up and took him to the hospital. His kidney was sliced, he had a concussion, and his bruises were deep and angry. Although Ronnie was hospitalized for three days, he kept his beating a secret from his mother— but not John the Hatter.

When Ronnie was healed and ready to go back to school, John the Hatter and two wiseguys named Roberto and Paulee arrived in a black sedan to pick him up in his slum. At school, the three men barged into the principal's office, dispensed a vicious beating—and swatted his insolent secretary's bare ass, just for good measure. After that, Mr. T was never seen again, Kennedy's manuscript says.

Things were looking up. Later that day, Ronnie retrieved a solid gold watch from his locker and gave it to Mr. Black for saving his life.

Then he met Sally Springs.

And almost predictably, when he got home his mom and dad—too poor to put food on the table—presented him with a brand-new bike for getting straight A's.

Life was suddenly good again.

In the summer of 1958, according to Kennedy, John the Hatter traveled home to Chicago, leaving twelve-year-old Ronnie in charge of his pool hall. As a gift to his beloved surrogate father and fedora-topped avenger, Ronnie hired a muralist to paint the pool hall's walls with images of John's favorite antique cars, and he added several new poker tables. The renovation was such a success, the pool hall's business skyrocketed, reaping almost $10,000 in a few days.

When John the Hatter's always dapper, vaguely menacing friends flew to Casper, Wyoming, from New York and Chicago, they were impressed by the loyal kid who had transformed John's sleazy, small-town, underground billiards hall into a classy joint. They even offered Ronnie money to come to renovate their own big-city saloons, restaurants and social clubs, but he had his hands full with seventh grade.

The rhythms of little Ronnie's life swung to and fro like a twitchy pendulum on an impatient clock racing faster than time itself. The same day he was offered a job as an interior designer for the Mob, he returned home to find deputies escorting his sister to their squad car. Like most little boys in similar circumstances, he ran inside to snatch his father's antique double-barreled shotgun.

> I pulled back both hammers. I said, "Let my sister go!" The lawman said, "You better put that gun down." I turned the old shotgun towards the garbage cans and pulled the trigger at one of them. The gun went off with a loud boom and hit the garbage can. I pointed the gun quickly back at the lawman. I said, "I'm going to count to three. If you haven't let go of my sister by then, you can kiss your ass goodbye." I said, "One. Two . . . then all of a sudden they both let go. I told them both, "Raise those arms above your head and keep them there." My sister ran over to my mother, crying something awful. I told them lawmen, "Just keep those hands raised in the air and keep your mouths shut. . . . Don't you know it's against the law to come on someone else's property without a search warrant, and then end up assaulting someone like you have just done with my sister?" Neither of them said one word. The one that was beating my sister was the sheriff of the county . . . I said, "There's two things that make me angry. One is a principal that likes to beat on students with a wooden board. The second is a sheriff that likes to assault girls on people's own property. Who do you two think you are?" The sheriff said, "The law. You better remember that." I said, "Well, Mr. Lawman, you better remember this . . ." Before he could blink an eye, I took the butt of the shotgun and hit him square across the bridge of the nose.

While the cold-cocked sheriff bled into the dust, his deputy apologized to Ronnie, who eventually demanded—and got—the sheriff's resignation.

A few days later, John the Hatter took Ronnie on a grand shopping spree to the finest boutiques in town. With three clerks waiting on him hand and foot, Ronnie demanded the clerk give up his own fashionable tie, and adding insult to injury, he forced the clerk to order pizza delivered to him at the shop, too. That night, John took Ronnie to Casper's finest restaurant, the Skyline, which sat ten stories in the air atop the tallest hotel in town. They feasted on big steaks, and life was good.

But the pendulum twitched again. The next day, John the Hatter suffered a heart attack. Rushing to the hospital to see him, Ronnie intimidated several nurses and a doctor into admitting him to John's room, where the Hatter lay comatose.

For eleven days, he slept on a cot, reading aloud to John from books about old cars and Chicago, as his stand-in father barely clung to life. His only break from the deathwatch came when a friendly, eighteen-year-old nurse named Anne showed him a place where he could take a refreshing shower.

Anne took me to this lounge. No people were around. The showers had doors . . . Anne said, "I will be right back. Go ahead and get in the shower. I will get you some shampoo." . . . I didn't notice Anne, but she came back. She was in the shower with me bare naked. Anne was quite beautiful. She said, "I needed a shower, too. I hope you don't mind. I locked the door so nobody could come in." I said, "That's good." She said, "Would you wash my back?" I said, "Sure" . . . For my age, I was extremely mature, including sexually. I said, "Anne, I'm still a virgin." Anne said, "You don't have a thing to worry about." We must have been in the shower for at least two hours. I leave the rest to the imagination of the reader.

In the coming week, thirteen-year-old Ronnie's virginity literally went down the drain as his reputation spread. He showered with no fewer than ten more lusty nurses. "And they all gave me their addresses, telephone numbers," he writes.

But Nurse Anne wanted a life with little Ronnie. If John the Hatter hadn't aroused from his coma at the moment she was proposing, things might have turned out differently for the little kid from a Wyoming ghetto.

But John awoke, and Ronnie had work to do. He pulled some strings with friends in the sheriff's department and got a permit to run the pool hall while John recovered. He did a land-office business and when John came back to his business after two weeks' recuperation, little Ronnie had $10,000 in small bills—the enormous profit from Ronnie's tenure as manager—stacked on his desk.

One day, a visitor came to the pool hall.

It was Sally Springs.

After he got over his boyish surprise, he got her a beer. He let her beat him in a few games of pool as they flirted flagrantly and then he invited her to dinner. He knew a romantic place.

As the elevator doors opened onto the top floor of the town's tallest hotel, Sally swooned. Lucky, the maitre d', led them to Ronnie's "usual" table, overlooking the town and the sunset. Slipping a fifty-dollar bill into the man's palm, Ronnie ordered the best wine he served.

Sally said, "You have a lot of power to come into this place, order wine and things." I said, "No, Sally, I would rather think of it as trust." Sally lifted her wine glass and said, "To our friendship that is just beginning." We touched glasses. From that moment on, Sally could not take her eyes off me.

When dinner ended, Ronnie slipped another twenty to Lucky. Then the chivalrous, romantic Ronnie kissed his virginal Sally goodnight and sent her home. Another knight's task awaited.

His mother had come home in tears because a shopkeeper had insulted her, overcharged her, and kicked her out of his store.

Once again, I felt a rage burning inside of me. Who are these people and where do they get off being so mean to certain people? The people that this shopkeeper made a point of hurting or cheating were kind, loving and caring people. I could no more let go of what this man did to my mother than I could stay away from the river . . . I went to the garage, got the baseball bat and headed for the store.

I said, "Do you like hurting people for no reason? Is that the kind of sorry human being you are?" He said, "I don't like beggars and thieves coming into my store." I said, "Is that what you think my mother is?" He said, "Worse. She was short."

He was a big man, but that meant nothing to me. . . . Then all of a sudden, he grabbed a can of food off the shelf and threw it at me. That stopped any intentions I had of just turning around and walking out the door . . . I took the bat and hit him across the arm. I hit him across the kneecap. I said, "Hey, you are the garbage of this world, but the mistake you made was hurting my mother, and nobody on this earth will get away with that as long as I'm around" . . . I trashed almost everything he had in his store. Afterwards, I told him "If you turn me in to the police, I promise you I will be back . . . and I never break a promise." I loaded up two sacks of groceries, which I felt he cheated my mother out of, then walked out the door.

As the summer of 1960 waned, Ronnie and a friend named Jack embarked on one more big adventure: A trip to the Van Rooms, the most infamous whorehouse in Casper's red-light and bootlegging district, the Sandbar. Jack was Ronnie's age, but he'd apparently been to the cathouse before. Inside the former boarding house, with its stunning chandeliers, perfumed parlor, ceaseless jukebox and half-naked working girls, Ronnie confessed to never seeing anything like it.

The owner's name was FeFe Belondin. I guess she was French. She walked up and said, "What's going on, Jack?" He said, "I just brought a friend in to have a look around, maybe get his virginity taken care of." FeFe said, "you know if the cops come and catch him in here, I'm in deep trouble." I said, "Ma'am, I don't think so. The cops don't want any trouble with me. A while back, I'm the one that took the shotgun to the sheriff, beat the shit out of him, then

made him retire. Also, my godfather is John the Hatter."
FeFe said, "I heard about you! You're the Savior Boy!"

FeFe Belondin had a proposition for young Ronnie—and his new bike: She'd pay him to deliver mysterious packages to certain customers, and then bring back the fat envelopes they gave him. It didn't take him long to realize he was delivering cocaine door-to-door and returning with literally thousands of dollars. And the customers were all judges, prosecutors, cops, prominent businessmen and politicians.

> Twice each week I would stop at the Van Rooms, pick up the package with the address to deliver it to. It seemed like the packages were going to the rich side of town. I was very curious about what was in the packages, but I didn't open any of them up yet . . . I didn't know what cocaine did to a person when you sucked it up your nose.

Ronnie learned the power of coke after he filched some from one of his packages and shared it with a half dozen strange black men, who got high and mugged him. Naturally, he went home and picked up his trusty baseball bat, with which he beat his assailants senseless.

Even if his life as a drug courier was occasionally dangerous, Ronnie's junior-high romance with Sally blossomed. They went for picnics in the park, played pool, rode double on Ronnie's bike, and went on dates subsidized with hundred-dollar bills dispensed by an approving John the Hatter.

But the love affair was about to be tested, and at thirteen, Ronnie's peculiar life as a child anti-hero would take an abrupt detour.

On the first day of eighth grade, Ronnie learned that his one-time savior, the black janitor, had died. The principal, Mr. T, had inexplicably and ominously returned.

And Sally was nowhere in sight.

Ronnie dashed to Sally's house. Her biological father had just been killed in a car crash, and her stepfather was moving the family to California in two short weeks. In the privacy of her bedroom—and with food delivered by her mother—Ronnie consoled her all night. He took time out for school the next day, but immediately returned to Sally's house that afternoon.

I ran up the stairs. She was still in bed asleep. I gently laid down beside her. She opened her eyes. She said, "I knew you would be back." I said, "How could I not be back. Especially when I happen to have fell in love with you?" Sally said, "Say that again." I said, "Sally, I love you!" Sally started crying, looking deep into my eyes and said, "I love you, too, my Ronnie." Sally got out of bed. She had no clothes on, then locked her bedroom door and came back to the bed and sat beside me. She started unbuttoning my shirt, then pulled it off. She took off my shoes. Then my pants came off. I was as naked as she was. Sally pressed herself close to me. I could hardly say no to her, I loved her. I knew it the first time I saw her. Sally said, "I'm a virgin just like you, but now it's time to do something about it, and I want it to be with the man I love." For the first time in my life I experienced what real love was like. We stayed together the whole night. I spent the next couple weeks staying all night with Sally.

The day finally came. It was time for them to leave. I said, "Sally, this is not goodbye, nor will I say it." Sally said, "I will be back as soon as I can." I left not looking back.

Suddenly, the cosmic pendulum whacked little Ronnie Kennedy. When he returned to school, the principal and a squad of cops were waiting for him. In his locker, they found a package of drugs. Luckily for Ronnie, the judge dismissed the case.

On the way out of the courtroom, I briefly stopped where the principal, Mr. T, was sitting. I said, "Your day is coming sooner than you think, so you ponder those words, you insane bastard." I knew this principal had to be dealt with, but getting rid of him was the only way to go. This was a mean man, completely prejudice, not to mention a coward. There had to be a way to get rid of him permanently.

Because he'd missed so much school while jailed for a bogus dope charge, Ronnie was not allowed to graduate from eighth grade, even though he had straight A's and school remained "a love in my life."

One day, John the Hatter handed him a registered letter from Sally's mother.

It dropped me to both knees. I was bent over and couldn't hold back the hurt I was feeling. John walked over and said, "My God, what is the matter?" I said, "Sally is in a coma. She is not expected to live. . . . I got to get to California to be with her." John said, "How are you going to get that far?" I told John I would walk if I had to. "In case something happens to me, I just want you to know that I have come to love you as a son loves his real father." John said, "Come back to me soon, son." All I knew is that I had to get to California. I didn't have hardly any money at all. I had to think of some way to get more money. Then it come to me. [sic]

On one last cocaine run, Ronnie stole an envelope containing up to nine thousand dollars, FeFe's drug money. He told his mother he must go to California to comfort Sally, who had given birth prematurely to a little baby girl who died—Ronnie's daughter. Then he lit out on a four-day bus ride to Long Beach, California.

Once in California, Ronnie kept a faithful vigil at Sally's bedside for a week. On the seventh day, Sally awoke.

I said, "I knew you would come back to me." She whispered, "I do love you." I said, "I love you more than life itself . . ." Sally told me something very strange. She said, "I knew you were here. I could hear you talking to me in my dreams as if you were right here with me." I said, "I was with you. I'll always be with you."

Ronnie stayed in California another ten days while Sally recovered, then began the thousand-mile trip home, mostly on foot, giving him time to think of a way to square things with FeFe. He knew people had been murdered for less than stealing a drug-dealer's cash. Once home, he armed himself with a large Bowie knife, purely for defense, and went to see the old prostitute.

The first thing that FeFe said was "You poor boy!" She walked over to me and put her arms around me, pulled my face to her breasts. She said, "I talked to John. He told me all about what happened. It must have been terrible for you" ... I spent the next two hours explaining what I wanted her to know. . . . FeFe was in tears. FeFe said, "You are one of the best men I have ever met." And all the girls were setting around listening to my story, half of them were crying and wanting to hold me. For being only thirteen years old, I was a handsome looking boy, perhaps that was part of my luck. Every girl in the place wanted to take me in one of their rooms and give me love and comfort.

Ronnie's long memory and seething resentments served him well. One day later that summer, he spied a man beating two small children—the same man who shot him in the back as he tried to steal some shoes a few years before. As had become his habit, he retrieved the baseball bat from his father's shed and, with his friend Jack's help, hunted the man down at a local market.

Pretending to steal a shirt, Ronnie sprung his trap as the store owner came for him.

I waited until he was only a couple feet away from me, then I hit him square across the chest. That let some of the air out of him. He started to stick his hand under his shirt. . . . So I hit him right across the back of the neck, then across the arm. The gun fell to the ground. "Jack, this is the man that shot me in the back when I was eleven years old. He tried to kill me." . . . I took the bat and beat the hell out of his right hand. It was busted up real good.

I bent down and said, "You don't remember me, do you? But I do you. I still have the bullet to prove it and your gun to match it with. Your days of working at this store, in this town, are over. You've picked on your last little boy, you coward. If I ever come back to this store, see your face anywhere near or around it, I will put you in a wheelchair for the rest of your life."

I never grew up with a mean bone in my body. I was always a quiet boy, very good natured, would do anything to help someone. I just went through so much unnecessary hurt by people which I never deserved in my life. All I could do was fight back the best way I knew how. It wasn't revenge, nor did I fight back with the intent to actually hurt someone really bad, but rather to teach them a lesson. About half the time, it did.

Snooks served him well, too. One day while swimming in the river, Ronnie was swept away, and Snooks chased him down the bank, leapt in and came up beneath him, like a living life vest. They paddled to shore, and Snooks had saved little Ronnie's life (one of several times, according to his autobiography).

But Ronnie's greater guardian, John the Hatter, was leaving the boy's life for good. The tough-guy with a heart of gold, the pool hall proprietor who'd become everything Ronnie's real father wasn't, the touchstone of Ronnie's troubled youth, his role model of hard-fisted generosity—was going home to his native Chicago to live out his golden years.

"It was not easy for me to sell the place, but I don't want to end up dying in this part of the country where I wasn't born," John said. "It saddens me that I will be leaving you behind . . . I never had any children but I gained a son. You

are the closest I have ever come to having a son of my own."
I said, "I am your son. I love you like a real father."

He pulled out some papers. "For the past couple years, I
have been putting extra money away in a savings account
for you for your college education. You can't make it in this
life anymore without an education." He handed me the papers, then said, "It's yours to do with whatever you want, but
it is my desire you use it for your education."

Two weeks went by fast. It was time for John to leave. I
jumped on my bike and headed for the airport . . . I just
barely made it in time. John was walking toward the gate
where he would board his plane. I shouted. He stopped. "I
love you, my father," I said. "I love you, too, my son." I
watched him board his plane. I never much in my life allowed myself to get attached to very many people. The
hurt of losing them was too much for the human heart to
handle. I knew in my own heart I would never see John
again.

When Ronnie finally looked inside the pouch of papers
John gave him, he found John's beloved gold pocket-watch
and a bank passbook containing fifteen thousand dollars.

His anchor gone, Ronnie drifted. Worse, word came that
Sally had been sent to France, without further explanation.

One Sunday night, a couple friends invited him to a party.
He jumped in the backseat of their car, but they weren't
heading toward any party. Instead, they were casing a local
liquor store, Oil City Liquors, a neighborhood joint where
his father often drank.

After dark, his buddies smashed the front window and
grabbed all the liquor bottles they could reach, dumping it
all in their trunk. When cops stopped the car a few blocks
away, the other boys ran, leaving Ronnie to face the rap.
Ronnie claimed he never even got out of the car, but it didn't
matter: In juvenile court, he narrowly dodged the reformatory, drawing three years of probation.

But a fourteen-year-old kid has no chance against a system
that's intent on skewering him. Lured into a beer-chugging

contest by a pretty girl, he realized too late he'd been trapped by evil, unseen powers, who quickly had him arrested and sent to the Wyoming Boys' School, the reformatory more than a hundred miles away in Worland, Wyoming.

> I was always able to rise above most things. I had a good heart. I loved people. It wasn't my fault if they didn't feel the same way.

So he ran. His desperate flight took him to Montana, where he hid out with friends. He also met a pretty young country girl who showed him more than Montana's big sky.

> Her name was Pam. She was a polite girl, kind of pretty. We became real good friends. She took me to this one place that had a creek . . . She just took off her clothes until she was bare naked and jumped in. I got undressed and jumped in the pond . . . After we got out of the water, we just laid in the sun naked to dry off. Then one thing led to another. We ended up having sex on a daily basis.

Until the man who was hiding Ronnie made a pass at her. Rebuffed, he snitched on Ronnie to Montana cops, and Ronnie was soon extradited back to Wyoming to serve his time at reformatory.

For four years, he endured beatings and other humiliations as he grew to young manhood. On the day he was released, the warden handed him a shoebox stuffed with letters from Sally, all unopened and all deliberately withheld from him. Sally had come home from France and was living in Bakersfield, California, and he knew what he had to do.

Now eighteen, with money he saved from reformatory, he bought a wrecked 1930 Ford coupe for five hundred bucks and immediately began customizing it into the baby-blue, silver-metal flake, baby-moon hubcapped, double four-barrel carbs and fuel-injected, blue tuck-and-rolled leather, hot-rod chariot he'd drive to rescue Sally once and for all. His license plates said it all: SALLY.

After bribing a Department of Motor Vehicles clerk two hundred dollars to overlook a failed driver's test, he got his license and immediately lit out for California, to Sally.

But every journey was an adventure for Ronnie Kennedy.

Somewhere in the vast emptiness of the West, an arrogant Jaguar sprayed gravel on Ronnie's dream car, breaking a headlight and chipping his magnificent paint job. Surging to one hundred twenty miles an hour—with more speed still in her—he caught the Jag and forced him off the road. Ronnie and the Jag driver squared off on the dusty shoulder.

His lady friend got out of the car with him, walked over and looked at the car. I said, "It's crazy drivers like you that get people killed. Well, you owe me at least fifteen hundred dollars for the damage you caused to my car. Besides, you're drunk as hell, you freak." He said, "My insurance will pay for the damage." I said, "Not good enough!" The lady said, "Harold, it was your fault. You pay him." Harold said, "Hell, no!"

"Well, Harold, let me show you what I can do to your Jaguar with my bat," I said. I started walking towards his car. He said, "Wait, I'll pay you." He started to reach under his coat jacket . . . I said, "What I should do now is give you an old-fashioned ass-whipping, but out of respect for your lady friend, I'm going to spare you the pain, and her the embarrassment. Lady, thank you for your intelligent understanding of this matter. Also, you're much too pretty of a lady and too smart to be with a punk like Harold. Why not find yourself a man who will respect you? Harold, this better be the last time I hear from you. Do I make myself clear?" He said yes. I winked and smiled at his lady friend. She nodded her head, smiled back. To me, that meant Harold just lost his woman.

Although he was on his way to his beloved Sally, Ronnie also found irresistible romance on the road. At a small town somewhere in California, after eighteen straight hours on the road, he stopped at a roadside café, where he ordered the day's special from a pretty young waitress, who also brought him coffee to wash down a few more hits of speed.

Ronnie was ready for the last leg of his journey, but he knew the sad and lonely waitress, who just turned twenty, wanted a ride in his extraordinary car—and maybe more. Ronnie's odyssey was put on hold.

I suppose common sense would have told me to go on and forget about other people's dreams. I just couldn't do that, not if I could make one person's life happy for a moment. She was an attractive girl, she was nice, polite. I thought what the heck. It's only going to be an hour out of my life to make one person's dream come true.

She took me to an ocean front highway, and said, "I like fast." . . . She reached over and turned on the radio. She was kind of moving with the music, it was nice to see someone like having a good time in her dream ride. I followed her directions [and] we started going up this small mountain road . . . and we got out of the car. Then out of the blue, she said, "You're different than other guys I have met. You're thoughtful, polite, caring and good-looking." . . . She bent over and kissed me on the cheek. We sat and finished the last beer of the second six-pack. Then she said, "Do you have time for me to show you one more place that I've never shown anyone else before?" I knew I really shouldn't [but] this girl just seemed like it was forever since she had done anything nice in her life. My good-hearted nature was getting the best of me again . . .

She directed him down several secluded roads over rolling hills, to a hidden, wildflower-strewn meadow. They spread a sleeping bag in the thick green grass beside a placid, warm-water pond, drinking more beer and smoking marijuana. It wasn't Heaven, but it was close.

The air was fresh. You could smell the awesome fragrance of the flowers in the air. It was everywhere. I reached over and picked a handful of wildflowers. I put some in her hair, some around her body. I said, "Now you look more beautiful than nature itself." I lost track of time, where I was at. She dropped off all her clothes then said, "Let's go swimming."

[After swimming] she stretched out on her back letting the sun dry her off. I got up for a few minutes, grabbed as many flowers as I could. I pulled the flowers off their stems, then I don't know why, I just started decorating her body like an artist. When I was done, I said "Now you are one with beautiful Mother Earth, but you are more beautiful." . . . I guess I knew what was going to happen next, whether I liked it or not, because I was just as much to fault as her. Besides, how in the hell could I say no, or have ever put myself in such a position. I had too big of a heart. At least I made somebody truly happy.

We got back to town; she gave me a phone number and told me to call her. She said, "You're one of a kind. I wish you were mine." I said, "You take care. I will try to see you again sometime soon." . . . It was time for me to head on for Sally.

Ronnie's reunion with Sally in California was joyous. After making passionate love that had been forestalled by separation and four years in reformatory, Ronnie proposes to the woman who had never given up on him, and she accepts. They immediately set out for Las Vegas, where they exchanged quickly improvised vows at a roadside chapel.

We were at long last married, and the two happiest people on the face of the earth. God knows I loved Sally more than life itself. I had never seen such a happy, love-filled look in my Sally's eyes before. They were gleaming with total love for me. I could feel her love going right through my soul. We had to consummate our wedding. That we did for four days.

Sally's parents blessed the new couple with a twenty thousand-dollar check, but Ronnie was still flush. After a quick run to Reno to get Sally's name stenciled in gold lettering on his coupe's door, they headed south to Mexico. In his autobiography, he recalls bribing someone three hundred dollars to get passports at Tijuana.

As they journeyed across the Mexican countryside, dancing in village fiestas and taking Polaroids of themselves making love in rural hideaways, Ronnie began to sense something sad in Sally. He didn't know what it was, and couldn't guess, but after making love atop an idyllic Mexican hill one afternoon, she told him: She was pregnant.

Their Mexican honeymoon stretched into a lengthy vacation, then into a way of life. Once they reached Mexico City, they decided to stay, not as citizens but as lovers in the world. After two months there, Sally's health declined.

I began to notice that Sally's eating habits were not just a normal thing. It began to scare me. Then she started having extremely bad headaches, and other pain in different parts of her body . . . There was something Sally knew that she wasn't telling me. She finally told me they had found some lumps under her breasts quite some time back.

It didn't take me long to get back to Long Beach, California. I took her to the same medical center she was at the last time I came to see her. . . . They found out that Sally was pregnant, but the baby was only five months old. . . . The doctor said "Sally has cancer. It has spread to the point where we don't know what can be done about it." I said, "What about our child?" The doctor said, "The baby is what caused the cancer to spread faster. We don't know for certain, but there's no indication the child is alive. It doesn't have to be removed because of Sally's condition . . ." I asked the doctor, how long does Sally have left to live? He said, "Two, maybe three weeks, at the most."

The test results [later] showed the baby passed away inside of her during the fourth month of her pregnancy. That really tore me apart. I wanted this baby to be alive. I wanted a part of Sally to be with me. It was a baby boy, and that just made it worse.

Sally died in Ronnie's arms on June 6, 1965.

We went to Sally's funeral. It was outdoors, and it was my request that it be held like that, and it be an open casket. I wanted the sun to shine on her beautiful face one more time. I placed pictures of us in with her, my wedding ring, and other things. I bent over and kissed my special angel on the lips for the last time in this life. I wished that our second child would have lived. It was buried inside of Sally, she would take care of him even in death.

This was the ultimate hurt of my life, for which I would never get over. That which I loved most on this earth was gone, and I knew she could never be replaced. . . . I went to a secluded spot. I gathered up everything that belonged to me and Sally, put it all in a pile, then lit it on fire. I wanted to remember Sally the way she was in life. It was the ultimate love between two people.

Among the items he burned was the twenty-thousand-dollar check from Sally's parents. Even though he'd been an opportunistic thief and impoverished child for most of his eighteen years—even though he believed the world owed him more than it could ever pay—it didn't seem right to keep it. And when he returned to Wyoming, Ronnie even had his dream car crushed, erasing all earthly evidence of Sally once and for all.

Ronnie sunk into a haze of drugs, booze and partying. He hadn't been home long when a friend introduced him to an outgoing and petite teenager who was more interested in flirting than school. Janie, as he came to know her, quickly fell in love with him and, soon, she was pregnant.

The only problem was: Janie was only thirteen. Luckily, her parents loved nineteen-year-old Ronnie immensely, and they gave him a chance to avoid a statutory rape charge: Marry Janie or go directly to jail. They married in 1966 and a son was soon born. They lived rent-free in a bungalow behind Janie's parents' house in north Casper. He was fulfilling

Sally's deathbed wish: That he find someone to love, have children, live long and well.

Ronnie had his family, and he claims he had sixty thousand dollars hidden in a secret bank account, but he was selling drugs to make ends meet. Plus, FeFe had kept him on her payroll as a drug mule.

> I wanted to make this marriage work, even try to love Janie, but she backed away from it. I started going to parties all over town. I always knew where they were at, but they were the good ones, not the flunkies-type parties. I was always welcome to any party I went to. I was drinking a lot, doing lots of hard drugs, going to bed with untold numbers of women who finally got their chance.

In 1968, he and his wife divorced. He made a few gentle, loving attempts to reconcile, but she pushed him away. He moved back with his parents. In less than two years, Ronald Kennedy had loved and lost twice. Two marriages, two endings.

> The truth is, when I met Janie, I learned that I could still love, but the hurt from losing that love only shattered my heart and soul more than it already was. It's not hard to say, "I love you," but if you really mean it, then that love becomes a permanent part of your soul. I will always miss you Janie, even love you, because you were mine, virginity and all. The greatest truth of all is I know, Janie, whether she knows it or not, still loves me.

He didn't know it, but the storms in his life had not yet passed.

Less than a year after he divorced Janie, in early 1969, Ronnie married another woman, Nancy. (That marriage would fail in less than two years, too, and when it did, Nancy won everything he owned: a 1956 Mercury.) At the same time, his older brother James was convicted of first-degree rape after he and a buddy named Jerry Jenkins abducted a young woman and sexually assaulted her in a forcible gang-bang.

And a week before Christmas in 1969, Ernest Leroy Kennedy died of complications from his chronic alcoholism. The father whose body and dreams were wounded irreparably in a workplace accident, whom Ronnie defended as a kind but troubled soul, was gone. He was sixty-five.

> We were all with him. I was next to his bed, had my arms around him tight. We talked for a few minutes, then he passed away. I was so mad, angry, hurt. I loved my father so dearly. I didn't want him to leave us, but he was taken from us anyway . . . I tried my best to give my father a grandson, or granddaughter, but it never happened. Nothing in my life was meant to be.

While he served a "bullshit" prison sentence for burglary and receiving stolen goods, Nancy ran off with another man. After five years and three wives, Ronnie was alone again.

> I often wondered why I couldn't make a marriage work. It wasn't because I didn't try. I did. Maybe I tried too hard. I stopped my alcohol use and drug use during both times I was married. I never had a problem finding a woman. They were there for the taking. But marriage was something else. Perhaps deep down inside I just didn't show them enough love, the kind of love that I had for Sally, but then I really didn't know.

In the autumn of 1971, Ronnie returned to Sally's grave in California, where he left flowers and a letter before returning to Wyoming, never again to leave. In Casper, he took a job as a bartender and soon became the darling of the local drinking set—and women.

> I had lots of fancy moves. People liked to come in and just watch me. They would buy their share of drinks, but more

so because they liked me. Business started picking up at
the place more than it ever had. It always seemed like
there were more women in the bar than men. I worked almost every day, except Sundays. Never a working day
went by that I wasn't propositioned by some woman. I was
only human when it came to all the women that come in
the bar. I picked who I wanted, then it was strictly understood that it wasn't nothing more than for pleasure, fun.
Most of them I picked to go out with had their own drugs.
They got what they wanted most, and I got what I
wanted.

But there was one who caught his eye. She wasn't pretty,
but she was friendly.

I judged people by their actions and what was in their
hearts. I always had a sense of knowing whether a person
was sincere . . . Booze was a powerful drug. More often than
not it brought out the bad in a majority of people. As for
myself, I was always a mellow person when on drugs or
drinking alcohol. It never made me mean. It just made me
forget the past, all the hurt I endured throughout years in
my life. Drugs did have a different effect on me. They
caused me to totally blank out everything to the point
where I would not realize where I was at or who I was with.
I took the best drugs money could buy. Most women that I
went out with found me to be extremely enjoyable, something that I didn't even remember the next day.

Drugs ended Ronnie's bartending career, too. But not because he was taking them. He got fired, he claims in his autobiography, when he confronted a powerful South American
drug lord who was planning to smuggle drugs into the
United States.

So he became a pool hustler, a talent he picked up as a kid
at John the Hatter's pool hall. He continued seeing the "sincere" young woman, continued his drugging and continued
moving sideways in his life until late July 1973.

One morning I woke up. Later that day, I found out we were married. I had no recollection of the marriage at all, but she had the marriage license to prove it. That changed things quite a bit. I thought about getting the marriage annulled, but then I could do that most anytime. The marriage didn't mean anything to me to begin with, so I didn't see what it could possibly hurt. I don't recall even giving her a wedding ring to this day.

I often wondered what my purpose was on this earth. It certainly didn't turn out the way I hoped it would. I always ended up losing someone that I loved. Sally was the turning point in my life. When I lost her, a part of me died right along with her. I stayed with her because I had nothing better to do in life.

I had no idea what kind of tragedy was going to strike next in my life, but if I was a betting man, I would put money on myself that something was going to happen eventually, without me even seeing it coming.

ALL SOCIOPATHS SHARE three common characteristics: They are very egocentric, devoid of compassion, and incapable of remorse or guilt.

But the violent ones are made even more frightening by their ability to camouflage their twisted natures. They are the nice guys next door, the sincere liars who can appear utterly normal. They are charming pretenders who live behind appealing facades. Among them is the serial killer who is later described by stunned neighbors on the evening news as "a nice boy who'd never hurt a fly."

The diagnosis has evolved over the years. In 1952, the American Psychiatric Association officially changed its lexicon, replacing the word "psychopath" with "sociopath," which suggested the condition was more a social affliction than a psychological one. The two words are still used interchangeably, although they have subtle differences. In 1968, the American Psychiatric Association again changed its dictionary, blending both terms under the softer umbrella of "antisocial personality disorder," or APD.

"Antisocial" doesn't mean the sociopath can't socialize, nor is it a casual term for shy, reclusive or inhibited people. Rather, it connotes a rebellion against society. The sociopath can be an expert charmer and manipulator whose main goal is to dissolve the ties that bind one person to another.

Pioneering psychologist Alfred Adler defined a sociopath as someone who preys on society to help satisfy his desire for personal superiority. In addition to the other well-known traits, he believed sociopaths were often incapable of expressing a normal emotional range, a characteristic known as "flat affect."

Aside from their extraordinary egotism, and unhealthy sense of personal responsibility and morality, the worst sociopaths tend to be highly impulsive daredevils who are quarrelsome, manipulative and ceaseless liars who swear they're telling the truth. They believe rules—like promises—were meant to be broken.

They usually can't sustain relationships; in fact, their lifestyles tend to be parasitic and sexually promiscuous. They are good at feigning love. They brag about their many sexual conquests and prowess. They are more likely to have a series of short marriages than anything long-term.

In a single, brilliant burst of charm, they can usually get what they want. They revel in the illusion they are powerful. The grandiosity of their self-image is boundless, seeing themselves as consummate thinkers, lovers and leaders.

They are prone to hostile and sometimes violent behavior, from schoolyard brawls to domestic abuse to rape . . . and murder. Alcohol and drug abuse is common. They are likely to drop out of school. They might not work at all, but if they do, they are frequently absent and quit jobs abruptly, often after a short time. Why? They often believe they have little control over their own destiny.

A violent sociopath is often gratified by hurting someone for absolutely no reason. So juvenile delinquency and early behavior problems are common among antisocial people, leading to an adult routine in which crime is merely a way of life. If caught, they rarely "learn" from their punishment.

And no misbehavior is their fault. They will blame society, parentage, even the victims for their wrongdoing. Serial killer John Wayne Gacy, who killed thirty-three people, once said, "I was the victim. I was cheated out of my childhood."

More men than women are clinically antisocial, and more from lower socioeconomic groups. And if there's a history of antisocial personality disorders in their families, the risk is even higher.

Still, socio- and psychopaths aren't always easy to spot. They are often excellent actors, always appearing charming, glib and calm. Their dark side can remain safely hidden.

And while many theories exist about how and why APD blossoms in some people, there is no definitive answer in either nature or nurture. Maybe it's caused by abusive, neglectful parents, or maybe the brain chemistry is flawed from birth. But one thing is known: Socio- and psychopaths typically reject therapy or medication, and few are ever "cured."

Three psychiatrists declared Ronald Kennedy a classic violent sociopath, including one hired by his own defense.

But none of them declared him legally insane. He knew his crimes were wrong and that he faced certain punishment if he was caught, they said. While he might have serious mental issues, he was clearly just a criminal who couldn't blame his transgressions on a scrambled brain. Just a vacant heart.

And nobody was happier to be judged sane—even if it was "criminally sane"—than Ronald Kennedy himself.

In fourteen hours of jailhouse interviews in 2003, Kennedy was engaging and amiable, even charismatic. I was occasionally susceptible to his manipulations, and for hours after our conversations, I wondered if he knew how outlandish his stories were, or if they were utterly true in his brain. But my questions about his sanity invariably aroused him to rail against anyone who suggested he was mentally ill, even the lawyers who were trying to save him from the gas chamber with an insanity defense.

He simply didn't think he was crazy.

Still doesn't.

◆ ◆ ◆

RONALD KENNEDY'S MEMOIR represents the life he wishes
he'd led.

A generous reader might say his memory was just a little
foggy, perhaps misremembered. In fact, it's a patchwork of
fantasies stitched together by a slender thread of half-truths
and richly re-imagined incidents—and a few familiar scenes
from Hollywood movies like *Cocktail, Old Yeller* and *Pretty
Woman*—in his life.

The real facts are not disputed: Ronald Kennedy was
born in Casper, Wyoming, on July 17, 1946. His family of
eight was desperately poor and lived in a claustrophobic
row-house—a former bootlegger's shack—in north Casper,
literally the "wrong" side of the small-town tracks. His father was mostly unemployed and alcoholic, and his mother
often worked two or three menial jobs to feed and clothe the
family.

The rest provides nothing more than a glimpse into the
sinister and disturbing mind of a sociopathic killer.

Some of Kennedy's distorted yarns are benign. For example, his account often confuses the years he was probably
in different school grades. And north Casper was home to
many families on the slack end of the town's socioeconomic
scale, but it was by no means a violent, impotent slum where
dead bodies littered every dark corner—I lived there briefly
when I was a newlywed young reporter fresh out of college.
It was, by and large, home to both young working-class people who often come and go in a boom town, and long-time
families that never rose above their modest circumstances.

Always a player in every drama, Kennedy claims to have
watched a black woman empty her handgun into her abusive
husband during a crap game in a north Casper park in the
spring of 1959. Although he said the fight erupted because
the woman was flirting with him, he claims the killing taught
him the value of human life.

Kennedy's account is rooted in reality. On March 16,
1959, a black man named Robert Conley was murdered in a
crap game. But that's where the facts and Kennedy's fantasy

diverge. Conley was murdered by another player, a young black named Johnny Smith, who vaporized Conley's brain with a single shotgun blast to the head. The killing happened in a two-room apartment, and was witnessed by a third man—not Kennedy—who was the only other person present. Smith was sentenced ten days later to twenty- to twenty-five years for second-degree murder.

No other similar killings appear in police or coroner records, so it's likely the real crap-game killing story was simply "re-imagined" by Kennedy as a way to cast himself in yet another intimate drama.

Many of his other stories are more complex, offering a glimpse into the machinery of his mind rather than true history. From a bleak childhood to many conflicted relationships, Kennedy's imagination usually trumps truth.

His father Ernest was not emotionally and physically crippled by a workplace fall. He was simply lazy and addicted. In 1965, Ernest Kennedy told his son's probation officer that he was unemployed because he suffered from arthritis and muscle spasms. No mention of a cataclysmic accident.

Nor was Ernest a loving father with a "delicate condition." He was physically and mentally abusive, not a warm man. He was arrested several times for violent behavior. Once, while some of his children watched, he stabbed his wife Hilda in the side with a carving knife, and then went to bed.

And when Ernest died of a hemorrhaged ulcer at age sixty-five in December 1969, he didn't die in his son's arms. At the moment Ernest Kennedy drew his last breath, Ron was serving twelve to eighteen months in prison for burglary and receiving stolen property.

During interviews, Ronald Kennedy claimed he was sexually abused for years, starting around age six, by the drinking buddies his father brought home. He does not relate those incidents in his autobiography.

Nor does he include those childhood rapes among his first sexual experiences. He variously describes losing his virginity to a much older neighbor girl, and to the nurses tending John the Hatter.

Ah, John the Hatter. The pool hall owner with the tarnished heart of gold, a fat wad of cash and an underworld cachet, the man who became a surrogate father to the wayward Ronnie, is an invention, too. But he has roots in reality.

Casper sported two pool halls during Ronald Kennedy's youth. One was owned by a Greek immigrant named Joe Jackson, who ran billiards tables (and some back-room poker) in the basement of his hat shop. He'd come directly to Casper from Greece in 1918, and lived the last forty-five years of his life in a small downtown hotel room.

And that's where he died in May 1978, alone and penniless in his squalid room in a decaying hotel. Nobody had even cared to look in on him, and his body festered for several days. He was eighty-one and all but forgotten. A few of his Greek friends in town pooled their money to buy him a cheap casket and a grave in that part of the Highland Cemetery where other Greeks were buried.

None of his friends ever recall seeing a kid hanging around the pool hall, much less Ronald Kennedy. Joe was a gentle man, but not a collector of strays, a shadowy underworld figure, nor wealthy.

But what son—even an unofficially adoptive son—would forget his father's name was Joe, not John?

Fefe Belondin was real, but again, maybe her relationship with little Ronnie was imagined.

The Van Rooms were an open secret around town, and by 1973, Fefe had been running girls there for almost twenty years. In her first six years operating the erstwhile "boarding house" in the infamous red-light and bootleg district known as the Sandbar, cops raided it 136 times, raking in more than $13,000 in fines for prostitution—yet the Van Rooms only got bigger, more profitable and more notorious. When a half-hour with one of Fefe's girls cost twenty dollars, that added up to a lot of entertainment.

Her girls tended to be prettier than itinerant, freelance whores. Many of them worked the circuit that stretched from Denver to Seattle, moving down the line every few months in a perpetual quest to be "the new girl" with new stories and no history. It was profitable for Fefe's business too, in the same way ripe, fresh, sweet, fragrant fruit was profitable for a greengrocer.

Feisty Fefe ran the place from 1959 until it was bulldozed by urban renewal in the late 1970s. A chain-smoker and near-teetotaler who loved crystal, French perfume and grape soda, she would often greet johns at the back door in a skimpy bikini stretched tight across her Rubenesque bulk, holding one of her brightly dyed poodles. She loved tinting them with food coloring to celebrate various holidays.

Improbably proud of her chosen career, she was forever battling the town fathers and the cops. Often arrested on prostitution-related charges, Fefe usually fought back so passionately with her own lawsuits that her main prosecutor eventually retired and became her defense lawyer.

Her sense of humor was rivaled only by her knack for nomenclature. In court papers over the years, she gave her name as Sunny Day, Stormy Night, Josie Jones, Marion Miller and Rita Rea, among the many aliases she used. Her real name remains a mystery, although when legal matters were most serious, she preferred to be called Rose Suszenski or Helen Smith.

But everybody in town knew her as Fefe.

Fefe Belondin died in the 1980s in Seattle, an elderly old whore with painted poodles. Her life had been long and colorful, with few consequences money wouldn't solve. Even today, the mention of her name elicits smiles among Casper's old timers.

But for all the seaminess of Fefe's work, even the cops knew a peculiar set of principles guided her enterprises. Among the inviolable rules every girl learned, sometimes at the expense of her job: No kids in bed and no drugs.

The likelihood that Ron Kennedy was a prepubescent, pedal-pushing drug courier for a cocaine-peddling madam in the late 1950s—twenty years before the cocaine epidemic exploded—is slim. A romantic fantasy for a lifelong criminal, but unlikely.

It is more likely, however, that violence played a recurring role in Ronald Kennedy's childhood, although probably not as noble and chivalrous as he described it. Even friends and family describe him as lean and sneaky, more likely to ambush than confront.

His gallant defense of his sister—in which a twelve-year-old boy cold-cocks a good ol' boy sheriff with a shotgun butt and intimidates armed deputies into retreat—sounds like a bad movie script. His various brutal attacks on evil shopkeepers, dirty cops, sadistic store detectives, bullying gangs, even a junior-high principal, always involve high drama and high principles—and dialogue straight out of old hardboiled detective novels.

While he describes himself repeatedly as a good-natured, placid soul, he also says he never hurt anyone who didn't have a lesson coming. And Ronnie Kennedy was the one who could teach them.

He imagines his exploits have earned him the reputation as a kind of knight in tarnished armor, even a "savior." Further, he describes witnessing a murder and being shot while fleeing a petty crime as a child.

But no evidence exists in any record anywhere that any of these assaults ever happened. In one case, his mother explained in court that the "bullet hole" scar on his back was really caused when young Ronnie fell across the barbed-wire fence that encircled the family's front yard.

DESPITE HIS CLAIMS, Ronald Kennedy wasn't smart. A classroom was the most unnatural place he ever found himself.

He dropped out of school after eighth grade, although he claims sheer love of learning allowed him another year in a different school that apparently went unnoticed by school record-keepers.

He was a below average student, often failing. He skipped school regularly. Separate intelligence tests in 1958 and 1969 placed his IQ between 81 and 84—dull normal.

Although he claims he had straight A's in junior high school, despite the immense harassment, he never earned better than a C, according to court documents.

THROUGHOUT HIS MEMOIR, Kennedy describes himself as good-looking and irresistible to women. In almost every encounter he describes with a woman, she falls deeply, madly, passionately in love—or lust—with him. A dozen nurses in a hospital shower, waitresses in roadside diners, elegant barflies, the anonymous girlfriend of a Jaguar driver, a bordello full of kind-hearted hookers and their chunky madam, a Montana country girl, a thirteen-year-old vixen, girls who traded drugs for sex, four or five wives, even the victim of his most monstrous crime—all were supposedly mesmerized by him.

His sexual encounters all read like fevered adolescent fantasies. In each, he is a potent stud who needn't even wink to cause a woman to swoon, and every one of them surrenders her body and soul to him, whether he wants the soul or not. He even describes some encounters as good-will gestures to improve the lives of sad and forlorn girls.

But a frightening subtext emerges when the tittering dies down. Several of his spontaneous sexual conquests involve bodies of water and occur in remote, isolated places—just like the crime against Becky Thomson and Amy Burridge that might have gone unpunished except for an accident of fate. A haunting possibility arises: Might Ronald Kennedy be describing, in his own deviant way, other old, undiscovered rapes?

Was a California waitress named Darlene raped beside an idyllic pond in the mid-1960s by a drifter? Was a Montana girl named Pam raped near a swimming hole around that same time? Does Kennedy's narcissism outweigh his discretion, forcing him to tell the stories again and again with his special, deluded twists?

We are unlikely to know.

Nonetheless, Kennedy has had a few provable romances besides his several marriages.

His first, Jane, was thirteen, Kennedy nineteen, when he got her pregnant. Their child was raised by her parents, got involved with drugs, and later went to prison. When she filed for divorce in 1968, Kennedy virtually abducted her and held her as a sexual hostage for a night, claiming the law stated that having sex would render the divorce action moot. It didn't work.

And some romances blossomed *after* he went to prison. He continues to correspond with a former female prison worker who had a previous romance with a known rapist/killer in Colorado. And he was married for almost ten years to a childhood friend who married him in the joint, where they enjoyed conjugal visits before divorcing in the early 1990s.

But even today, he exalts one love above all others: A sweet, angelic, faithful girl named Sally, a doomed vessel into which he poured every last ounce of his love and devotion.

Too bad she never existed.

ALTHOUGH KENNEDY LATER admitted in interviews that he had given Sally a false name in his manuscript rather than sully her memory, he reluctantly said he was revealing her true name: Sally McClew.

But no student named Sally Springs or Sally McClew ever attended any Casper school, according to school census reports between 1955 and 1965. A girl named in Kennedy's seventh-grade class is alive and well today but doesn't recall ever speaking to the skinny little kid who'd grow up to be one of Wyoming's most infamous killers.

No Ronald Kennedy ever got a marriage license in Las Vegas, according to the clerk's records in Clark County, Nevada.

No girl with these names died in California during the entire 1960s, according to the California Vital Records Office. And calls to all the cemeteries in Long Beach and Bakersfield, California, found no such burials.

When pressed during interviews in 2003, the ghost of Sally Springs—the woman to whom Kennedy's life story was dedicated—grew even fainter:

> Q: *All right, here we go. Ron, these are tough questions. I'll tell you right up front. Sally Springs: You know, she plays a pretty pivotal role in your life story. You sorta . . .*
> A: *Who was that?*
> Q: *Sally Springs.*
> A: *Sally Springs?*
> Q: *Yes.*
> A: *I don't know that name.*
> Q: *Okay. (pause) Do you remember the girl you fell in love with at Dean Morgan and married?*
> A: *Yes.*
> Q: *Okay. What was her name?*
> A: *Sally?*
> Q: *Sally . . . what was her last name?*
> A: *Sally's last name? (long pause) My girlfriend, yeah, the one that I married. Yeah, I didn't put her real name in the autobiography. . . . Yeah, I was kinda afraid of using her real name because of privacy things for her and the baby. And if she had any surviving kin still left, which I don't know. I haven't heard from her mother in years, so I have no idea.*

Either the real Sally has been erased from all the records and memories where she once existed, or Ronald Kennedy invented his perfect love from thin air. If she is a waking dream, she represents everything Kennedy never knew in his tormented real life: Trust, beauty, loyalty, unconditional love, virginity, commitment, intellect, eroticism, innocence, comfort and acceptance.

Their love story, as he tells it, embodies the high romance of novels and Hollywood, from deathbed vigils to starry-eyed dinners on top of the world to stolen moments in exotic places. Kennedy plays the role of the heartbroken lover left alone in a cruel world, Romeo to Sally's Juliet, who lives and dies twice.

But Sally also represents an easy excuse. After her, even if she never existed, he can rationalize his lack of intimacy, true love, connection and empathy for another human being.

He once had those things, he asserts now, but he spent them all on one woman.

Even if she only existed in his underfed mind and bankrupt heart.

THE LAST CHAPTER of Kennedy's memoir, written in 1999, is devoted entirely to his account of the 1973 abduction of Amy Burridge and Becky Thomson, and the subsequent rape and murder at Fremont Canyon Bridge.

In short, he says he didn't do it.

In his memoir and our 2003 interviews, Kennedy admits he was there but maintained he took no part in the crimes, which he blames squarely on Jerry Jenkins, dead since 1998.

His story, which he never told to police, his own defense lawyer or a jury, differs significantly from Becky Thomson's testimony and Jerry Jenkins' confession to police—eerily similar stories, even though they would not and could not have collaborated to frame Ronald Kennedy.

Instead, he claims corrupt cops, populist prosecutors, judges biased against poor people, sensational media and even his own defense lawyer entrapped him in their web.

The "truth," according to Kennedy, goes something like this:

Spending a leisurely Monday morning at his mother's home shooting up heroin, Kennedy was rousted by a guy named Jerry Jenkins, his brother's friend whom he didn't like. They'd never been buddies, never hung around together. But Jenkins needed a favor, and Kennedy believed in helping people. Jenkins had skipped work for several days, and he needed somebody to go to the service station where he worked and pick up his paycheck, which he needed to buy milk for his new baby daughter.

After Kennedy got the paycheck, he was forced to join Jenkins on a day-long drinking and drugging spree. He begged Jenkins to take him home, but Jenkins threatened to kill or maim him if he didn't shut up. Knowing Jenkins to be a vicious, bloodthirsty man with a violent past—he claims he once watched Jenkins gouge out a woman's eyeball with a can opener in a tavern—Kennedy went along.

> Jerry started going through downtown, every woman he would see he would make nasty remarks to, like: "Hey you, wanna go fuck?" They would take off as fast as they could.
> It was probably around 6:30 p.m. when Jerry said he needed to stop and get some cigarettes. We pulled into the Thrift [sic] Store. At the same time, two girls pulled right up beside us in a station wagon car. Jerry kept looking at them. The girls got out of the car, went into the store. . . . Jerry got out for just a minute, but I had no idea why.

Jenkins had flattened the girls' tire. He offered to help them while Kennedy sat in Jenkins' two-door Impala, reeling from the drugs and booze forced upon him.

When the two girls climbed into Jenkins' back seat, Kennedy recognized the older one as a former girlfriend, and they exchanged pleasantries. Today, he's certain the only reason Becky Thomson got into Jenkins' car is because she knew Kennedy from their year-long romance, which he claims began when they met at a roller-skating rink a couple of years before.

But the shamelessly licentious Jenkins had other plans. They drove around town. Becky became so upset that Jenkins pulled off the road and beat her. When Kennedy tried to intervene, he claims Jenkins merely grabbed his hand and flogged the girls with it.

When they arrived at the Fremont Canyon Bridge, Kennedy had no idea where he was. It was dark, and he was nauseated by his overdose of pills and booze.

Kennedy puked on Jenkins' front seat, and Jenkins exploded. He dragged Kennedy from his car and beat him senseless.

Little Amy Burridge saw her chance to escape. She

leaped from the car and ran into the blackness toward the canyon. Jenkins chased her, but he was too fat and slow, so he gave up after a few steps.

In interviews thirty years later, Kennedy recalls what he says he feels most guilty about: Not being able to help the girls.

> You know, the thing of it is, Becky Thomson came around the car, and she knelt down beside me when I was laying half out of the car and half on the ground, OK? And, uh, I can recall something like her saying, "You've got to get out of here. We've got to get out of here. You got to get me out of here. You got to get me out of here." I think that's what's being said, I can't be 110 percent certain. I think that's what's being said. "You've got to get me out of here." I couldn't even get off the ground. I was just so danged violently ill from everything that was poured down me from beginning to end. No food in my stomach, no anything.

The next thing he remembers is waking up in an alley near his house the next morning. On the way to pick up a prescription for his wife around noon, he was arrested. The framing of Ronald Leroy Kennedy had begun.

Thirty years later, Ronald Kennedy still denies everything. And more.

He doesn't believe Becky Thomson ever fell into the canyon. She faked her injuries, he claims. He claims his defense lawyer was hand-picked by prosecutors to lose the capital case against him and Jenkins. He claims Jenkins was part of the conspiracy to frame him, even though Jenkins faced the same grisly fate in Wyoming's gas chamber. And he claims his romance with his victim, Becky Thomson—whom he also suggests stalked him after he was married—was covered up by her family and the legal system to make a stronger case against him.

In 1991—just before one of their many appeals for a new trial—Jerry Jenkins signed a notarized affidavit in prison, claiming he did the crime alone and Ronald Kennedy was totally innocent. The notary public who endorsed the confession swears it was Jenkins who signed it.

Jenkins later told his ex-wife the affidavit was a sham, a jailhouse deal with Kennedy while they were seeking a new trial. He told her that Kennedy had promised to help Jerry in some unspecified way if he only would take the fall for the crime. So Jerry signed the affidavit, assuring his ex "none of it matters and it isn't important and they'll see it doesn't mean anything anyway."

Was Jerry Jenkins once again invoking his perverse sense of honor, accepting total blame for a crime he didn't commit alone—just as when he took a beating for the car wrecked by his mother's drunken lover?

More importantly, in more than fifteen years, why had Ronald Kennedy never shared it with anyone, even though such a document, if genuine and true, would have exonerated him?

I just . . . I dunno. You know, I wanna tell you something. I feel like you're my friend, okay? I haven't had too many friends in my life, okay? I'm to the point where I do trust you. But you know I've lived with so much hurt in my heart over this case, and over what happened, I feel so much hurt inside me because of what's happened to these two girls, that it's there day after day, it's been there for thirty years. I love children with all my heart, you know, and always have, and now one's gone. And even though things turned out the way they did, I still feel just as guilty about that as the person who did it. [*Kennedy begins to get tearful, voice shaking*] There wasn't anything I could do to stop it or prevent it. And there shoulda been something I coulda done, you know. I don't know what that would have been. These two girls don't deserve to be dead. I'd rather be dead in their place, you know. That's two precious lives that are gone and can't never come back again, especially little Amy. She can't never come back again, you know. I live with the guilt of that in my heart day after day after day, you know. For this little girl, for God's sake. It's not a fun thing to have to live with.

THAT'S HIS STORY. I promised I would tell it.

But I came back to this unwelcome memory wanting to know why this crime happened. I wanted to believe there was a reason—not an excuse—that such a monstrous thing would happen.

I wanted to hear remorse. I wanted to hear a rapist and a killer say something—anything—that sounded like regret. I wanted some tiny detail that had never been told, but would allow a whole town to exhale, finally.

Or maybe I just wanted him to say one true thing, so I didn't have to believe in monsters.

But none of those things happened.

In fourteen hours of interviews and an autobiographical manuscript the length of a typical supermarket paperback, I got little more than a glimpse inside an unrepentant murderer's rancid mind and took a tumble in his perverse logic. If truth and repentance ever existed there, they had long since rotted away.

Ron Kennedy and Jerry Jenkins took many things from me—my friends, my sense of security, a certain amount of childhood innocence. Decades later, as I inventory what's left, I find a surplus of memory and only a thin residue of forgiveness. Kennedy and Jenkins made me an unapologetic supporter of the death penalty. They were not innocent of their crimes. I suspected it then, and I know it now. They should have died in the gas chamber, and part of me is angry they didn't. They robbed the best part of my mercy for them.

But I'm not in the absolution business. I'm a newspaperman, a storyteller.

And that's why I came home. I didn't know it at the beginning of my journey, but I do now.

I desperately wanted to look Ron Kennedy in the eye, to listen to his version of things, and to give him a voice no-

body had ever given him. If I couldn't do that, I wasn't the newspaperman I thought I was, or wanted to be. If I couldn't do that, he had poisoned me.

Above all, I wanted to know if I was a good enough journalist that I could set aside the memory of a profound event that introduced me to fear and the existence of evil, and despite how it changed me, to tell Ronald Kennedy's story as fairly as possible.

Whether I succeeded, these pages must tell.

Chapter 10

CLOSURE

On a sunny morning a few days after Becky died, Mike Carr scrambled down the treacherous north wall of Fremont Canyon, to a half-hidden spot just beneath the bridge. The air was so still, he could hear the insects swarming. The calm was ironic, he thought, considering what had just happened on this spot.

He'd read the newspaper accounts of her death, and although he didn't know her, he grieved. Like Becky, he'd grown up in Casper, although he was about ten years older than her. And he knew, like almost everyone else, what had happened to Becky and Amy nineteen years before. But unlike Becky, he'd gone off to seek his fortune in the outside world, first joining the Marine Corps at the height of the Vietnam War, then as an artist. After a while, he became a civilian Navy employee, at first as an illustrator and later an analyst. On vacation, like he was now, he almost always came home to Wyoming.

Despite his day job in the fluorescent corridors of the military, he was first an artist. At night, he was painting the life-sized outlines of imaginary corpses in the alley beside his Washington D.C. carriage house—one for each of the 552 murder victims in the District in 1992. He called them "urban petroglyphs," symbols of social, artistic and historic synergy. The images, which resembled investigators' grotesque chalk outlines, were painted in white acrylic house paint, purposely ephemeral. He knew the paint would fade like memories over the years and he intended his outlines to parallel life.

As Carr dragged some stones away from the base of the cliff face so he could work, the clarity and heat of the day struck him. How very different, he thought, from the darkness that drove Becky to this place.

He opened a gallon of white acrylic house paint and daubed it against the ancient rock. As he painted, an occasional stone would slough away from the cliffs and fall into the sluggish green river. He sensed he wasn't alone; the canyon itself had a life.

Unwittingly, Carr had chosen the exact spot where Becky had spent the frigid night after her rape and plunge from Fremont Canyon Bridge, half-naked, gravely injured and frightened. It had been her sanctuary.

When he finished, he stepped back. There on the canyon wall, in a spot Becky herself might have touched in her agony, were the outlines of two girls, holding hands as they fell from a mythic height.

The image was incomplete. Between the two figures, Carr added a simple poem he'd scrawled on his drive to the bridge that morning. *Two souls lost to us*, it began.

Mike Carr left the canyon and never went back. His expression of grief was among the more public in a community that suffered its losses stoically. No foundations were established, no teddy bears or flowers left in a makeshift memorial, no counselors visited the schools, no monuments were erected in the city park—although the county erected a small chain-link fence to prevent any future accidents on the bridge approaches. Death was like the seasons: It visited with regularity and energies must be saved for the next. Remembering was enough.

Over the years, wind and weather took their toll on Mike Carr's pictograph, and the rock canvas is pocked as if some idiot hunter on a distant cliff sighted his rifle on them. But a faint outline remained more than ten years later, visible only to the few souls who might brave the steep climb to the isolated spot.

Like memories, paint fades.

Life continues.

+ + +

THE PSYCHIATRIST BECKY Thomson believed had raped her
while she was drugged with a "truth gas" ultimately faced at
least three lawsuits by former patients who said he had im-
proper sex with them. They were all settled out of court between 1990-92, each for six-figure amounts. The psychiatrist
also lost his Idaho medical license, and then fled to Texas.

In 1993, almost a year after Becky's death, he was extradited back to Wyoming to face fifteen sexual assault charges
in criminal court. In a plea bargain, he pleaded no contest to
two second-degree rape charges in exchange for only five
years of probation (during which he couldn't treat any female patients) and a fifty-dollar fine.

Had Becky been one of his unknown victims? Had she
been raped once by two thugs in a lonely, horrifying place,
then again in the safety of a clinic by a doctor she had
trusted to help her?

It's impossible to know, unless the doctor himself admitted
it. Becky's lawsuit was discussed with a lawyer, but she died
before it was prepared. She certainly fit the profile of the doctor's typical victims—attractive and troubled women with long
dark hair. And the assault she described to friends, even though
remembered through a pharmaceutical fog, sounded like some
of his known victims' accounts of the doctor's assaults.

Soon after his conviction on sex charges, the psychiatrist
left his prison counseling job and no longer provides psychiatric services. He still lives in Texas.

TONI CASE, THE girls' mother, lives today in California. Her
husband Jack, the stalwart oilfield roughneck who stood by
her and his stepdaughters during the 1973 ordeal, died in
2005.

In their modest garden stands the metal cross from Mexico that first marked little Amy's grave. When it was replaced by a stone marker that bore the words of an old song,
"Once in Love with Amy," Toni planted the iron crucifix
among her other flowers.

Photos of Amy and Becky remain in a box in the closet, but their memories are close at hand.

Toni lies in bed some nights, trying to visualize the breadth of Amy's shoulders, the hard muscles in her calves, and the color of the hair on top of her head. She remembers that Amy smelled like sweet, fresh air and dust. She still keeps Amy's old pajamas in a wicker basket near her bed, but the smell has long gone from them.

She tried to climb down into the canyon after Becky's death, but she could only scramble halfway down the precarious slope. Becky once told her that during the night after her rape, she kept looking at the bridge, expecting to see her mother. "It was the first time you were never there for me," she said.

Toni had also heard about the pictographs painted down there, but she simply couldn't get down that far, physically or emotionally. She came out of the canyon, went directly home to California, hid in her house, and didn't answer the phone or the door for six months.

Among Becky's possessions were dozens of copies of the petitions signed by people all over Wyoming to keep Kennedy from getting paroled. Literally thousands of pages. She'd made copies, and copies of copies, and then more copies. When Becky died, there were stacks and stacks of them in her closets. Toni kept them for a while, devoting an enormous amount of space in her own closets to them, but eventually she couldn't bear to see the petitions anymore and threw them out.

Becky and Amy were the glue. It seemed they might all hold it together in the painful days after Amy's death, but when Becky died, the family fragmented. Toni's surviving daughters drifted away, and while modest repair has happened, the family simply has never found complete comfort together again.

After her death in 1992, Becky's ex-husband assumed custody of the toddler, only two at the time, and moved. He declined to be interviewed for this book, saying he was not yet ready to expose his daughter (fifteen years old at the time of this writing) to the whole tragic story of her mother's life, rape and death.

DAVE DOVALA—THE small-town cop who interviewed Becky Thomson the morning she was found, who escorted her mother to the morgue, who dramatically busted Ron Kennedy on Casper's main street, and who eventually gave Becky Thomson away at her wedding—retired from the Casper Police Department as a commander in 1987 and took a new job with the Natrona County Sheriff's Office.

Four years later he was elected sheriff, and he served two four-year terms. When he retired for good in 1999, he was sixty-one. The blue-collar son of Ohio had been a Wyoming cop for thirty-eight years.

The abduction of Amy Burridge and Becky Thomson, and the subsequent rape and murder, remains the single most vivid memory in his long career. Partly because he'd grown close to Becky after the crime, and partly because of its monstrosity. As hard as Dovala had worked to keep his emotions subdued at the time of the crime, he couldn't keep them down forever. Even a veteran cop deals with his feelings eventually.

And for Dovala, a grandfather of eight who still lives in Casper, Wyoming, it comes in second-guessing.

"The lesson I learned is not to get so close," he said in 2005. "But it would have been difficult not to."

AFTER LEAVING CASPER at the end of Kennedy and Jenkins' trial, public defender John Ackerman became dean of the National College for Criminal Defense at the University of Houston, a job he held for seven years. Entering private practice in Houston in 1982, he was elected president of the National Association of Criminal Defense Lawyers in 1982-1983 and briefly served as a criminal court judge in Houston by appointment from Texas Governor Ann Richards.

In 1976, he successfully defended Indian activist Russell Means against murder charges stemming from a protest at Wounded Knee. "I think I am the only criminal defense lawyer in history to have acquitted a future presidential candidate of murder," he says today.

His career has now come full circle from the Kennedy and Jenkins case. In 1997, Ackerman defended accused Yugoslavian war criminals on rape and murder charges at the International Criminal Tribunal in The Hague, Netherlands. He participated in the appeal of four Bosnian Muslims and Croats who had held various command positions in the Celebici prison camp, which had a reputation for atrocities against Bosnian Serbs, including murder, torture, rape, physical beatings and other inhumane treatment.

The so-called Delalic case acknowledged rape as a form of torture, making it a violation of the Geneva Conventions.

Shuttling between Houston and Eastern Europe—a fast track routine interrupted only briefly by cancer surgery—Ackerman and his lawyer-wife, Barbara Baruch, assumed the defense of Radislav Brdjanin, a Serbian leader facing life in prison for planning ethnic cleansing of Muslims and Croats from the Prijedor and Sanski Most regions of northwest Bosnia.

In the course of his work, Ackerman co-authored a book, *Practice and Procedure of the International Criminal Tribunal for the Former Yugoslavia.*

Don Chapin remains a lawyer in Casper, and son Charlie, who witnessed his father's personal and professional anguish, grew up to become a lawyer himself. Father and son now practice law together.

JACK BURK WAS not re-elected after the Kennedy and Jenkins trial. He was outgunned by the wealthy scion of a well-known ranch family, so Burk opened his first private practice at the age of forty-seven. Along the way, he and his wife Wanelda had four sons, and he never stopped playing his beloved Dixieland jazz. He retired in 1992 when diagnosed with throat cancer. He moved to San Diego, briefly returned to Casper, then shuffled off to idyllic Camano Island, Washington.

Jack Burk died of esophageal cancer in his home, with his family at his side, on December 12, 1995. He was cremated and his ashes buried in Lynwood, Washington. He was sixty-eight when he died, and in all his years as a lawyer, he never handled another case as momentous as the prosecution of Ronald Kennedy and Jerry Jenkins.

And until the day he died, a photograph of Fremont Canyon Bridge hung in his office.

His deputy prosecutor, Dave Lewis, is now in private practice in Jackson, Wyoming.

SOMEBODY ONCE TOLD Darci Jenkins that if she believed in good, she must also believe in evil. It was like standing in front of a mirror. It didn't matter on which side of the mirror you stood. One couldn't exist without the other.

Darci didn't want to believe it. No matter which side of the mirror she saw, she knew only one image was real. Only one could be touched, held, hurt and loved.

The other was an illusion.

She always saw herself on that side of the mirror.

In some ways, Jerry had always been on the other side, an illusion.

She left Wyoming and settled in Texas after Jerry went to prison. Darci met her current husband in 1975, with whom she had two more children. She now lives in Nevada near her other children, who have given her seven grandchildren.

And she finally got her place with "some animals." Darci is now happily married and keeps her own horses, which she says provide solace, companionship and therapy.

CHERA JENKINS, JERRY and Darci's oldest daughter, remained Daddy's girl to the end.

She never found a rhythm of her own. At fifteen, her life

began to fall apart. She ran away, dropped out of school, and got pregnant a couple times. She never stuck around home long enough to seek help, although Darci begged her.

She married at twenty-two, but two months after the wedding, she got out of bed at 2:00 a.m. and left for good.

Secretly, she went searching for the father she lost, the guy who ate candy for breakfast and rolled around on the floor with her. She visited him a few times in prison and wrote many letters to him, sending pictures. She had a relationship with her father that her little sister never did. Nobody knows the depth of Chera's and Jerry's relationship, but the contact made both of them happy.

In 1995, during an argument in a shopping mall, Chera's boyfriend pushed her hard against a glass window, dazing her. On her way out of the mall, she collapsed and later died of internal injuries, maybe a bruised brain, a damaged spine, or a bad heart. Nobody proved it conclusively. The boyfriend served eighteen months for involuntary manslaughter, and then disappeared for good.

The coroner gave Darci Chera's purse, which contained two letters from Jerry. Before that moment, she hadn't known Chera had been in contact with her father.

Today, Darci is raising Chera's son as her own. He wants to be a lawyer when he grows up.

IN 1997, NEWLY born-again and recently diagnosed with cancer, the former Jane Kennedy contacted Ron Kennedy for the first time in almost twenty-five years. In a letter to her imprisoned ex-husband, Jane condensed almost thirty years of their son's life into a single paragraph. After his mother and father divorced, their son was largely raised by his grandparents, who changed the infant's name long before his father's infamous crime. Jane was going through another divorce herself—at least her third—and sensed the end of her life was near. "I must tell you," she wrote to Ron in prison, "that at this time I am uncertain as to how much contact I wish to have with you. It's very new and strange to me, although 'the powers that be' guided me to do this."

Jane died in 2001 of cancer. She was forty-nine.

OF THE FOUR people whose lives converged on Fremont Canyon Bridge on September 24, 1973, only Ronald Kennedy survives.

He remains in the Wyoming State Penitentiary on a medium-security cell block. He is the second most senior inmate.

Amy Burridge died that night in 1973. Becky Thomson was next in 1992; Kennedy believes that when she was about to tell the world about her love affair with him, she died mysteriously at Fremont Canyon Bridge. He still suspects foul play by the same sinister forces that robbed him of his innocence and freedom. Jerry Jenkins died in 1998, leaving Ronald Kennedy the only person who knows what happened.

After finishing twenty-nine years of rape and assault time, he only began serving his life sentence for the murder of Amy Burridge in 2002 and will come up for parole every five years starting in 2007, although nobody—including Kennedy—ever truly expects he will be freed.

Several law enforcement sources whisper that there's solid evidence of at least one contract to be paid fully to anyone who kills Ronald Kennedy if he ever walks out of prison. Even Kennedy and family members have heard about it, and fear it; his mother once advised him to never hope to leave prison, where he was comparatively safe, for a free life in which he faced the death penalty he never received in prison.

Why? Few crimes in Wyoming's history compete with his for monstrosity, cold-blooded randomness, its assault on innocents, and the resulting public outrage. And since a governor must grant parole, politics will likely trump mercy. In short, even if a Wyoming governor truly believed Kennedy had paid his blood-debt to society, he would likely suffer a swift political backlash in the intensely personal world of Wyoming's handshake politics.

The 1901 long-shot assassination of young Willie Nickell by infamous stock detective Tom Horn is long forgotten. But this crime is no place to look for mercy: Horn was hanged. Yes, an innocent child was killed, but Horn's case has become more a piece of Wyoming's colorful outlaw history than a foundation-rattling moral lesson.

The 1982 ambush-execution of abusive father Richard Jahnke by his two frightened Cheyenne children is far more current. It spotlighted domestic abuse and became a book, *The Poison Tree,* and made-for-TV movie, *The Right to Kill?* But oddly, in this case, the killers had the public's sympathy, not the victim. In the end, few people seemed particularly disappointed in the victim's death.

The secret serial rape of many unwitting patients by Dr. John Story in the tiny sugar-beet town of Lovell also caught the attention of the outside world. Crime writer Jack Olsen detailed the peculiar series of sexual assaults in his book, *"Doc,"* prompting many readers to wonder how a doctor could possibly rape his unsuspecting patients while they submitted to routine gynecological exams over more than twenty years before he was convicted in the 1980s. The strange case of Doc Story was perverse and chilling, but in the end, all of his victims—some of them elderly—went on with their lives.

The 1998 crucifixion of gay student Matthew Shepard on a buck rail fence near Laramie by two homophobic slacker punks comes closest to the monstrosity of the crimes against Amy Burridge and Becky Thomson. While gay hate-crimes unfolded with regularity elsewhere, the circumstances and settings of this one shocked a cable-news nation. The resulting news deluge became more about homophobia in the Heartland than about the grisly killing of an innocent boy who never hurt anyone.

When his murder morphed into a story about Wyoming's alleged gay bias—at least that's how it was perceived in Wyoming—hungry reporters and breathless gay activists seemed to lose sight of the ghastly crime and how it shocked Wyoming, too. It was good footage and fund-raising fodder for gay-rights groups, but fewer gay hate-crimes have been committed per capita in Wyoming than in San Francisco, Miami or New York City. Countless television movies, plays and news broadcasts later, Matthew Shepard became an inanimate symbol, and his humanity all but dissolved in the circus that followed.

Few people in Wyoming today—or anywhere, for that matter—could name Matthew Shepard's two killers. Not so with Ron Kennedy and Jerry Jenkins, whose names flow in the blood-memory of Wyoming.

One reason is the place: Fremont Canyon. The frightful gash in the remote prairie is an example of Wyoming's co-existent beauty and menace. The bridge is so nightmarishly high it clenches the gut just to see it in daylight. When Kennedy and Jenkins chose it to dispose of their victims' bodies—just as Matthew Shepard's killers chose a rustic rail fence—they unwittingly chose a context that would seal their own fates.

And when the broken Becky Thomson surmounted the seemingly insurmountable canyon walls, the crime suddenly assumed mythic proportions.

Another element that sets this crime apart is its entanglement in the great crime-and-punishment issue of the day—the wisdom of the death penalty. Society promised Kennedy and Jenkins would die for their sins, but in the abstract angst over how a culture deals with its worst offenders, the two killers enjoyed gratuitous mercy. The very system of rules and order they had defied saved their lives.

So Kennedy and Jenkins became symbols of a national agony, too. They represented every irony, every flaw and every clemency in American justice.

But there was more.

Most crimes contain clues that explain them. For horrified and powerless bystanders, their atrocity is somehow mitigated by understanding how and why they happened. True-crime books—like trials—often serve the purpose of connecting all the dots, as if by explaining, the wounds will be healed.

But the clues to Ron Kennedy and Jerry Jenkins' crime are obscure. Amy and Becky were mere strangers to the two men when they got into that car. Amy died a tormented death because she was simply in the way, dropped off the edge of the world with no more remorse than if she were being dropped off at school. The public never heard the icy calm in Kennedy's voice when he assured Jenkins that he needn't worry about the little girl, whom he'd just thrown to her death moments before.

The crime's randomness, ferocity, sadism, raw terror and bloodcurdling setting are all out of proportion to a common "drive-by" rape.

All the more curious is the fact that the Wyoming Department of Corrections initially refused my repeated requests to interview Kennedy, who was eager to be interviewed. A prison spokeswoman cited an open federal complaint Kennedy had filed against the prison, concerns for the safety of both inmate and journalist, and fears that Kennedy might say something hurtful to the victims' family.

After numerous appeals over several months, the WDOC relented, permitting only phone contact with Kennedy. Under no circumstances would I be allowed to look him in the eye—nor he to look into mine. Fourteen hours of phone interviews followed, but the prison never yielded on a face-to-face visit, even though Kennedy himself also pleaded for it. Instead, he claims an unnamed prison official warned him privately to measure his words carefully and not say anything that might reveal too much.

The prison had allowed this infamous rapist and killer to keep pets in his cell. He had been allowed to marry and have weekend sex on prison grounds and to attend dances with his wife. He was granted extraordinary freedom to cavort with children on his sister's front lawn during a secret furlough to his victims' hometown.

But still, the prison deemed a face-to-face interview with a newspaperman inappropriate.

While the prison did not ask the victim's blessing for Ron Kennedy's furlough in 1985, a prison official sought an opinion from the victims' family on whether I—or anyone—should later be allowed to interview him. No details of that conversation were ever shared.

The Wyoming Department of Corrections is jealous of its total control and its secrecy. Even though the department's policies specifically permit media contact with inmates, it's just for show: Only one face-to-face interview has ever been allowed at this writing, and then only at the request of the inmate's victim. Whatever its motives, Wyoming's cowboy-correctional system remains cagey, parochial and seemingly more motivated to protect its closely held power than to protect the law-abiding public.

Nonetheless, Ronald Leroy Kennedy shows no inclination toward explanation or apology. The outlines of the truth might be generally known, but the last unknown details of the monstrous crime are likely to die with him, unspoken.

DANNY NEMITZ, AMY'S best childhood friend, still weeps when he talks about Amy. He is haunted by hypotheses: If he had ridden along with Amy and Becky when they asked him, would this eleven-year-old boy have been able to save them? Would he have been dumped off the bridge, too, or would his mere presence have deflected the pernicious intentions of Ron Kennedy and Jerry Jenkins, who might have seen the abduction of three people as too much of a risk?

Nobody knows. But Danny, like others, can't stop the questions from creeping up on him in dark moments.

Now in his forties and managing a tire store in Houston, Texas, he has his own children. And he thinks about his best friend Amy all the time when his children are late coming home or when he sends them out into the world alone.

He regrets something else: Not expressing his remorse to Amy's family. He was too young to know the protocol of death. But when his older brother Rick was killed in a refinery accident many years later, he realized the value of just saying, "I'm sorry" or "I will miss her."

The other children closest to Amy and Becky grew up and scattered from the old neighborhood.

Most started their own families. Some took jobs far away, and some came back, yielding to the pull of the last comfortable place they ever knew.

Some just left for good.

Tommy Browning grew up to be a pitcher for the Cincinnati Reds, and on September 16, 1988, he became only the fourteenth pitcher in Major League history to throw a perfect game. Others went on to be executives, housewives, preachers, itinerant laborers, analysts, miners, insurance sellers, shopkeepers, truck drivers, soldiers, carpenters, teachers, oilfield workers, even authors.

Some have died and are past caring, but the rest remember.

They remember how suddenly the limits tightened. One could no longer ride her bike past a certain street, just a few blocks away. Another had a curfew before dark. Parents who had allowed extraordinary latitude abruptly shortened the leash. Many remember the photos in the paper of the bridge and the canyon walls, illustrating vividly where the bodies slammed into the water or the cliff face.

But they also remember—and still feel intimately—how their carefree little world grew more treacherous and unfathomable, literally overnight. Their small town, bounded by sandlots and frog ponds, earthen forts and public swimming pools, had betrayed them. The dark was no longer a time for adventure, but for fear.

But they also think about forgiveness, fear and regret in equal parts.

"I'm the one who loses if I can't forgive," says Tami Smothers Rudkin, one of Amy's classmates and closest friends. She is now a pastor at a community church in Casper. "If I can't forgive, [the killers] take the best part of my life. If I can't do that, they win."

"I was so afraid to go out in the dark after that day, and still am today," says another childhood friend, who now lives in Billings, Montana, with her own family. "I have a night light in every room of my house and will not go outside at night. Even camping I sleep with a flashlight."

"We let Amy play the outfield for both sides and hardly ever let her bat," my younger brother recalled recently. He became a gas company executive in Florida, with three children of his own. "She didn't mind. She was stuck way out in the middle of the sagebrush tracking down lost balls or just guarding them from rolling in the alkali wash. She never complained. She just wanted to be involved in the game. I wish now we would have let her bat."

What do children learn from tragedies they could never have imagined or anticipated? The kids from the old neighborhood recite their lessons in their own ways and their own words, but they say the same things:

We're not just vapors.

Every day must count.

Trust isn't always unconditional, but it can be.

And whether we know it, somebody will remember we were here.

The daughter of a tow-truck driver in Riverside, California, Missy Kirk doesn't talk much about her past, except to say "I have lived an unjust life." Clearly, it hasn't been perfect. Once, finally defeated by insurmountable sadness, the trained nurse almost drove her truck deliberately off a seaside cliff to end her life.

Even if the physical Missy Kirk didn't perish, her old spirit did. As many people in crisis do, she reached out for answers in unexpected places. Missy Kirk found hers in God.

In 1996, Missy traveled to India in search of meaning. She'd only been born again a year before, but she put her nursing skills and her heart to work in Mother Teresa's homes in downtown Calcutta just before Christmas, just before Mother Teresa herself died.

On the flight home, she sat beside a pastor who was reading a book called *Finding the Courage to Overcome the Past* by Texan evangelist Max Lucado. The first chapter was entitled "Not Guilty," a sermon based on Becky Thomson's haunted life and tragic death:

Canyons of shame run deep. Gorges of never-ending guilt. Walls ribboned with the greens and grays of death. Unending echoes of screams. Put your hands over your ears. Splash water on your face. Stop looking over your shoulder. Try as you might to outrun yesterday's tragedies—their tentacles are longer than your hope. They draw you back to the bridge of sorrows to be shamed again and again and again.

If it was your fault, it would be different. If you were to blame, you could apologize. If the tumble into the canyon was your mistake, you could respond. But you weren't a volunteer. You were a victim.

Sometimes your shame is private. Pushed over the edge by an abusive spouse. Molested by a perverted parent. Seduced by a compromising superior. No one else knows. But you know. And that's enough.

Sometimes it's public. Branded by a divorce you didn't want. Contaminated by a disease you never expected. Marked by a handicap you didn't create. And whether it's actually in their eyes or just in your imagination, you have to deal with it—you are marked: a divorcee, an invalid, an orphan, an AIDS patient.

Whether private or public, shame is always painful. And unless you deal with it, it is permanent. Unless you get help—the dawn will never come.

You're not surprised when I say there are Rebecca Thomsons in every city and Fremont Bridges in every town. And there are many Rebecca Thomsons in the Bible. So many, in fact, that it almost seems that the pages of Scripture are stitched together with their stories. Each acquainted with the hard floor of the canyon of shame.

When Missy read the story, she wept. "The reality is that I was a Rebecca on a bridge, once, long ago," she says today, "and instead of being at the bottom of an ocean cliff, God had other plans."

So in 1998, she founded Rebecca House, a modest home on the Columbia River in Portland, Oregon. In the north end of the original house's attic was a stained glass window she designed. Etched in black across a mosaic of green glass are the words: Rebecca House.

Missy is now building a new Rebecca House, but its purpose remains. It is a refuge, a sanctuary. Her "guests" are not all haunted by the same ghosts. They are diseased and dying, abused, forgotten, poor or lost. Anyone whose life has become his greatest burden.

Like Missy. Like Becky.

"I felt that I easily could have been Rebecca on that bridge," she says now. "Her body was physically taken that day, her spirit released. However, until my last breath, the legacy of her life is going to be alive in me. I promised her that very moment that we are going to be a team, we are going to live a life of significance in trying to help others."

For Missy Kirk, Becky Thomson inspired a life's work, even though she'd never learned another thing about Becky nor even seen a picture until a curious writer called five years later.

"You see, Rebecca has passed the baton to me," Missy says. "I'm kind of picking up where she left off. It is my hope that someday I will look into the eyes of Rebecca's daughter and tell her about the extraordinary woman who gave birth to her."

Not every defeat contains a hidden victory. Not every storm cloud has a silver lining. Sometimes, we simply embrace the good that follows evil as reassurance that humans are basically resilient and virtuous. Of course, we wouldn't need such proof if humans truly were resilient and virtuous, but faith is a funny thing.

An artist expresses public grief by painting a memory . . . a woman founds a sanctuary for the temporarily defeated . . . a child grows up to understand how compassion is a comfort . . . all because they had to believe something good must arise from something very bad.

Pain is the price we pay for memory. It's some kind of sin to forget what hurts, as much as it is to forget what makes us smile. Suffering has its meaning, and memory has its graces.

I've gone to the Fremont Canyon Bridge many times, and I might someday go again. Not soon, but someday.

The last time was the thirtieth anniversary of the actual crime, September 24, 2003. At the moment I realized the moon, temperatures and sky were to be exactly as they'd been that night, I knew I had to spend that night under the bridge. I wanted to feel for myself some of what Becky felt.

I took no food or water, no blankets or matches. Unlike Becky in her thin sweater, I wore denim jeans, a shirt and hiking boots. Unlike Becky, I chose to be there and had prepared my mind for it. And unlike Becky, I climbed down to the spot in the canyon's fatigued twilight, while I could still see a path.

I huddled against the rock wall exactly where Becky had hidden. I could reach up in the dark and know I was touching the white-paint outlines Mike Carr had painted there years before, but before ten p.m. I couldn't see my fingers two inches in front of my face. As the night wore on, I spoke my thoughts into the tape recorder; listening to it now, I hear a quavering, uneasy voice that is mine, but not mine.

I began to tremble even before the sky had gone completely black, partly from the pervasive cold and partly from haunted edginess. My gut was knotted, steeped in icy adrenaline.

Sometime in the middle of the night, bafflingly, my watch stopped dead. I lost track of time, except for the moment. At times, I heard distant howls, rocks falling into the water fifty yards off, and an inexplicable hum that seemed to rise from the water. Just like the night of the crime, the temperature dipped below freezing, and although I wore far more clothing than Becky, I shivered throughout the night. Without a watch, without a sense of time, the next identifiable moment would be daybreak, but not until false dawn had tricked me into false hope.

I knew I couldn't replicate Becky's experience, even if I'd leapt naked from the bridge in pitch dark. I was not battered, raped, naked. My bones weren't broken into smaller pieces, paralyzing me. I knew the spot where I lay. I needn't fear my little sister's corpse lay someplace nearby and that her killers prowled above me. I knew I'd survive.

I shared only Becky's loneliness, the razor-slice of the air, the suffocating darkness, the mysterious sounds up-river, the eviscerating length of night, and the treachery of false dawn.

In the morning, I could climb out using healthy hands and two strong legs.

And as I clambered up the canyon's unstable wall, I picked up two steel-gray stones, etched by layers of untold epochs. They stood out among the other dun-colored granite and sandstones sliding slowly toward the water, so I put them in my pocket as a remembrance.

Today, they sit above my word processor, where I can see them every day.

One is slightly larger than the other, but both are heavier than you might expect. The smaller one is smoother, more symmetrical, less vexed by the unimaginable, incessant forces that reduce every large stone to a small one. Its angular lines are even and concentric, like a precise topographical map of a tiny coffin. It came from near the water's edge, among the wild cinquefoil and the sound of trickling water.

The larger one was higher up, maybe halfway between the slow water below and the world above. Although they are likely to be exactly the same age, the larger one is riven with irregular seams and encrusted with primordial accretions. It's grossly asymmetrical. Its tiny troughs are deeper, its surface coarser. To me, it seems older, or at least more tormented.

What were they? I took them to my local rock shop. The lady behind the counter perched her glasses on her nose, weighed them in her hand, examined them under a magnifying glass, and praised their unusual beauty, but she didn't know what they were.

Yet these two stones are clearly pieces of the same ancient monolith, related as if by blood, separated by time and by uncontrollable forces of nature. Maybe they fell into that gorge at the same moment in geological time, or maybe the gorge came later, but they are clearly made of the same stuff. And long after the blood wind has swept away my bone-dust, after all memories have dissipated, these stones will remain. Just stones.

Stones needn't hope to be remembered. Stones don't die. Stones don't cry.

People do.

In another story many years ago, I invented a myth about an old frontiersman who is visited by a mysterious Indian spirit under each full moon for nearly a year. Each time, she leaves him a smooth black stone. Each stone represented an intimate past: memories, dreams, sins, journeys. But the last stone was different. It symbolized life as-yet-unlived.

My two stones embody two unlived lives, but it's only a meaning I give them. They are merely stones.

We are not stones. On stones, we carve the words that summarize our lives. With stones, we declare lifelong love. From stones, we take metaphors and meanings. Within stone walls and fences, we sometimes hide.

The fear of evil, like grief, must be reduced to its proper weight in our hearts. The memory of it never goes away, but we find a way to live with it. The children in our neighborhood now have children of their own. Most have continued living, wiser and chastened. Some of us went on to successes that let us see the place in prouder, happier ways, but all of us live with this one tragedy tucked away someplace in our hearts.

Uncomfortable with a mystery, I showed the stones to my ninth-grade earth-science teacher, who has taken children on summer field trips into Wyoming's outback for more than forty years. He had seen that kind of stone before, though not commonly.

"It's what is referred to as banded iron," he told me. "The mineral is hematite. It comes from the Wind River Mountains. I have picked up pieces along Trappers Route near Government Bridge and from the shoreline of Pathfinder. Someday I'm going to track it on up the Sweetwater and then check to see if it is along the Platte above Pathfinder. One of those wonderful someday projects. It takes a beautiful polish."

Hematite is an iron ore. Its name comes from the Greek word haematites, which means "blood-like," because its powder is rich red. Ancient legends say hematite was formed under the great battlefields of history when blood seeped into the ground. Egyptians believed it cured madness.

Humans have always invested memory and hope in stones.

Becky Thomson and Amy Burridge were not stones. They were softer and sentient. They weren't made to survive for millennia, just longer than they did. They were gone too soon, leaving only stones and memories for us to visit.

On a frosty February morning, thirty years after the crime, I visited Amy and Becky's grave. A fresh snow had fallen overnight. Approaching the grave, I saw one set of footprints from the path to the grave, where someone had lingered and walked back to the path. I don't know who visited that morning, but it suggests the memory remains fresh.

Their story continues to echo in the small town of my childhood, and in many hearts, because in death they, too, were invested with memory and hope. To me, they were literally the girls next door, but to everyone who felt the sudden, chilly wind of fear in the hours, days and months after the crime, they represented every girl next door. Their fates were entangled in our fears.

Becky lived behind invisible stone walls. Part of what she lost on Fremont Canyon Bridge was the ability to trust deeply enough to let someone touch the core of her. Her solitary trauma set her apart from everyone, and she was ill-equipped to dismantle—or even learn to live with—the stone wall she'd built in one night around herself.

Then, on another night, she leapt from her stone fortress and plunged to infinity.

I have known this story for more than thirty years, and I found a place for it on a shelf in my heart where it wouldn't be forgotten, but where it also didn't trip me up every single day of my life. When I first began to write it down, I mistakenly thought it was about the coming of evil to my town, but I was wrong.

The crime remains an open wound in Casper, Wyoming, more than thirty years later. Most of the locals know—or think they know—the facts of the case, and "newcomers" hear about it eventually. Many view the legal system with equal parts of satisfaction and betrayal. It certainly worked by determining the guilt of Kennedy and Jenkins, but it failed to keep a crucial promise: To execute them.

Without question, if Ronald Kennedy were allowed to walk out the front gates of the Wyoming State Penitentiary today, someone with a very long memory would be waiting.

To me, this began as a story about how one crime has suppurated in one community's memory for more than thirty years, an open wound only barely healed by time. I envisioned a social study of my hometown, my friends, myself. I wanted to explore the reason why, after more than thirty years, only a few words or names—Kennedy, Fremont Canyon, the girls who died at the bridge, Jenkins—still elicited visceral reactions. How could such a savage thing become part of a whole town's collective DNA?

But in the end, this isn't the story I thought it would be. It's not just about a town that suffered a grievous wound or a grotesque epiphany.

Evil had existed in Casper, Wyoming, long before me, and all around me. I hadn't seen, heard, tasted, felt nor smelled it, but it was there. Ronald Kennedy and Jerry Jenkins were from that town, just like me. They'd always been there.

This is the story about evil coming to me, to my heart. It would have come sooner or later anyway, as it does for each of us. Whether it settles in like dust or blasts through like a tempest, we cannot avoid it. We can only build our homes and our hearts strong enough to weather it when it comes, and hope the damage is reparable.

It was also the moment death became real to me. I didn't think of myself as immortal or indestructible, but until that day, I didn't consider the finality, the absolute black vacuum, of dying. Suddenly, I was afraid of it, and I still am.

Survival is an instinct, not a choice. Perhaps Becky's courage came from fear: She was afraid to die. Her only hope—hope distilled to its ethereal essence—was the very next breath. Not tomorrow. Not next week.

Maybe solid ground is just an illusion. A friend who was herself a victim of rape asked me: What if we are always falling—or at least forgetting to fly or glide—and holding onto each other is the closest we ever get to something remotely solid?

We want to feel the earth beneath our feet, to dig our toes deep in it, to stand up on our own while we touch someone.

But will we all fall eventually? If, like gravity itself, evil is a force of nature, can we avoid a freefall over a whole lifetime?

Probably not. But we can acknowledge that it's a messy world, and humans weren't intended to live behind stone walls, so we must find our place in our messy world and take action seeking justice when we find evil, rather than surrender . . . or not truly live at all.

Endnotes

1. (Page 67) In true Hollywood fashion, Cattle Kate and Jim Averell eventually became grossly distorted "heroes." In 1953's *The Redhead from Wyoming*, Maureen O'Hara played a lovable saloon queen named Kate who unwittingly helps her old flame, an ambitious gambler named Jim Averell (played by western star William Bishop), in a cattle rustling scheme that sparks a Wyoming range war. In director Michael Cimino's colossal 1980 flop, *Heaven's Gate*, Ella Watson was portrayed by the fetching Isabelle Huppert as an exotic European immigrant. Averell, played by Kris Kristofferson, was laughably re-created as a lawman. And together, they were (in Cimino's pipe dream) champions of the 1892 Johnson County War — which actually happened three years after the real and anything-but-heroic Cattle Kate and Jim Averell were lynched more than 150 miles away.

2. (Page 80) Twenty years later, David Kendall became the personal lawyer for President Bill Clinton and Hillary Rodham Clinton and represented him in the impeachment inquiry resulting from investigations of his Whitewater real estate scheme.

3. (Page 108) In 1973, long before the advent of forensic DNA analysis, investigators could only determine blood type from semen, and only then if the donor were a "secretor." Even if enough semen had survived Becky Thomson's

ordeal, the best prosecutors could show was that it came from a man whose blood type was consistent with one or both of the suspects'. In the end, investigators had too little to form any conclusive evidence.

4. (Page 152) In 1912, the condemned man Joseph Seng distinguished himself as the catcher for the prison's baseball team. Another prisoner later wrote in his diary: "After they hanged the catcher, the team was never again worth a damn." Since 1965, Wyoming has executed only one inmate. Shortly after midnight on Jan. 22, 1992, Mark Hopkinson died by lethal injection at the Wyoming State Penitentiary for ordering an informant's 1979 assassination from his prison cell while awaiting trial in a fatal bombing.

5. (Page 170) Killer Billy James Cloman had a federal rap against him at the time of his 1973 murders, so he served time at Leavenworth from 1980-84. While imprisoned there, he was found guilty of another assault with intent to commit murder, and seven more years of federal time were added at the end of his back-to-back life sentences in Wyoming, should he ever serve them out. Turning 50 years old in 2005, he's been at the Wyoming State Penitentiary since he was sent back from Leavenworth in 1984.

Acknowledgments

This book emerges from what seems like a lifetime. But in truth, it is the product of many lives, many hearts and many memories.

Most of my sources are mentioned by name throughout the book, and I wish to thank them for their valuable assistance with this story. Rather than repeat their names, I prefer taking this space to express my profound appreciation for their sometimes painful, sometimes poignant, always significant contributions. Others shared stories or documents, but for their own reasons asked not to be identified, and I owe them equal thanks.

Of the many others who responded to my requests for help or information, I am particularly grateful to the Case family; Dr. John MacDonald, the retired director of forensic psychiatry at the University of Colorado Medical Center and himself the author of a dozen books on criminal psychology; archivist Kevin Anderson of Casper (Wyo.) College; Pastor Tami Rudkin, Catherine Martin, Brandi Wollerman Forgey and Pam Cooper-Shiba; Gen Tuma, Clerk of Seventh Judicial District Court, Casper; Clerk Gerrie Bishop and her deputies of First Judicial District Court, Cheyenne; Wyoming defense lawyers Richard Rideout, Mike Krampner, Dallas Laird, John Whitaker and Ronald Pretty; Dr. James Thorpen and Gary Hazen of the Natrona County (Wyo.) Coroner's Office; Bonnie Weiss-McDonald; news librarian Kay McCullough; George Kay of KTWO-TV; Dr. Thomas E. Nunnally of

Auburn University; Bonnie Paulley; sextons Rita and Mandy Butler of Memorial Gardens; Genie Maples, whose intimate insights found their way into this narrative in many places; Elaine Hough; Ken Trimmer; Bill Hambrick; Roy Jenkins and other members of the Jenkins family; the Kennedy family; Kay Coleman; prison spokeswoman Melinda Brazzale; Bill Vandeventer, for room, board and friendship on the many long road trips to my past; and to my old friends from the neighborhood, with whom I share a painful, indelible memory.

Special thanks to my agent Gina Panettieri, New Horizon Press Editor-in-Chief Joan Dunphy and Production Manager Chris Nielsen for seeing value in this achingly tragic story. They made it possible for you to hold it in your hands now.

The support of family and friends is necessary for any major undertaking. As always, my thanks to my children, Matt and Ashley, for their faith and support; my own brother and sisters for their recollections and advice; and Mary Vandeventer for suffering long hours of my thinking aloud, and still copy-editing the manuscript expertly.

My reporting also distilled a variety of media reports in the *Casper* (Wyo.) *Star-Tribune, Cheyenne* (Wyo.) *Tribune-Eagle, The Washington Post, Associated Press,* and *First for Women* magazine.

What you just read really happened. No names were changed, no known facts deliberately tainted. All dialogue is fashioned from testimony, public statements and interviews where sources were asked to reconstruct conversations as precisely as possible.

However, in one segment, the chronology of events unfolded slightly differently than the narrative. The police interrogation of Jerry Lee Jenkins actually occurred in three separate interviews over two days immediately after his arrest. The questions and answers are exactly and accurately reported here, but for clarity, the three interviews were merged in the narrative.

Ron Franscell
October 2006